TWO PRINCESSES:

THE TRIUMPHS AND TRIALS OF GRACE KELLY AND DIANA SPENCER

By

Kevin Noa

Best Wishes

Kevin Noa

ISBN: 1-4033-3956-2 (e-book)
ISBN: 1-4033-3957-0 (Paperback)
ISBN: 1-4033-5115-5 (Dustjacket)

This book is printed on acid free paper.

FIRST EDITION

1stBooks – rev. 09/26/02

DEDICATION

To my big brother Glenn, who is now in Christ's Kingdom

Acknowledgements

From the night I awoke in November of 1996 with the disease that changed my life, interstitial cystitis, to the day I completed this book in April of 2002, I have so many people to thank for making this labor of love possible.

I'd like to begin by thanking Judy Marshall for giving me her copy of *Grace*, by Robert Lacey, which set this whole adventure in motion.

To all my teachers throughout the years of my education: these include my fifth and sixth grade teachers, Miss Mary Ann Andrews and Mr. Richard Dorherty; in high school, Mr. Alexander Baldwin Sr., the father whose sons all went on to careers in acting; in junior college, my American History professor Dr. John Cable, who praised my writing skills on both my essay tests and assigned papers; in senior college, Dr. Harold Lerch and Dr. Ruth Alexander, who also reinforced my ability as a writer. These men and women laid the foundation for making me the writer I became.

The staff of several libraries also must receive recognition in my years of research. Those include Nancy House and the librarians of the Haverhill Public Library in Haverhill, Massachusetts, and the librarians of the Merrimac, Massachusetts and Pollard Memorial Library in Lowell, Massachusetts, who also helped me in my research. Special thanks goes to Evan Towle and the librarians of the Temple University Archives, who had both Princess Grace's newspaper articles and photographs ready to go during each of my visits.

Through the many letters I wrote, most of which went either unanswered or with regrets, the ones who did share their experiences of either princess' life with me gave this book its authenticity.

For the sections about Princess Grace, my heartfelt thanks go to Judith Balaban Quine, who was Princess Grace's closest and dearest friend. Judith's love and respect for her best friend were evident throughout our interview. Also, Mrs. Adele Richards, whose interview told me of the love of dried flowers and friendship she shared with Princess Grace.

For the sections about Princess Diana, a debt of gratitude I can never repay goes to Reverend Dr. Tony Lloyd, who linked the vital theme of spirituality and the calling of service to Christ between each princess. If I had had only one choice of whom to interview from among Princess Diana's family or friends, I still would have chosen Tony. Their work together in the Leprosy Mission went beyond the call of duty, as did so many of Princess Diana's humanitarian causes. In that regard, the staffs of the AIDS Foundation and Centrepoint homes for "teens at risk" were also helpful in providing me with beneficial literature.

Another appreciative thanks goes to Paul Burrell, Princess Diana's butler, whose letter to me displayed the love, devotion, dedication and loyalty he gave to Princess Diana through her professional life.

Among my fellow teaching peers who helped make this book a reality are the following. Dr. Ellen McDonough, the computer and technology teacher at The Bailey School, Barbara Leary, librarian at The Bailey School, and Margaret Towers, reading specialist at The Bailey School, whose Saturday yard-sale excursions provided me with many books on the two princesses.

Also a thank you goes to software engineer Richard Plourde, who helped with some of the technical picture files and other computer related things.

The editing of this book was done by two women who are as competent and professional as they come. First, Dr. Glenda Ouellette, who did the rough editing and punctuation, and Arlene Robinson, whose top shelf expertise polished the text of this book like a new car in a dealer's showroom. I was truly blessed to have each of these extraordinary women involved in this project.

From my parish I give thanks to Father Leo Gagnon, whose expertise helped me tie the two princesses together spiritually. Also Larry Woodworth, a staff sportswriter for the Portland, Maine *News*, who was instrumental in coaching me in how to conduct my interviews.

Other friends who were there with their support and encouragement throughout this undertaking are: Eleanor Otis, William Mullen, Rita Roper, Helen Noone, Charles and Rita Malmsten, Peter and Mary Karalekas, as well as my cousin Carol Rowehl and her husband John Kahler.

I must also thank my primary care physician, Dr. William Jackson and my urologist, Dr. James Shula. Without their care for me through the dark days of my disease, I would not have been able to pull myself together and face the struggles of interstitial cystitis.

Finally I must thank my family of which I am so proud. My daughter, Kelly, and her husband, Dr. Michael Francoeur, along with their two children, Christopher and Kaylin; my son Keith Clark, who passed the tests of Parris Island and served proudly as a United States Marine for five years and now works at the American Embassy in Berlin, Germany along with his wife, Katja. My parents, Gerdi and Elsie Noa, whose unconditional love made me the man I am today. And finally to my wife, Cheryl, who has seen me through my own triumphs and trials with the love and devotion she shows me each day. All of these people have been instrumental as I walk my faith journey with the Father, Son and Holy Spirit by my side and within me. They have all made my life the gift I am forever grateful for.

Table of Contents

Introduction

It is mid-August 1997, and the summer heat of Northeastern Massachusetts has taken a break. Dog days of 90-plus degree temperatures dry the landscape, parching lawns and flowerbeds thirsting for the steady rains and waning sun of September. The cooling atmosphere brings back the full color and stature of the gardens and grounds, just briefly, before the cold winds put each parcel to sleep.

The deep green luster of the spring's blades of grass now shows tarnished amber from these days of inferno. Flexible emerald lawns brought by the warm May rains now crackle and crunch with each step. Footprints that once disappeared in an instant from the once supple turf now slowly strain their way back to conform to the other blades of grass surrounding them. Children run and play while gusts of wind send dust clouds through the air of arid ball fields and playgrounds.

The steady drops pattering on the roof of my house set a perfect backdrop for my next read—a biography about the beautiful movie star who left the world and homeland she knew to become a princess. *Grace*, by Robert Lacey, became my focus for the next several days. From the first few chapters I read that day, more pages, information and details rolled along from my shady lakeside spot like the soft waves hitting the shore. For the next four years I would become totally enthralled in Grace Kelly's life, as well as the life of another princess.

A dire, world-moving event set my undertaking in motion. On August 30, 1997, a speeding car entered a tunnel of death. With unyielding force, it crashed head-on into a square pillar that ended the life of "the people's princess" whose stature set new standards by which women will be measured, just as a similar tragedy had taken Grace Kelly's life fifteen years before. So moved was I by the circumstances surrounding each of their lives that I wrote an editorial conveying my feelings for these two extraordinary idols. Even before the column was published, my decision to write this book was made.

Similarities and differences abound between these two breathtaking princesses who captivated the world in the second half of the twentieth century. Although they grew up in different environments, cultures, and eras, their status reached a level that few celebrities or heads of state could compare to. Diverse in some ways and similar in so many, the magnitude with which their charm and decorum influenced the people of two separate continents was astounding. Their lives mirrored each other's, both personally and professionally, in the experiences they encountered. It was as if their destiny, and even their fate was the work of a power higher than themselves. In agreement with designer Oleg Cassini, who loved—and lost—one of them, "Fate does not provide such a coincidence in life without reason."

Their style and glamour effortlessly gained recognition in the fast paced, technologically modern media. They drew praise, compliments, and adoration. But above all else, they drew attention. At their peak of popularity, the attention they drew became a chronic annoyance for one of them and a life-ending tragedy for the other.

Grace Kelly and Diana Spencer's public personas were role models and fantasy-ideals for both men and women. Each having all the riches and rewards life had to offer, at times their lifestyles were perceived as utopias. Envious women in each hemisphere, whether well off or struggling, couldn't help but admire the ideal balance of career and motherhood each seemed to accomplish.

This was not the total picture, however. Like anyone made of flesh and blood, they had their crosses to bear. The two lives were not lived in a never-ending state of Eden; Grace and Diana had more than their fair share of problems, both personal and professional, which plagued them throughout their lives. Periods of melancholy invaded and, at times, overran the tranquil peace each hoped for. Yet these challenges, as grave and lonely as any misfortunes in life, built strong characters that cleared many hurdles.

Their similarities continued in their charitable works. Always purposeful in their actions, they poured their hearts and souls into many projects and enterprises with an abundance of energy. The motivation with which they pursued these interests helped soothe them therapeutically, even as they gave back to those less fortunate. Those traits were building blocks for the legacy each left behind.

This, too, is where the media had its lone positive effect on each icon's life. The media's negative side, however, seemed to be as cold and cruel as an abusive parent. The double-edged sword of fame is razor sharp on the side of privacy invasions, and becomes a piercing intrusion on the celebrated victim's life. These wounds test the will, character, and patience of all those who gain notoriety, infiltrating every aspect of the existence of all those whose stature places them in the limelight.

By the end of the last millennium, this media scrutiny had evolved to such a degree that those who pursued the rich and famous would go to any lengths to gain monetary rewards of collecting—or creating— tales of celebrities: stories and pictures, written or on film, had become a lucrative industry unto itself. More than at any time in the history of mankind, privacy invasions unfailingly accompanied fame and glory. Many famous people were not ready for the immense melees and temptations fame incurred. This led to the self-destruction of many who couldn't deal with media's overwhelming persistence.

Like other bigger-than-life celebrities, these women waged a never-ending battle to try to keep a stable balance with the media. Grace Kelly was able to control this better early in her stardom. Later on however, she succumbed to one of the prime temptations of celebrity status, that being several torrid romances and love affairs. These were the beginning of various torments she was to experience throughout her film career, marriage, and even into the lives of her children.

Diana Spencer, from the onset of notoriety, was a steadfast prey for the media. The shy, innocently coy girl, barely out of her teens, became the single most sought-after personality ever. Diana surpassed any and all before her. The age of technology and media tabloids, consumed with the monetary rewards that a single camera shot brought, engulfed her endlessly until tragedy ended her life.

This book will show the many comparisons and contrasts between these two phenomenal women. Although they shared only a few precious moments with each other during their lifetimes, they formed a special bond due to the similar lives they led, with all their highs and lows, as well as the tenderness, compassion, and empathy each gave our world. Through my research I was overwhelmed by how many of the dramas Grace and Diana lived that could be identified with the other. Every aspect of their styles and strong characters, as well as their vulnerabilities, showed a human quality that transposed each of them beyond any normal assessment. The trials and triumphs that each of these striking, effervescent, hopeless romantics endured throughout their lives will be studied frequently in coming generations. *Two Princesses* will show the many roles each experienced, such as strolling down an avenue, displaying glamour and appeal with the stunning gifts of radiance God generously bestowed on them, or comforting a downtrodden member of society. In either light, they moved the world with a purposeful and determined direction.

The poignant way each of them suffered at times showed the reality that fairy tales are reserved for the pages of books and the imaginations of children. Grace Kelly and Diana Spencer lived their lives in spotlights few know while going through this world. They loved and were loved. They hurt and were hurt; they ran a wide-ranging span of emotions, finally surrendering to the hand Fate can cruelly impose at any given moment in life.

Chapter I - They'd Only Just Begun

Little girls they laugh and sing
Little girls will always bring
Joy and fun from near and far
With several moments as shining stars.
Sometimes sad and sometimes hurt
The sorrow fades when comfort lurks,
But thank heavens as they grow
The things they seek will always show
A pride enriched from where they came
From lessons learned and love sustained.
Imaginations that dream of days
Of glory, fame and shining rays;
For children know this beginning of life
Has so much promise to reach new heights.
KJN

Both Grace Kelly and Diana Spencer had happy, normal childhoods through the formative stages of infancy to early primary school. Like all healthy toddlers, they were playful, curious, happy—two bundles of energy. Each came from affluent families, and both girls grew up in large homes showing off extravagant decors: stately dwellings detailing the artifacts, treasures, and affluence of the Kellys and the Spencers.

Diana was nurtured by her sisters from the beginning. One of the Spencers' maids said, "Sarah and Jane loved their baby sister, and treated her as if she were their own living doll until they were sent away to boarding school six years later."

Their homes provided an abundance of space to explore while exhibiting the sheer joy and pleasure of their early stages of life, their feet moving little bodies in the pace and rhythm essential to growth and development, their imaginations choreographing the free-flowing motions that are second nature to babies and toddlers.

More important though, each girl had one critical ingredient that is vital to early childhood: love. The two girls' nuclear families were stable until each of them reached school age. At that time, while Grace's family remained intact, Diana's would separate.

1

Grace Kelly was born in Philadelphia on November 12, 1929. She grew up in a beautiful section of the city called Germantown. Pride beams from this neighborhood, whose tree-lined streets are decorated with a variety of hardwoods and evergreen trees. A collage of shrubs, ivy, and other foliage set a backdrop for the brick- and stone-faced homes set well back from the roads and sidewalks.

The pride each resident feels for the neighborhood Grace Kelly grew up in was proven to me by my first glimpse at 3901 Henry Avenue. When I asked a passer-by if this was Grace Kelly's former home, she answered "Yes" but offered no more. Her simple answer was spoken with conviction in this corner of the "City of Brotherly Love," where this hidden suburb, away from downtown Philadelphia, is a quiet haven for those who dwell there.

The former Kelly home is one of a number of large houses on the busy Henry Avenue. The house is somewhat rundown now and in need of a good going-over. However, in the Kellys' glory days, it was one of the grandest homes in Philadelphia. Grace's father, John (Jack) Kelly had the three story red-brick home constructed as a symbol of his success, and his intent is still clearly demonstrated in this handsome edifice. Standing at a high point on a large corner lot, the regal house is preceded by an extensive front yard. Ivy groundcover, along with seasonal flowering and evergreen shrubs, take up a large portion of the square landscape, accented by a cherry blossom tree, which was in full bloom during my visit in the third week of April 1999.

The house is designed symmetrically, with each side mirroring the other. To the left and right of the second floor, two identical walkout porches extend beyond the chimneys, and two round-routered pillars support the colonial-style front entrance. The copper entrance roof shows a green patina from years of weathering. Six-over-six double-hung windows sit on large, thick sills, their white casings and sash accented by black shutters on each side. The steeply pitched slate shingled roof exhibits three dormers equidistant from one another.

The large backyard features a three-car garage and more varied foliage. Here, Grace and her siblings played games, and grew flowers and vegetables with their mother. The tilling and cultivating in the backyard of her childhood home would lead to Grace's lifelong love of flowers and gardening—so much so that, as Princess Grace, she would become one of Monaco's authorities on floral design.

♛ ♛

Diana Spencer was born on July 1, 1961 at Park House, which is located on the Royal Family's Sandringham Estate in England. Diana was not totally English; she had Irish ancestry and affluence on her mother's side of her family. Diana's grandmother, Ruth Gill, had come from one of the richest families in Ireland and, in centuries past, raising sheep had been quite lucrative for Diana's Irish ancestors.

♛ ♛

As the two girls reached school age, problems arose that would have a profound influence on each. Grace's parents remained together throughout their lives. Diana was not as fortunate. In 1967, the love, warmth, and security of a stable family for Diana and her siblings were broken when her parents went their separate ways. She was to experience a trial far too many children have had to endure over the last few decades of the twentieth century: divorce. The breakup of her family would wound her deeply, and she carried the scars left behind into adulthood.

The two princesses' fathers were very diverse. Jack Kelly was a champion athlete and stoic Irishman, a rock-solid, competitive individual who had made his fortune with sweat and manual labor. Grace's grandfather, John Henry Kelly, emigrated from Ireland in 1867. He married Mary Costello in Vermont before settling in Philadelphia. Mary Kelly became the driving force in her family, and was the one who motivated her sons to strive for a better life.

Jack Kelly began working at Dobson's Mill at the age of nine. Later, his brother Patrick managed to raise enough money to start his own construction company, and Jack then went to work in what was to become the family business. A bricklayer by trade, Jack helped mold the family company into a successful enterprise during the later stages of the Industrial Revolution.

Each day after work, the athletic young man would go down to the Schuylkill River and practice his passion: rowing. His chiseled frame exhibited a chest, shoulders, and arms that pulled and stroked oars with unyielding precision. According to an article published in *Yankee Magazine* about rowing, "When the oars come up out of the water and turn 'palms up,' flat, facing heaven, it seems in the brief pause like a prayer, an offering, a supplication." In concert with this description of the sport, Jack's domineering personality and athletic talent propelled him to win a gold medal for America as a champion single scull rower in the 1920 Olympic Games.

He was a man who expected orders followed when given, and with his Irish ancestry, made no bones about his lack of respect for royalty or Englishmen in general. These feelings were deeply rooted in his knowledge of the suffering and plight of Irish immigrants who had to leave their homeland because of the famine and tyranny imposed upon them, where for decades families starved in the lanes of Irish cities, with those lucky enough seeking hope, opportunity, and salvation in America. This knowledge left its mark on him; people in the arts or those who had not earned their wealth themselves definitely took a backseat in his view.

His loathing of the British was extreme, perhaps partly because he had been excluded from the Henley-On-Thames Regatta (a British rowing competition for the elite and wealthy) in 1919. Jack Kelly was to have his day, though. Upon winning the Gold Medal in 1920, he sent the king of England his green rowing cap.

In opposing character, Diana's father, Johnnie Althorp, was a completely different kind of man from Jack Kelly. The future earl grew up in the bloodline of nobility that had passed through the centuries in Great Britain. The family was of nobility, yes; but they were of no real bloodline to any of England's royal family.

Even so, Johnnie Althorp was the country gentleman, a man of leisure. While Jack Kelly might be out estimating jobs and conferring with foremen, Johnnie Althorp would be hunting, fishing, playing cricket, or just enjoying the comforts of life. Money was never a problem, and he had no great desire to make his mark on the world in any way.

Diana's parents married young, and were very much in love during the early years of their marriage. However, her mother,

Frances, wanted more out of life emotionally, socially and creatively. Even after bearing four children, she was still a radiant, active young woman, and boredom finally drove an inevitable wedge between them, and they drifted apart. Eventually, Frances' social circle found the heart of another man more to her lifestyle. His name was Peter Shand-Kydd. Although their affair was kept under lock and key for a time, it was eventually uncovered.

At first, Diana's parents only separated, but their parting began the inevitable stages of upheaval and anger. Diana and her younger brother, Charles, who was only five, left home with their mother and moved to London. Here began a short term of peace and normalcy, which was only to last until Christmas. Then the fuse reached the powder keg.

On bringing the two youngest children home to spend the holidays with their father and their two older sisters, Diana's father refused to let her mother return Diana and her brother, Charles, to London. So here now were two young children, separated from their primary nurturer and caregiver. Naturally, like so many other innocent children put into this situation each and every day, behavioral changes became apparent.

This was only the beginning of the four children's separation from their mother. Frances' mother, Ruth, in an outrageous display of erroneous tradition, sided with Johnnie. This stacked the royal deck against Frances, since Ruth was closely connected to the royal family, and was also a very close friend of the queen mother. As a consequence, Frances lost custody in the final divorce decree; in effect, motherhood lost to the politics of British royalty, thus proving that in England as well as America comedienne Lenny Bruce was right: "In the halls of justice, there is only justice in the halls."

So at the age of seven, Diana's life became part of the shuffled and entangled world of a broken family. She was never to suffer the financial difficulties so many children do as the innocent victims of divorce, but the emotional burdens were hellish. Those, no amount of money can repair.

In interviews conducted by Andrew Morton before her divorce, Diana told of the dark periods in her childhood, when she and her siblings gave many of their nannies a rough time. Also, like so many

5

young children of divorce, the constant shuffle between parents was confusing, entangling and frustrating for everyone.

As Diana's nuclear family eroded like a stormy coastline, Grace Kelly's remained as solid as New Hampshire granite. A strict Catholic upbringing was the order of business for Grace's early life. Her mother, Margaret, who became better known as "Ma Kelly," was like most American women of her era: firmly in charge of her household, a regimented German American who, like her husband, had the enduring competitive streak that gave their family its stoic character. A very attractive woman, Ma Kelly was also both practical and frugal. Knitting and gardening were two of the many positive activities she taught her girls. Grace, who fell in love with flowers as a child, would accompany her sisters in clipping the neighbors' flowers and selling them for their mother's charity.

Margaret Kelly was raised a Lutheran, but converted to Catholicism when she married. Before her marriage, she was a physical education teacher and competitive swimmer, two extremely strong disciplines. As a physical education teacher and former swimming coach myself, I can assure you Margaret Kelly's adolescence and young adult life was filled with a persistent drive. In the era where male chauvinism was still the rule, Margaret Majer Kelly became the first woman to ever teach physical education at Temple University. Athletics, especially single scull rowing or swimming, have no shortcuts. Whoever touches the wall or crosses the finish line first wins the race. If an athlete fails to train to their potential, it will show at the sound of the starter's pistol. The individual athletics of Jack and Margaret Kelly created an infrastructure that ran an upper-middleclass American home with discipline and strict values.

Not that Henry Avenue was a utopia. Jack and Margaret Kelly were very overbearing and inflexible. Margaret Kelly's thriftiness went a bit overboard. Even with the substantial amount of income her family had, Grace at times wore hand-me-downs. Their parents' characteristics would affect Grace and her brother Kel a great deal as they grew up.

Of the three girls, Grace's sister Peggy was their father's favorite. The affectionate "Baba," as Jack called his oldest child, was lavished with praise and compliments regularly. In contrast, Grace was the meekest of all the Kelly children. Her nose ran a great deal in childhood, too, causing her parents and other adults to question her fortitude. She would prove them all wrong later on.

Although the Kelly family framework allowed Grace and her other siblings to feel safe and secure, it restricted the freedom and creativity all growing children yearn for. This was one of the many obstacles Grace had to overcome in her rise to stardom. In certain ways she was fragile, struggling with childhood asthma at times. In other respects though, she was tough as nails; during her entire childhood, she had to compete with her other siblings for her parents' love, affection, and emotional support.

Judith Quine, Grace's closest and dearest friend, knew the intimate workings and emotions of Princess Grace better than anyone. As one of many examples, Grace's gravitation toward the arts was never understood by her father, and puzzled him throughout his life. Judith related the similar feelings in her own relationship with her father as she said: "We daughters who didn't want to develop exactly as our fathers saw fit were mysteries to them. It wasn't that we weren't loved. It was just that we had chosen the wrong way, a way they couldn't understand."

Although the competitive athletic psyche of Jack Kelly couldn't grasp his middle daughter's dreams, it did instill in Grace the determination she would need to compete and strive for what she became. You do not reach the heights of stardom and acclaim Grace did without tremendous drive and tenacity. In a coincidental way, Jack Kelly provided those traits Grace needed to compete in an industry that only a select few become part of.

Grace's early education was to give her the self-control she would need to deal with the rigors of her adult life. She attended Ravenhill, a devout Catholic parochial school in Philadelphia under the direction of the Sisters of the Assumption. The school was located just up the hill from her home on Henry Avenue, across the bridge over the Schuylkill River. The beautiful campus, which has now become a small college, was kept immaculately orderly and clean by the French nuns. Down the hill from Henry Avenue, meandering toward the riverbank on Midvale Avenue stands St. Briget's, the neighborhood parish of East Falls. This is where Jack Kelly grew up. The homes, tenements, a few stores and some of the empty mills form a village which St. Briget's stands at the center of. The majestic stone exterior is a smaller replica of some of the more massive cathedrals of America and Europe, a beautiful tribute to the Catholic Church etched on the hillside, with the running waters of the Schuylkill within view. Two towers peak on each side of the facade, lowering down to the three bright red entrance doors. Intricate stained-glass windows run down each side of the building. The light gathers and shines into the church, displaying the various tributes and scenes of Christ. A gothic-style bell tower looms in the rear, rising above the steep pitched roof. Inside, the well-worn oak floor firmly holds the pews in place, and carved marble Stations of the Cross are displayed on each wall. A beautifully detailed spiral stairway leads up to the balcony. The baptismal font where Grace became a child of Christ is tucked just beyond the stairway. Marble steps lead up the grand altar, which were still surrounded by the lilies of Easter season at the time of my visit.

This is where Grace became the devout Catholic she remained her entire life: where she received the sacraments of baptism, first communion, and confirmation in her religious education classes. The French order of nuns was strict in what was expected of each girl: uniforms kept neat and orderly for each activity; white gloves and folded hands, with each girl walking to chapel in silence, genuflecting to the tabernacle and making the sign of the cross before kneeling for prayer as they pledged their devotion to Christ each day; doctrine that saw each girl through their first Eucharist, Reconciliation, and Penance as they followed the examples set by their Messiah. They were also there to learn the love and disciplines of the Trinity. As the *New Catholic Vision* stated so well:

> "Every faith journey begins with God knocking at the door of the heart ever so gently. The knock may be a spiritual hunger in the soul, a call to love in the heart, an illness that invades the body. If we open the door, God will take us by the hand and lead us into the unknown ever so gently. Then at some memorable moment God will surprise and bless us beyond our wildest dreams."

The respect and devotion for the sacrifices and forgiveness of Christ's kingdom were prioritized throughout Grace's primary education. This is where Grace became acclimated to the class and manners she showed her entire life.

Diana's early education began on the Sandringham Estate with her first governess and nanny, Gertrude Allen. Learning in a small group of five or six children encompassed the traditional way on the royal estate. But this all changed when her parents divorced. While living with her mother in London (before her father gained custody), she attended school there. After gaining custody, her father sent her to the Silfield School at King's Lynn. She remained there for two years, until her parents' divorce was final.

The nuns who taught Grace, as well as the teachers who educated Diana, found them average students. Grace seemed better adjusted though, which was logical under their circumstances. Even so, the world of fantasy and make-believe became a refuge for each of them. In their own little worlds, they spent many hours in their rooms: Grace setting up her dolls with the calling of the stage and fame; Diana seeking comfort from all the stuffed animals she cherished that would mold the unyielding love she showed to the unfortunate throughout her life. Unquestionably, the hearts of these two girls synthesized and furnished a devotion that in turn fostered a compassion culminating in the way they touched people throughout their lives.

Childhood for the two future princesses was like that experienced by healthy young apple trees, with each encountering some winter storms, each set of roots firmly secure in the rich earth, and with tender, beautiful spring blossoms sending off the sweet aroma promising future fruit. Their adolescence would further promote the abundant harvest that would yield such magnificent achievements.

Even with such bright futures to come, the adolescent and teenage years of Grace and Diana were typical in most respects, filled with all the vibrant, energetic things preteens and teenage girls engage in such as fashion, makeup, mirror-time and boys—schoolgirl thoughts that flashed across the mind in a never-ending sequence of activities, projects and endeavors.

Naturally, some awkward moments came where puberty told each that womanhood was just around the corner, as maturity slowly but surely set its course. This is where the characters and personalities of each of them began to incubate for what was to come later on. They didn't know what lay ahead for them, but those years continued building the skyscraper each would become.

In 1969, Diana's parents' divorce became final. Shortly after this, Diana's mother, Francis, and Peter Shand-Kydd, were married. The harsh changes in Diana's early life had some effect on her, as she admitted later on, but she made the necessary, painful adjustments and went on with her youth.

In 1970, a year-and-a-half after her parents' divorce became final, Diana was sent to Riddlesworth, a boarding school in Norfolk with a reputation for stressing academics and giving each girl preparedness for the future. Like many aristocratic offspring, although Diana was by no means a scholar, the rules, regulations, and traditions of a regal education always influence the quality of aristocratic values. Diana's priorities were not academic; athletics and socialization took precedence over textbooks and studies. However, romance novels always churned the fervent hormones of the future Princess of Wales.

The two future world-renowned icons differed somewhat during their teen years. They each had their friends and schoolmates, including the occasional innocent romantic attraction, but Grace's beauty was evident from the minute she reached puberty. Diana, like many others, did not have profound or striking beauty as a teen. Her beauty was to grow with age, with each year bringing more radiance and sex appeal. In spite of Grace's early blooming, emotional insecurities ran through both girls' minds. Grace always craved the affection and warmth that her parents never committed to. Jack Kelly gravitated towards his son, to the point where he made the crucial mistake so many fathers make of trying to live their lives through their sons. His main goal was to make Kel an Olympic champion, as he had been. To that end, Jack Kelly pushed Kel until the goal was obtained. This was to have catastrophic consequences for Kel later on. Added to this was how Jack's single-minded determination affected the girls emotionally, especially Grace. Her father's neglect of her interests would carry a psychological consequence for her.

Diana's emotional problems also carried over from her childhood. Diana's early teen years were emotionally disorganized; the constant shuffling back and forth between home and boarding school kept her on an emotional roller coaster. On the few occasions she did get to come home, the comfort and security she gained there were banished at the end of holidays when her father returned her to school. Some of these became traumatic scenes, with Diana pleading and begging her father not to send her back. Loneliness cast a shadow over Diana while growing up that never completely ebbed, and carried on throughout most of her life. Like those of notoriety before her, the popularity she eventually achieved brought a dark side that forced her to retreat into a vacuum, making her sense of isolation worse.

Like many in early adolescence, she wandered emotionally. This would change, however; Diana's growth and development brought her both pleasure and pain, a natural stage for the future princess in the journey she traveled. All was not doom and dread in her adolescence, though. In fact, there were many happy times for Grace and Diana both. They were teenage girls, after all, and fun (and a bit of mischief) went along with being energetic young ladies. Grace was more outgoing. However, the shy Diana had her escapades as well.

Along with fun times, Grace learned that hard work and diligence were vital characteristics for success. Things that interested her were given priority status and labored at until her goals were achieved. This is where her burning desire for the theater began to kindle. From the beginning, acting and dancing were labors of love for the beautiful teenager. She made a full commitment to each role she was chosen for, and was always punctual. Even though she was given little encouragement from her family to pursue her dreams, she never wavered. Lines and scripts were in her blood, calling and beckoning from both the stage and the audience.

With bounding energy and talent during high school, Grace played successful leads in *The Taming of the Shrew* and *Peter Pan*. Her focus here pinpointed the way toward what was to become her first career.

At about the same age, Diana seemed destined to flounder and flip, somewhat like a freshly caught fish on a boat deck. Worthy of note, Diana and Grace shared a talent and love of dancing, especially ballet. With all the mixed-up topsy-turvy emotions so prevalent in Diana's adolescence, ballet was a constant passion that became a lifelong love. She truly loved ballet. Even more, she had real affinity for the dance. Ballet was an emotional and therapeutic release for her; the physical movements, rising heartbeat, respiration, perspiration and endorphin levels eased the pain and calmed the nerves of her fragile psyche. A career in ballet was out of the question, though—at five-foot-ten, Diana was much too tall to pursue the dream of being a professional dancer.

Because of their academic weaknesses, neither future princess was destined for college or university. This was to play a pivotal role for both of them.

Although Grace received a disciplined and well-rounded education at both Ravenhill and the Stevens School, she was weak in mathematics. She wanted to attend Bennington College in Vermont and study dancing; however, she was refused admittance because of her weakness in math. But the beautiful young woman was undeterred, and with the influence of her Uncle George, an accomplished writer and actor, she was able to get an audition at the American Academy of Dramatic Arts in Manhattan, New York. As her entrance audition, Grace read from her Uncle George's play, *The Torch Bearers.* She was accepted into the academy and, even though their attitude was indifferent, her parents agreed to send her. Her father's reservations were matched by her mother's cavalier demeanor. Ma Kelly placated her husband with the philosophy of letting Grace get her lofty dreams out of her system. In fact, Ma Kelly was confident that her daughter would be back at Henry Avenue, safe at home, in a couple of weeks.

This was by far the greatest underestimation Mrs. Kelly would make of the sniffling little girl who was to prove herself a potent adversary in the pursuit of her dreams. And so the City That Never Sleeps would admit another candidate who would someday grow into one of the most renowned women of the twentieth century.

Diana's time at Riddlesworth went along at an even keel. Not accomplishing anything extraordinary, along with her proficiency in ballet, she also excelled in swimming, which was to become another refuge from the demons that plagued her for so long. It was here that her love of children and compassion for the underdog became a permanent attribute of her character, and these helped shape a self-image that would lead to the grace and style she exhibited later on. Fiercely competitive, she found a direction and sense of accomplishment in the sports and arts she enjoyed. All these things began weaving together to form the looks, personality, and charm of the future Princess of Wales.

Diana, like Grace, never had to worry about anything financial while growing up. Even so, her broken family encountered many other upheavals. The biggest of these was the arrival of a stepmother into the lives of the Spencer children. In the early 1970s, Diana's father began a relationship with Raines Cartland. None of the children took to her at all, especially Sarah and Jane. As expected, there were many confrontations involving rude behavior and rejection. Raines had a forceful, "takeover" personality that turned Diana and her siblings off completely. Without much success, their father tried to keep peace, but like so many other broken families, the coming of a replacement parent became a no-win situation. Boarding school for the three girls then became a cease-fire for some of the volatile situation.

In 1975, just before Diana turned fourteen, Diana's grandfather died and her father became heir to the family's estate at Althorp, as well as inheriting his grandfather's title. This was another change Diana and her siblings had to adjust to; they were used to their home at Park House. The transition might have been easier on the children had Raines not been in the picture; however, like it or not, Althorp was to become the family home, and their father the new Earl Spencer. For Diana, Althorp would become the final sanctuary after fate's cruelty ended her life.

At fourteen, Diana followed in the footsteps of Sarah and Jane by entering the West Heath School. As at Riddlesworth, Diana did not excel academically. Again though, the seeds of the mark she was to make on the world were sprouting. The headmistress at West Heath, Ruth Rude, recalled how Diana spent many hours helping and working with the handicapped children of West Heath. Overall, West Heath held many fond memories for Diana. Work that consumed her time and kept her busy (as well as some normal teenage pranks and antics), and gave her an adequate secondary education.

After failing her O-exams twice, which dashed any hopes of higher education, Diana talked her father into letting her attend finishing school at Institute Alpin Videmanette in Switzerland. The school did not stress academics, so she was relieved of the pressures of subjects she didn't like. There are conflicting views as to why Diana left finishing school after only one term. Some authors claim she was homesick. Even so, the headmistress of Institute Alpin Videmanette, Heidi Yersin, said Diana was never homesick and enjoyed her stay, even though it was brief. Instead, she only registered for one term to fill in the remaining school year after failing her O-exams.

This was the time when Diana began the infatuation with her sister Sarah's boyfriend Charles, the Prince of Wales. Although she had admired him for some time and saw him when he was invited to Althorp for shooting, admiration and longing for the royal life were now beginning to take hold in Diana.

Grace Kelly and Diana Spencer's adolescences were building blocks for what the future would hold for them. Here, in the years spent between anticipation and anxiety, they struck the chords that would play the melodies of their lives. The youths each experienced many vibrant adventures, as well as some doldrumed plights. Along the way, the journey was molding them with the elegance they would eventually display to the world. The foundations and framing were complete. Mitering the precise finished work would come quicker for Grace. However, when completed, Diana's display would show more beautifully than any seen before.

Chapter II – Different Roads Traveled

At the end of their secondary educations, Grace and Diana's lives went in different directions. There was a little more than a year's difference in their ages as they embarked into the working world.

Diana, with no real formal training, became employed in a series of what would now be called entry-level jobs. These included being a mother's helper, and cleaning houses. Although these were jobs for women without advanced educations, Diana performed them well. She was always excellent with children and, as she progressed through her destiny, it became one of the focal points in her life. She had thoughts of becoming a dance teacher, but gave up that idea. Again, like so many other young adults, she was wandering and traversing through an unknown path, living an ordinary existence with no true direction or goals, until fate would knock with sledgehammer force.

Grace Kelly's path to success was something to admire. Even though she was never given encouragement to pursue her dreams, this did not dissuade her in the least. Her parents sent her off to New York, much like Diana's parents had sent her to Switzerland. The outcome, though, would be completely different.

👑 👑

After being accepted, Grace entered The American Academy of Dramatic Arts in the fall of 1947. The Academy, considered top-shelf in all of its training and disciplines, fed right into the years of persistent regiments Grace had received from her Catholic schooling. Here, young aspiring actors and actresses found out quickly if they had the talent, patience, and willpower to make it in the highly competitive world of entertainment.

New York City became Grace's second hometown. But more than that, as the years went by New York would be the site of some of her fondest memories. From the moment she arrived in New York as a young woman, an electric exhilaration sent surges of current through her entire being. Even more than her training and eventual stardom, New York's limelight and glitter became the fruits and rewards Grace enjoyed, and the roots she set so firmly in Manhattan in the early

1950's stayed with her the rest of her life, becoming a part of the girl from Germantown that she freely accepted and relished—an endowment for the first of many legacies she would leave in this and other world-class cities.

The life force behind the Academy was Charles Jehlinger, a white-haired, passionate man who demanded nothing short of excellence from his students. Just like the famed coaches Bear Bryant and John Wooden, the students were taught that constant drilling and repetition were the fundamentals that lead to achievement. As with the pursuit of excellence in athletics, inspiration and perspiration went hand-in-hand in all endeavors involving the theater and acting.

To reach the pinnacle of any career involves talent, a bit of luck, discipline, patience, and hard work. No one is successful unless all of the ingredients are in the recipe. From Marjorie Rawlings to Bill Gates, greatness is achieved by talent and actions. Grace Kelly's talents were within her, and this is where they would be nurtured.

She was up to the task. In fact, Grace loved the Academy. The discipline and structure were no problem for her. In fact, they enhanced and optimized the learning and techniques she would acquire. She was determined that she was not going to be "just another pretty face," and here in New York her skills were crafted like a fine jewel until ready for display. To create the legendary voice, walk, and allure that would envelope stage and screen, she put forth endless efforts to detail. Her effort yielded phenomenal success; throughout Grace's career her charm and sophistication, which became two of her trademarks, were equal to any other starlet of the era.

It was during this period in both women's lives that even more similarities—and differences—became evident. Photographers' cameras immediately focused on both Grace and Diana when their notoriety became evident. While Diana's beauty grew slowly, like first-year roses climbing an arbor, with Grace the photo-attraction was immediate. This is understandable, since even in her teens, Grace had the more mature look, with skin as smooth as freshly troweled plaster canvassing the other beautiful features of her sensual face. Her large, piercing-blue eyes, perfectly shaped nose, and assiduously formed cheekbones and jaw line complemented a smile either brightly beaming, coy, or provocative, which could even further arouse male hormones with a glancing profile. That seductive expression, engaging in intrigue with closed enticing lips, completed a portrait that was one in a billon.

While Diana was still tied to her trust fund and her parents' financial support, Grace was becoming more independent financially. Grace Kelly's career got a jumpstart when a friend of Grace's, Carolyn Scott (who would eventually become one of her bridesmaids), got her started in modeling. Grace was a natural, and was soon making good money while gaining experience. Yet most of her modeling jobs were for products, not fashion; agencies never had any notions of making her a runway giant. This was fine with Grace, however—she had her eyes firmly set on the stage and screen.

Financial independence gave Grace Kelly a deep sense of freedom and self-respect, even though her strict upbringing left an emotional bondage on her that she was never able to completely untie. In spite of that, gaining financial independence so young in life gave her a base she was able to work from in dealing with the world. Her parents were always going to be lurking in the background with anything to do with her personal life. However, that early success gave her the resilience she needed to meet and present herself to those in the thoroughly competitive world of show business.

It was clear that standing on her own two feet wasn't something she would have any trouble doing. Not that this was an instant ticket to the gates of any picture studio. Like any other candidate, Grace had to prove her ability and take some lumps.

👑 👑

Diana's task was different. To her, employment was merely a stepping-stone to achieving her ambition to become the Princess of Wales. Yet even though Diana's parents controlled her finances, they were not overbearing. For Diana, luck, intuition and opportunity would bring all her desires to reality.

Not wanting to return to return to Althorp and avoid the scenes created by her stepmother Raines, Diana followed Sarah and Jane to

London. This was Diana, pure and simple. The stores, theaters, and pubs brought energy and life to the young woman who belonged to the city.

Diana lived with her mother in London before venturing out on her own. There was money available in a trust left to Diana by her great-grandmother. With her mother's help, Diana bought an apartment in West London. As for basic living expenses, many well-to-do London mothers were continually searching for nannies. This suited Diana just fine, as she was so good with children.

To better understand Diana's pre-royal living environment, I visited the area where she had her apartment. Colhere Court is located off Old Brompton Road in the Southwest 5th section of London, a fairly affluent residential neighborhood where the buildings all resemble each other. Tree-lined sidewalks garnish the brick and sandstone exteriors, and the black iron rail balconies that would soon become notorious were set out from each flat. The small alley to the left of the building was where Diana parked her small car. This alley would become the battleground between Diana and the paparazzi each day after her romance with Charles was discovered, when she would be attacked by cameras and microphones.

But that would come later. For now, here is where Diana and four of her friends led the single life, bicycling to and fro around the busy streets, gathering a circle of acquaintances for evening social events. Dinner parties, movies, and the theater kept the regal young lady vibrant and content.

In spite of her early self-assurance to the contrary, a suitable career was a different and difficult nut to crack in London, especially with no formal or specific training. Diana didn't want to make a career of being a nanny so, with her love of ballet, she enrolled at the Betty Vancani School of Dance—not to become a dancer, but to learn to teach dancing. Her hopes to teach dance were dashed when she was injured while skiing. As Andrew Morton recounted in his book about her life, "Diana fell badly on the ski slopes, tearing all the tendons in her left ankle. For three months she was in and out of plaster as the tendons slowly healed."

After this setback, Diana found a position as a helper at the Young England Kindergarten. She was very competent in this environment; her natural compassion and tenderness were keys to the success she displayed with children. Later, she exhibited those same qualities when the curtain rose to her new audience—the world.

♛· ♛

While Grace Kelly would never attain total independence in her life, her second and final year at the American Academy of Dramatic Art was very productive for her. Her own hard work combined with the skilled teaching found there had carefully molded her into the distinguished actress she was to become. All that was required was the polish every professional needs to begin their career.

Before graduation, and chosen out of all the underclassmen at the Academy, she played the lead in *Philadelphia Story*. Here would also began the many confrontations Grace would have with her parents over her many boyfriends. Grace's parents were overbearing, overprotective, and bold. They did not mince words with anyone, and gave each boyfriend of Grace's the bottom line very quickly: their standards for their daughter's friends were high, and none of her boyfriends was likely to ever meet them.

Grace's first boyfriend at the Academy was Mark Miller. He and Grace were sweethearts who had fun and enjoyed each other. They also helped each other with their studies, particularly their vocal training.

Don Richardson, one of the teachers at the Academy, became involved with Grace during her second year. Like most women, when Grace and Diana fell in love with someone, they pledged their hearts. And so Don Richardson became the first true love of Grace Kelly's life.

When Grace finally introduced Richardson to her parents, they made every effort to destroy the relationship; Don Richardson was Jewish, and also several years older than Grace—a complete no-no in the devoutly Catholic Kelly clan.

On a weekend visit home to Henry Avenue, Grace's mother went as far as to search through Mr. Richardson's luggage to see what evidence she could come up with of how serious the romance was. When love letters and condoms were found by Grace's mother, her livid parents attacked full-force. Mr. Richardson, who had been staying for the weekend, was ordered out, and Grace's punishment was what we would refer to today as house arrest: For the remainder of the summer she was watched like a hawk by various members of her family at their summer house in Ocean City, New Jersey. She bristled at this level of control, but managed to remain loyal and obedient nonetheless. In the end, her parents' law was always obeyed.

This scenario was to play itself out many other times during Grace's acting career. Throughout her twenties, Grace would have torrid affairs with many rich and famous men. A few times she came within a whisker's width of marriage. In the end though, clearer-thinking impending grooms, her parents, or Grace herself would think better of this. Even when she lost, Grace gained much; with the hurt came fond memories, and her romantic wounds eventually healed—at least, until the next one-and-only came along.

While Grace found several throngs of love by her early adulthood, Diana was content with casual, nonchalant dating. Before purchasing her flat, she had a couple of boyfriends, among them George Plumptre and Daniel Wiggins. A trip to a show or theater, with handholding and a goodnight kiss, were quite sufficient. Whether the right young man never invaded Diana's comfortable space with enough impact, or whether she was just not interested in passionate romances towards the end of her teen years is hard to say. One thing is certain, though; when the Prince of Wales asked for her heart, she gave it to him totally and without reservation.

Diana was a very attractive girl in her late teens. No more, and no less. The striking, radiant beauty would come with age. Grace Kelly however, could pass for a sophisticated woman by the end of her teen years. This is not a criticism of Diana at all. On the contrary, it was an asset. If she had not come to such a tragic end in the best years of her life, I believe her stunning looks would have stayed with her well beyond most women's, and Grace's earlier blooming beauty might have faded had she lived to an advanced age.

The different directions each princess took were due to their upbringing, fate and intuition. Grace Kelly definitely experienced a more exciting and adventurous life as a young woman. Diana would have to wait. The future Princess of Wales was fortunate to have come from affluence, or she wouldn't have been able to afford the comfortable lifestyle her salary definitely did not pay. Grace Kelly assuredly had more drive and determination early in life. For her, success was going to be achieved like a river in spring being fed by all its tributaries.

Though Grace realized financial independence at a younger age, both she and Diana were to suffer bondage that would test the will and character of each. The young women would face challenges as they entered adulthood that would bring their sanities to the edge of destruction, and their strengths and fortitudes would be challenged many times. One thing for sure, though—each of them would experience milestones that most can only comprehend through their imaginations.

Chapter III - Young Star

While Diana was living life with her flatmates and caring for children, Grace was almost completely ready to embark on her first career. She still needed some fine-tuning and good fortune to complete the package; however, these would come through and launch the girl from Philadelphia to fame and stardom.

After graduation from the American Academy of Dramatic Arts in 1949 and the disaster at her home on Henry Avenue with Don Richardson, Grace Kelly began her acting career in summer stock. Television was still in its infancy, so this is how young, aspiring actors and actresses gained experience. Socially, her family still closely watched her that summer.

When the summer ended, she was finally able to go back to New York and get an apartment of her own. Knowing her parents were always intruding into her personal life, she nevertheless worked and dated a great deal. Again, all the men she had relationships with were much older than she. Usually they had been married previously, or were separated. This was a real sore spot for her parents; her becoming involved with older divorced men really made the Catholic Jack and Margaret Kelly smolder. But this was Grace's taste in men at this point in her life. She wanted to act, and was serious about her career and her future success. She was not interested in young college men who captained athletic teams.

Perhaps, too, she was seeking a father-figure to replace the void in her heart that Jack Kelly's distance created, and made Grace find older and more worldly men attractive. In retrospect, her preference fit her mature look and personality, the allure and affinity of her image revealed years beyond her chronological age.

Although still a teenager at this point, Diana began to have ambitions and dreams of becoming a member of the royal family. She confided these visions to her flatmates, and the visits she made to various homes of the royal family reinforced her aspirations. Nevertheless, there were still a few episodes to come before Diana was propelled to her destiny.

Grace Kelly was only twenty years old when she played Broadway for the first time. It was a play called *The Father,* in which she played the role of a tormented daughter. Considering her novice status and the fact that she didn't posses the voice or stage presence necessary to make a career out of the stage, the reviews were positive.

Luckily, television was just beginning to take off, and she was able to break into its early dramas. Between 1950 and 1953, Grace played many dramatic roles on television. Some early soap operas gave Grace good experience that would help her ascend to stardom. It was as if both Grace and television were growing together, and helping each other along the way.

Her first film role happened in the summer of 1950, a very small part in a film called *Fourteen Hours.* Although her work on it only lasted a few days, it got her some recognition, and she was offered a long-term contract with MGM…which she turned down.

Her father and uncle's business and life experiences had been lessons Grace learned well, but Grace was shrewd and cunning in her own right. She wasn't going to let Hollywood trap her into controlling every facet of her life. Her refusal to commit to MGM was a risk she saw as necessary, and one she was willing to take.

Grace Kelly's first real motion picture role was with Gary Cooper in the 1952 film *High Noon.* Cooper was the focal point of the movie in both scene and dialogue, and this epic and classic black-and-white western has gone down in fame with others such as *The Man Who Shot Liberty Valance.*

Rather than a small part, Grace's role in this project was as significant as any of the other characters except Cooper's. She was lucky in that the producer was looking for a rookie. "I wanted somebody unknown to play opposite Gary Cooper," remembers Stanley Kramer. "I couldn't afford anybody else. So I signed her." So the novice actress, just getting her acting feet wet, was cast with a group of costarring screen legends like Lloyd Bridges, Otto Kruger, and Lon Chaney Jr.

The young Quaker maiden she played is torn between loyalty to her husband and the nonviolent virtues of her religion. In the end, her love of her husband prevails, and she helps him win the gun battle he cannot run away from.

Aside from her fortunate casting, other significant forces came together during Grace's first starring role. The most important of these was becoming the client of agent Jay Kanter. Jay, who was Grace's agent throughout her entire career, was an excellent advocate, and always did a thorough and competent job for Grace. They became lifelong friends.

Even though my own personal viewing causes me to think otherwise, the published reviews for Grace's role in *High Noon* were not especially good. She was good at taking criticism, however, and knew she needed further training. For this she summoned the help of acting teacher Sanford Meisner. Under his tutelage she completed additional work. Meisner was very impressed with what a good student Grace was, totally dedicated to the cause. "She had played leading roles on television. She had had success in Hollywood and had been offered a contract," Meisner was quoted as saying. "But she put it all on hold. She said she was not going back until she had studied and learned to act properly—and that was after she had spent two years at drama school." With Meisner, Grace Kelly worked diligently and fine-tuned her craft until she was ready to become the star she had always dreamed about being.

After *High Noon*, Grace was offered another long-term contract with MGM. This time she accepted, on her terms. She had learned her father's business sense well. The All-American Girl knew how to sit up straight, look into the talent director's eyes, and negotiate.

The seven-year contract landed her third billing in an MGM extravaganza called *Mogambo*. Filmed in East Africa in 1953, this film had two of Hollywood's legends at the helm—director John Ford and leading man Clark Gable. The plot, like that of so many of his movies, revolved around Gable's charm, masculinity and sex appeal. In the film, Gable owned a company that trapped some of Africa's exotic animals, which were intended to be sold to zoos or collectors.

The scenery and action shots were well done. Some scenes showed native African tribesmen collectively bringing various rich adventurers down the river to seek the wild kingdom's treasures. The tribesmen followed their leaders' commands while singing and marching in cadence.

Amid the hunts and safaris, a triangular romance occurs between Clark Gable, Ava Gardner and Grace. Gardner plays the role of a sultry woman whose red-hot lipstick, tight jeans and clinging blouses would grab any man's attention. Grace's character is that of a clean-cut, energetic young wife, thrilled about traveling to Africa. Her naive husband, played by Donald Sinden, takes ill when Grace becomes attracted to Gable. A romance ensues…until Gable realizes what pain he's causing Grace's husband. When he tells Grace it's over, she lashes out with jealousy and rejection and shoots Gable, wounding him. Grace and her husband take their leave, and Gable and Gardner reunite at the movie's ending.

The irony of *Mogambo*'s plot is that much of the story was carried out in real life between Grace and Gable. A romance between "the king of leading men" and the young, beautiful newcomer in East Africa was too tempting for the tabloids to resist, and when rumors of the romance got back to the States, Mrs. Kelly was on a plane to London, where all the final scenes of *Mogambo* were made. Once again, Ma Kelly was on a mission to get to the bottom of Grace's latest dalliance.

The invasion of Grace's mother convinced Gable to cool the relationship quickly. Grace was devastated, but it seemed to be all for the best: *Mogambo* had launched her off the springboard and into stardom. Although another romance had come and gone, the future held more roles, on-screen and in the limelight, for the rising star.

MGM's landing a long-term contract with Grace Kelly was like a free agent like Kurt Warner leading the St. Louis Rams to the Super Bowl in 2000. From that day on, other movie companies had to pay MGM to use Grace in their movies.

The year 1954 was the pinnacle of Grace's acting career. The groundwork for all the awards and honors Grace would receive came from her successes in this single year. Too, this is when Grace became a leading lady and true star. The great director Alfred Hitchcock took an instant liking to her, and cast her in some of his best pictures. The years of education and dedication really began paying off for Grace, and the world found out that Grace Kelly was not just another pretty face. Her films with Hitchcock included *Dial M for Murder*, *Rear Window*, and *To Catch A Thief.* These films were by Warner Brothers and Paramount. Therefore, being under contract with MGM, compensation had to be paid to MGM—a very lucrative set of deals for MGM.

Hitchcock was the most influential man in Grace's professional career and, like most men, was captivated by her beauty. The key, though, between Hitchcock and Grace was the perfect match between director and star. They worked as well together as any other show business partnership. "The right leading lady and," according to Hitchcock, "the most co-operative actress he ever directed came along in the person of blonde Grace Kelly."

The young Grace was in awe of the love and dedication Hitchcock brought to his art form. His energetic passion for detail encompassed not only his formidable directing, but also creating scenes and choosing colors, wardrobe and designs. Hitchcock was just as masterful in his handling of Grace, and her confidence and self-esteem grew under his tutelage. No one was sadder than Hitchcock when Grace left the silver screen behind.

Dial M for Murder was Grace's first leading role. The plot revolved around a cool but jealous husband, played by Ray Milland. Grace played Margot Wendice, his naive but adulterous wife who is the victim of her husband's plot to have her murdered. In a true cloak-and-dagger scene, the murderer bursts from behind a curtain. His hands clutch a rope around Margot's neck as a struggle ensues. Gasping for breath, Grace's character grabs a pair of scissors and plunges them into the assassin's back, killing him. Mrs. Wendice becomes the victim again in this elaborate Hitchcock plot. She is tried and convicted of the scandal. Finally, the English inspector, brilliantly played by John Williams, solves the intricate conspiracy.

Again, a romance was to evolve between Grace and the leading man. Grace and Milland fell for each other, and hard. They didn't hide the relationship well, which became a double mistake for Grace. First, Milland was not divorced, which gave Grace her initial introduction to the gossip columnists' unfavorable narrations. Second was the all-too-familiar reaction of her father. Hitting the ceiling once again, he sent Ma on another mission to put an end to the relationship. Submissive as ever, Grace obeyed her parents.

This time, however, her parents' meddling had helped her dodge a large-caliber bullet that could have caused irreparable damage to her career. Had it been years later, after the tabloids and paparazzi really came of age, her reputation would have taken a nose-dive. Even though not living together, Milland's wife was quite angry about the relationship between Grace and her husband. With her help, modern tabloids would have had a field day with Grace.

Dial M For Murder was an excellent film. Like all Hitchcock films, its plot was as intricate and elaborate as any Sherlock Holmes tale. But there was something else significant for Grace on a personal level, aside from her relationship with Milland. That was her pledge of everlasting affection for the woman who would become Grace Kelly's best friend as star, princess, wife and mother. That woman was Judith Balaban Quine.

"Judybird," as Grace would affectionately call her throughout the remainder of her life, reached an intimacy with Grace that only two women can achieve, an intimacy of closeness and companionship which never wavered, and a sorority that spanned almost thirty years until Grace's tragic death.

Judy and Grace were introduced at Judy's marriage to Grace's agent Jay Kanter. "I met Grace Kelly three years before we sailed together to Monaco for her marriage to Prince Rainier," Judith said in an interview. "It was on April 15, 1953."

Their friendship grew and evolved over the next nine months, but became an unbreakable friendship during the return train ride from the opening of *Dial M*. As a cold rain pelted on the moving train, Grace and Judy had the first of countless intimate talks, which brought both fun and a release from the pressures they shared. Nestled together a few rows away from where Jay slept, Grace pledged her love, respect and friendship to the surprised Judith. "Judybird," she said emotionally, "I'm so glad you married Jay." Grace then went on to say how she was so glad her friendship with Jay had also brought the blessing of Judith. "But with you and Jay it's *completely* different because you know how much I love Jaybird, and now I want you to know how much I *really* love you and how close I *really* feel to you as a friend—not because of Jay, but because of us."

From that moment on, the two young women formed a partnership that saw each through joyful sharing as well as heartbreaking difficulties. They were there for one another without reservation.

Of all of Grace Kelly's films, *Rear Window* was everything her charm and beauty and acting skills encompassed. The entire film is

27

set in a Greenwich Village courtyard, a microcosm hidden away in its own space among the skyscrapers. James Stewart, a freelance photographer, is laid up with a broken leg. He passes the time waiting for his leg to heal by observing life out of his rear window. Here his naked eyes, binoculars and camera examine and canvas all the goings-on in the courtyard of brownstone dwellings. At first, his viewing displays the expected mix of activity, an energetic composite of rituals and responsibilities. Young shapely legs stretch and pivot to morning music while a pulley lowers a small dog in a basket to frolic among the tenants carrying out various chores. As hours pass, each apartment and back door are filled with distinct sagas and escapades.

Hitchcock's genius is further reinforced by the way he displays Grace's beauty. For me, the timing and sequence of her entrance was scintillating. Moving from the darkness of the apartment's entrance, the single light reflects softly, warmly manifesting the elegant radiance of her alluring splendor. This was reinforced for me in an article in *In Style* magazine. The Fall 1997 article commented on Hollywood's five greatest looks. Grace's entrance in *Rear Window* made the list as she "...hovers over James Stewart, in white chiffon and pearls."

Grace's upbeat personality and stunning fashions give the film a gregarious atmosphere along with its intrigue. The plot's climax is still vintage entertainment. Only someone of Hitchcock's caliber could make a film entirely set in one location and turn it into a classic. Of all Grace's films, I thought this one should have rated in the "top one hundred" of the twentieth century. Unfortunately, the critics left it out.

Grace Kelly was now ready to embark on the best work of her career. She was given the lead in the Paramount film, *The Country Girl*. Again she was cast with one of Hollywood's superstars, William Holden. Although Holden's part was significant, the male lead was played by the immortal Bing Crosby. Like most of her other leading men, Bing, who had recently lost his wife, was infatuated with her. Also in the great crooner's favor was that he was Catholic. All the other older men Grace had fallen in love with were usually still married, separated or divorced. This is why Jack Kelly especially had interfered so much in many of Grace's relationships. The strict Catholic doctrine had to be followed with no exceptions. Remember, this was in the 1950s, when the Catholic Church was much more conservative than it is today. Bing Crosby was the one man that Jack and Ma Kelly would have approved before the prince. However, Grace didn't have the passionate fire about him she had felt for the others. So, this also wasn't to be.

The Country Girl was a straightforward film. Its black-and-white backdrop displayed the problems and despair of Grace and Bing's roles. The story line was excellent, and the triangle of William Holden, Bing Crosby and Grace Kelly created a perfect chemistry. Grace and Bing played husband and wife living in a dreary apartment resembling Jackie Gleason's coldwater flat in *The Honeymooners*. The down-on-their-luck couple is befriended by Holden, who wants to give the anxiety-ridden, alcoholic Crosby one last chance at success on the stage. Grace is thrown into the middle of Holden's pressure and Bing's panic attacks. This was not a glamorous role. Grace, through much of the movie, looked more like a recipient of fashion from the local Salvation Army. Emotions and sentiments ran the boundaries in *The Country Girl*, with failure staring each of the trio in the face. All three were exceptional in their characters.

Grace starred with William Holden again in the Korean War film, *The Bridges at Toko-Ri*. I remember my history teacher showing us this film during high school. It was the classic tale of a Navy pilot and his family during the Korean War. Grace was only twenty-four when the film was produced in 1954. This was one of the times her mature and sophisticated look added realism to the part she played. The difference in age between her and the star of the film, William Holden, could have been problematic had she not had the conservative, military-wife look she played so well. One of the most captivating scenes of Grace's career was of her standing alone on the port dock. The aircraft carrier churning towards the open sea would carry her husband to his dreaded mission. The wind from the carrier's propellers whisked her hair and coat. There was an anxious tempo in her cadence until she reached the end of the pier and waved goodbye.

Together with a fabulous supporting cast including Fredric March and Mickey Rooney, this film showed a great deal of the life and dangers aboard an aircraft carrier. With the U.S. Navy's full cooperation, the film became a success.

29

William Holden was one of Hollywood's major leading men. William Holden was also one of Hollywood's thoroughbreds. Holden was talented, handsome, and distinguished, and Grace naturally was attracted to him, as he was to her, so a serious relationship between Holden and Grace ensued during the production of the *Bridges at Toko-Ri*. Again though, Jack Kelly's protective covenant eroded the relationship. Yet had it not been for the hawk-like patrol of her parents, always on guard duty for their famous daughter, Grace would never have become Princess of Monaco. She surely would have married one of the many men she fell in love with.

During her relationship with Holden, Grace repeated the mistake she had made with Don Richardson. William Holden, like Ray Milland, was a married man. Yet once again, she brought Holden home to Henry Avenue. This time the confrontation between Holden and Jack Kelly resembled a battle of gladiators in the Roman Coliseum. The non-Catholic, married Holden and the old man had a real go-around. In short, Holden's experience on Henry Avenue was in complete contrast to the hospitality Su-Yen's family displayed in another William Holden classic, *Love Is A Many Splendored Thing*.

During my research, I found one other interesting aspect of the relationship between Grace and Holden. Before his relationship with Grace, Holden had a serious romantic relationship with Audrey Hepburn. Hepburn and Holden fell madly in love during the filming of *Sabrina*. Hepburn wanted to marry Holden until he confessed to her he could not have children. "But I can't start a new family," Holden told Audrey, "I've had a vasectomy." I cannot believe that the Catholic Grace Kelly would have ever wed a man who could not give her children, either, and cannot comprehend what else she could have expected her parents' reaction to be.

Yet no matter what other factors may have influenced the outcome of this relationship, once more, Grace was reduced to tears. Finally, Holden, like all the others, knew it was hopeless and ended the relationship.

The year 1955 was a culmination year for Grace Kelly, a pinnacle not only in the films she made, but also in meeting someone who would become an exclusive and intricate part of her public life until her untimely death. This man was photographer Howell Conant. *Photoplay* magazine assigned Conant to do a layout on Grace for their

April issue. Conant was a young, talented and creative photographer. The session for *Photoplay* was a bit clumsy and not significant. Even so, Conant saw Grace's potential, and knew he had to do something to form a bond between them.

When Grace returned some costume jewelry she had borrowed from Conant, her eye caught the display of underwater photography he had in his studio. Fascinated by the pictures, Grace immediately asked Conant for further photo sessions. According to one account, "Soon, Conant was off on a Jamaican vacation with Grace and her sister Peggy, shooting for *Collier's*."

This is where the most alluring photograph ever of Grace was taken, the pristine aquamarine Caribbean waters providing a canvas for the once-in-a-lifetime depiction. Combining their skills and talents, Grace dove underwater several times. Conant, knee deep in the water, patiently waited for the perfect angle. Finally, on the eighth surface by Grace, triumph! Her blonde, wet hair was slicked back, revealing the compelling eyes whose blue tone matched the water. The half-profile expression revealed provocativness; her scarlet lips amplified perfect textured skin, softly beaded by drops of the salty water. Robert Lacey chose this picture for the cover of his biography on Grace. The black-and-white version is just as compelling in its own right.

Howell Conant became Grace's exclusive photographer after the initial successes. One article stated, "Grace Kelly trusted Conant; indeed, they worked like partners." He would be the man to gain exclusive, private and undistracted opportunities to journal the beauty and charm of one of the true icons of the twentieth century.

Grace reached the pinnacle of her acting career early. In 1955, she was nominated for an Academy Award for *The Country Girl*. Her competitors were Judy Garland and Audrey Hepburn, each of whom had also acted in fabulous movies that year: Garland in *A Star Is Born* and Hepburn in *Sabrina*.

The tension and drama were thick. When longtime friend Marlon Brando opened the envelope, he announced that Grace had won. So at the age of twenty-five, Grace Kelly won the top prize, the one all actors and actresses dream of. It was later reported that Grace was given the award not only for the film she had been nominated for, but for her work on all three films she had made that year—*The Country*

Girl and the two Hitchcock classics, *Dial M for Murder and Rear Window*.

Grace Kelly had gone to Manhattan to learn the craft she loved, and realized the ultimate award. The girl from Philadelphia had set her dreams and priorities before her and achieved them in eight fantastic and extraordinary years. What's more, she had lived a vibrant and exciting life with all the rest of those of notoriety in 1950s America.

The glamour and festiveness of the "City That Never Sleeps" played into Grace's success as well. Judith Quine gave compelling descriptions of the memorable times of the young, exuberant gang that had the world at their feet. Their group had many activities to choose from: daytime lunches and shopping; evenings filled with theater, dining, dancing; and all-night parties. That time in their life can be summed up very easily: They had a ball!

Grace Kelly reached a career zenith at a very young age, and the glory wasn't to flee for some time. She would end up making three more movies, two of which were quite good. The next two had a profound effect on the destiny the girl from Henry Avenue was to accomplish. In *To Catch A Thief*, Grace got a taste of what aristocratic Europe was all about, and she loved it. This set her on the course— and destiny—that she would later choose. In some ways it would be similar to the life she had, but in many it would be a sharp contrast, as she would find out.

To Catch a Thief was set on the French Riviera, where F. Scott Fitzgerald along with other famous writers and artists lived after World War I. Fitzgerald's epic novel, *Tender Is The Night*, described life among the villas and cabanas there, where residual monarchs and other bourgeoisie lucky enough to escape their countries' purges had come to live in after the Great War. There, money flowed and summers were filled with the good life that marked this unique territory with elite classes and material wealth. This would become home for the American movie star, and she would engage its inhabitants and win their favor.

With another great leading man, Cary Grant, *To Catch A Thief* also displayed the French Riviera's magnificent landscape. Narrow roads wound their way through the Maritime Alps and quaint villages, and steep slopes and winding curves descended down to the clear, placid waters of the Mediterranean.

During an action scene, Grace gives Grant the thrill ride of his life through the treacherous roads in the Riviera's hills. Ironically, one of these was the road from La Turbie, where Grace would meet her fate twenty-seven years later. Grace's character, Frances Stevens, handled the roads with precision. In 1982, the situation would be quite different.

The last man Grace had a serious relationship with before meeting her prince was Oleg Cassini. This man, who had become an icon in the world of fashion, was immediately attracted to Grace. Cassini had just seen her in *Mogambo* and was captivated by her, and also determined to win her heart. In fact, he was quoted as saying, "She is going to be my next romance."

Coincidentally, upon entering a New York restaurant after the movie, Grace was seated right near him, having dinner with Jean-Pierre Aumont when Cassini made his first approach. From that moment a romance and love story began that could have been chronicled in any great romance novel. Cassini, naturally charming, played his romantic desires like a Stradivarius. Flowers, notes, phone calls and dates followed for several weeks. Grace welcomed the pursuit with a coy flirtation as she slowly let down her guard and surrendered to love. The romance was consummated just before Grace began shooting for *To Catch A Thief.*

Their romance evolved steadily, and just before saying good-bye to Europe, they became engaged when Grace said, "I want to be your wife." Like all the others before Cassini, when the reality of the situation presented itself, the placid, tranquil Mediterranean waters churned with a distinctive chop until they reached the Northeastern Atlantic and Grace's homeland, and Ma Kelly was the first to criticize any intentions Cassini had. Even though Cassini was extremely shrewd and clever, Grace's parents once again turned on the fire hoses full blast to try and extinguish the flames of their love.

Like so many others before, Cassini got the "Kelly Clan Weekend from Hell" in Ocean City. The act was the same, with Jack Kelly alternately delivering racial slurs and ignoring Cassini altogether. Meanwhile, Grace displayed her usual frightened-child attitude and allowed her parents to walk all over Cassini. Grace's parents tried for another six-month moratorium to let Grace see things their way. The feelings they had for each other were too strong, though, and so their romance went on. When Grace had to go to Hollywood to film the final scenes for *To Catch a Thief*, they lived together in a house Grace rented. The engagement pressed on, with the pressure from Grace's family always lurking in the background.

The couple came within a whisk of marriage when Cassini found a priest in Virginia willing to marry them. In the end though, the pressure from so many directions made Grace change her mind, and Grace and Cassini went their separate ways. The endless wearing-down by those with influence finally won out again. When Grace became engaged to Rainier, she and Cassini said a final good-bye while riding the Staten Island Ferry, when Grace told Cassini she was going to marry Rainier. Cassini's reaction was much like that of Grace's sister Lizanne; he protested that she hardly knew Rainier. Grace's mind was made up, however, and it is reported that she confided to Cassini, "I have made my destiny."

Grace Kelly made two more films before leaving the glitter and glamour of Hollywood. The first one further reinforced the intrigue of royal life. It was an MGM production called *The Swan*. Here Grace played a princess who was hoping to be betrothed to a prince played by Alec Guinness.

The beginning scenes show various servants and attendants going about their duties, carefully and meticulously engaging in the protocols of the kingdom. Massive curtains are drawn and wardrobes are prepared while pewter and silver is polished and set with surgical precision. Guards and musicians flamboyantly fill the air with regal sounds and regiment, awaiting the arrival of Prince Albert.

Grace's character lacks self-confidence in her quest to impress Prince Albert, and there is no spark between the shy princess and the disregarding prince. Princess Alexandra is more at ease, and more attracted to her younger brothers' tutor, Dr. Agi, played by Louis Jourdan. In the end, the princess yields to loyalty, and the hand of Prince Albert.

The Swan was, in my opinion, mediocre. Grace's character trickled rather than flowed in what was trying to be conveyed about her. Louis Jourdan's character was much more believable than that of Grace or Guinness. However, playing a princess gave Grace an even more intriguing perspective of what the world of royalty could be. Even more ironic was the way the character of Princess Alexandra became much like Grace's life as a real princess, especially in her first two years.

One crucial mission *The Swan* accomplished nevertheless was to reinforce Grace's enticement for the royal life. Gwen Robyn believed Grace remained in character long after the completion of the film. According to Robyn, "Grace became the character she was playing. She was the Princess in *The Swan*—so it was easy for her to go to the next step and make it reality."

High Society was Grace's last film before she embarked on the royal life. She was already engaged to Prince Rainier at the time the movie was released, and this film served as her fond farewell to Hollywood. An all-star cast was assembled for the film, including Frank Sinatra, Bing Crosby and the immortal Louie Armstrong.

Adapted from *The Philadelphia Story*, Grace plays Tracy Lord, a rich, spoiled, and beautiful society girl. The film shows the pure splendor of what money brings: sprawling estates with decor and landscape that show the wealth of those who inhabit them; limousines, fancy sports cars, and boats at the beck and call of every member of American aristocracy.

A bit corny but entertaining, Grace is once again wooed by all the gentlemen competing for her affection. Her flighty character amuses herself and everyone else with various escapades and mischief. Grace even shows some singing talent when paired with Bing Crosby.

It was her choice, though, to take a bow and let the curtain fall for a final time. At twenty-six years of age, Grace Kelly walked away from what could have been an epic career. She was at the top in both appearance and ability when the hopeless romantic made a decision that would pass her parents' strict standards. Her decision sent her into a world that became a multitude of emotional triumphs and trials while demanding every bit of strength and fortitude she could muster.

Diana, the other hopeless romantic, waited in the wings for what was to be an epic story that would rewrite popularity's definition. Like what had already happened and would happen to Grace, Diana's story would eclipse all those before, transforming a commoner into a princess. These two beautiful young women were ready to embark on the paths they had dreamed of, and that fate was to give them. The naturally gifted twosome who, with just a turn and a smile, would make cameras, tape recorders, pads, pencils, and print register each occasion for all it was worth.

Chapter IV - Princely Pursuits

Grace Kelly and Diana Spencer each met their prince in comparatively different ways. Grace, raised an American, had not been raised in a culture of monarchy. Diana, though, had been born and bred an aristocrat of Britain, and was immediately spellbound by her new suitor and the life the situation presented her.

Grace Kelly's first meeting with Prince Rainier was of no significance romantically. However, the preparation leading up to it was hectic. Grace was in France for the Cannes Film Festival when the French magazine *Paris Match* wanted to do a photo shoot of Grace with Prince Rainier in Monaco. It would be another stop in an already hectic schedule; however, at the insistence of one of her old boyfriends, Jean-Pierre Aumont, she agreed to the shoot.

To complicate matters, there were strikes going on all over France and her hotel had no electricity. This meant the dress she wanted to wear that day could not be pressed. That left her to wear what Judith Quine describes as the "dreaded taffeta dress." "The taffeta dress was a ghastly little item Grace had purchased that we all teased her about," Judith relates. "It had a large dark background with monstrously large cabbage rose print all over it, a high neckline, a dropped waist and an enormous full skirt." After viewing the photographs, I agree with Judith's assessment; the dress was very unflattering to Grace, and made the stick-thin movie star look twenty pounds heavier, especially from the back.

While the dress was indeed less than she would have preferred, Grace wasn't overly concerned, figuring that the pictures taken that day would be no big deal in the long run. Little did she know the pictures of her first meeting with Rainier would follow her the remainder of her life and beyond.

Racing around from engagement to engagement all day, Grace and Rainier finally met at four o'clock in the afternoon. It had been a long day, and Grace was very tired and worn when they finally exchanged greetings. The photo shoot was done, and the prince showed Grace around the grounds. She was impressed by his private zoo, and his easy way with the compound's exotic animals. When asked later by Aumont what she thought of the prince, she simply said, "I think he's very charming."

Like Diana and Charles' first meeting, it would be a while before Grace would see Prince Rainier again.

Prince Charles had known and been friends with Diana's sisters since childhood. Diana's mother even used to take care of Charles during some social gatherings. In 1977, when the world was waiting for the most eligible bachelor to choose a bride, Charles began to date his former playmate, Diana's sister Sarah. Sarah was a very headstrong young woman, but Charles did not mind this trait. However, Sarah was never truly in love with him, and she wanted to be totally and passionately in love with the man she would marry. So the romance eventually lost its luster and ended. According to one account, she said, "If he asked me to marry him, I would turn him down. I'm not in love with him. I wouldn't marry anyone I didn't love, whether he was a dustman or the King of England!"

During the time that Sarah and Charles were dating, Diana was home from school for the weekend, the same time Sarah had invited Charles to Althorp for a weekend of hunting. During the morning shoot, Charles saw Diana for the first time since she was a little girl. That evening at dinner, he was formally introduced to her. This moment had no real significance as far as Charles was concerned. After all, at age sixteen, Diana was still a schoolgirl. They would not see each again for two years.

After not passing her O-exams, going to Switzerland and working her menial jobs, Diana was to cross paths with Charles once more, and then begin the romance that would make her the Princess of Wales.

Jealously wasn't a factor. By 1980, Sarah Spencer had married Neil McCorquodale, and this left Sarah and the rest of Diana's family to help her out in the pursuit of the prince. Without their help and influence, Diana surely would not have been successful.

In that two-year span, Charles had many girlfriends. Ironically, one of the royal matchmakers, Earl Mountbatten, had tried to set up Charles with Princess Grace's oldest daughter Caroline. Charles and the earl were visiting Monaco at the time, and the earl thought it might be a good match. Even so, Princess Grace wanted nothing of it because Charles was not Catholic. Grace's father's doctrine was quite intrinsic in her beliefs. She had nothing to worry about, though. According to one report, "They looked bored to tears all evening, and Prince Charles commented to us afterward that Caroline had more makeup on than heaven knows what." Some things, apparently, are not meant to be.

Charles had many girlfriends during his adult life. Some were short-term, while others became quite serious. The last relationship Charles had before his relationship with Diana was with a striking woman he had a great deal in common with. Her name was Anna Wallace. He had met her while on one of his many hunting outings, and she loved the outdoors as Charles did. With that common interest as a springboard, a romance flourished immediately. Anna could ride well, and loved the role women played in English gentlemen's hunting.

Charles was quite in love with Anna, and wanted her for his bride. When he proposed, though, she told him she'd have to think about it. Naturally, had she said yes immediately, the course of history would have been quite different. This, too, was not to be. The romance began to fade, and ended when at a social function Charles spent more time with Camilla Parker-Bowles than he did with Anna. The end of the romance left Charles emotionally drained and a bit sad; this opening gave Diana the motive and opportunity she'd been waiting for.

Diana was now becoming a young woman, and 1980 would be the year all the loose ends would come together. Both Diana and Charles attended a party in July given by Robert de Pass. After watching Charles at a polo match, Diana was seated next to Charles at a barbecue at the de Pass' country home. There, Diana consoled Charles on the death of his uncle, Lord Mountbatten, who had been killed in an IRA bombing while gathering in lobster traps. Charles was deeply touched by the concern Diana showed, of course not realizing that this God-given trait of compassion, which Diana was to display her entire life, was one of the biggest reasons the world would come to love her so.

Charles was so taken by the moments they shared that day that he invited her to drive back to Buckingham Palace with him. Charles had paperwork to do there, and had to leave early. Diana declined, not because she did not want to, but because she thought it would be rude to the de Passes if she also left early.

However, that summer barbecue would lead to Diana and Charles first official date. The Royal Albert Hall was playing Verdi's *Requiem*. This was one of Diana's favorite works. Chaperoning the occasion was none other than Diana's grandmother, Lady Ruth Fermoy. The evening went well, with them returning to Buckingham Palace for a cold buffet supper after the show.

Next, Charles invited Diana aboard the royal yacht *Britannia* during Cowes Week. Here Diana found herself a bit uncomfortable among Charles's friends. They were much older than Diana, and she felt awkward with the conversation and atmosphere.

In September, Charles invited Diana to Balmoral. This was the big test for Diana, and she knew it. How she would be perceived by the royal family at the queen's private estate could make or break her. Fortunately, the petrified young lady was able to stay with her sister, Jane, and her husband, Robert Fellows, who had their own quarters on the estate since Robert was the queen's private secretary. Diana again would be the youngest person at the weekend gathering, but the familiarity of her own family helped quell some of her anxieties.

The weekend was a success as far as the relationship between Diana and Charles was concerned. By now, however, the senses of the press—who could smell what was brewing better than a bloodhound—began their hunt. After the Balmoral weekend, Diana was pursued endlessly by the press and media. It would never end until her tragic death.

In October, Charles showed Diana Highgrove, the home he had purchased that past July. He was so impressed by her taste that he asked her to do all the interior decorating. Diana was flattered, but didn't think it was proper since they weren't even engaged yet. The game Diana wanted to be in was on, though, and things were falling into place. The momentum of their relationship was building strength, and the destiny Diana had felt inside her for so long was now reaching its climax. The circumstances, with all the pieces of the puzzle, fit into a dream that very few ever realize. However, these were not the only circumstances. Lurking in the shadows was another set of circumstances—circumstances that, when revealed, would be no match for the shy, innocent pawn Diana became.

♛ ♛

Grace Kelly's romance with Prince Rainier was not as complicated as Diana and Charles'. She didn't need family or friends to plot a course for her. Grace had her own identity already, and didn't require a support group of any kind.

After her meeting with the prince in the summer of 1955, Grace sent him a thank-you note. The disciplined star always adhered to decorum and polite behavior. The thank-you note sparked a fire in the prince that kindled quickly; soon Grace and Rainier were exchanging letters frequently. The French prince was a good letter writer with an excellent command of the English language. A great deal of his education had been in England, and his bilingual skills were superb.

Back in New York City, Grace confessed candidly to Judith Quine that she had been thinking a great deal about marriage and family. Back in the fifties, a woman's biological clock began to tick very early. Twenty-five would be scoffed at today. However, this was when women were still expected to play their role as wives and mothers, and begin their roles early in life. One of the first things Judith told me in my interview with her was how girls were raised to be matrons. "All young women wanted to be matrons after their formal education."

Careers and vocations were looked down upon. Bras still had more than a decade to go before they would burn. So, at twenty-five, Grace surely felt some internal pressure. Most of Grace's friends were married already and had children. The stress and apprehension made her blurt out to Judy Canter once, "You're all dropping them like calves. Before you know it I'll be everyone's spinster Aunt Grace."

Before leaving for the filming of *The Swan*, Judith and Grace had another of their many intimate talks. While Judith helped her pack, Grace broke down crying over not having married yet.

"Gracie," Judith remembers noting with surprise, "you're crying."

But seeing so many of her friends and family with families of her own had really gotten to her by the late summer of 1955. She confided in Judith that she longed for all that and more. "I want all of that," Grace had said.

Judith nodded. "I know, Gracie," she assured her, "and you'll have it." Then, as Judith relates, "She looked at me long and hard, as though wondering whether she could tell me a secret about herself. Then she [Grace] confessed, 'But I want more.'

"I nodded. 'I know, Gracie,' I answered, 'and you'll keep on getting that, too.'"

Reinforcing the stereotype and all the emotions building up inside her like a powder keg was her role of a princess in *The Swan*. Grace was right in the middle of rehearsal during her correspondences with Rainier. This was the true crossroads of the beautiful actress' life that would bring about the aspirations she desired.

Prince Rainier, like Prince Charles, was now over thirty and looking for heirs. Since the beginning of monarchies, one of the most sacred duties of the heir to any throne was to produce offspring. These were two young men who had been born and nurtured with all the protocol and customs necessary to assume their roles. They were both very serious about doing what was expected of them, and producing heirs was one of those duties.

The course was now set for what would make each couple "prince and princess." Some turbulence would still make the waters a bit rough on the way to their altars. The ship's hull was sturdy, though, and would carry them to the port of their destiny.

Chapter V - Engagements Festive and Volatile

The adventures of the two young women were reaching critical mass. The providence of each had run full circle, and was now ready to expose the epicenter they chose. The pace was quick, and momentum was at a level no one could halt.

In the late fall of 1955, after exchanging letters frequently, Prince Rainier wrote Grace Kelly and told her he was coming to America for a health checkup and wanted to see her. Rainier also had two Kelly family friends to help his cause, Edie and Russell Austin, who had vacationed with the Kellys in New Jersey for years. They were vacationing in Monaco at the time, and needed tickets to the sold-out Red Cross Ball. The mention of Grace's name to the prince quickly earned them tickets, and the Austins became one of the key matchmaking links for Rainier to visit Henry Avenue.

Grace was excited about the visit, but kept her demeanor coy to all her friends and relatives. The filming of *The Swan* was almost completed, and Grace invited the prince to the traditional Kelly family Christmas Day gathering.

Prince Rainier sailed from France with his personal physician, Dr. Robert Donat, and priest. In the late afternoon on Christmas Day, they arrived at Henry Avenue.

Grace was very tense. What was her father's reaction going to be to this one? She couldn't help but be anxious after all the disasters with previous potential husbands. Fortunately, the prince and Grace had a trump card in Father Tucker. He was an Irish Catholic priest— just the right man to charm Jack Kelly and keep any reservations he might have at bay.

After the ice had been broken and Grace's parents were comfortable with the prince, Ma Kelly invited the prince and Dr. Donat to spend the night. Father Tucker had other business, and had to leave. This gave Grace and Rainier the precious time they needed to package and seal their hopes. By the time the night ended, well into the single digits of the AM, Grace and Rainier were falling in love.

The next day, Grace and Prince Rainier took a drive in the country and had lunch. When Grace got back to Henry Avenue, she had a heart-to-heart talk with her mother about the joy and ecstasy she was feeling. Ma Kelly knew then that if the prince proposed, Grace would accept. Jack Kelly had previously stated that he would give his blessing if this was what his daughter really wanted.

Grace had to go back to New York after Christmas for the singing lessons required for her role in *High Society*, and Rainier accompanied her to the city. During their time together, Prince Rainier proposed to her, and she accepted immediately. Prince Rainier didn't give her any misgivings about the duty or protocol Charles would be been so paranoid about with Diana. Of course, this was only a small principality, not the United Kingdom. Also, Rainier knew Grace was a mature woman of the world, one who had the spotlight on her for the better part of six years. He was confident that whatever changes she had to make, she would. However, in many ways, the adjustments for the All-American Girl would be as challenging for Grace as they would later be for Diana Spencer.

Later retrospects on Grace and Rainier's feelings for each other during their short romance differ. Grace's younger sister, Lizanne, was taken aback by the announcement, saying, "Oh my God, Grace— you don't even know this guy." Lizanne's assessment was realistic; however, when Grace returned to New York to tell Judith and her other friends, she'd had time to digest the entire experience, and was by then firm and glad in the commitment she had made to Rainier.

Of course, Judith was the first to be told about Grace's impending nuptials. When Grace went back to her apartment in New York after Rainier and she became engaged, she left a message with Jay to have Judy call her. When Judith did, Grace told her she had to come for lunch the next day. Suspecting some important announcement, Judy tried to coax it out of her. Grace said, "I'm engaged to be married," then immediately hung up the phone. The rest of the night, Judy and Jay speculated about who Grace's intended could be.

Grace's euphoria predominated her behavior. Finally, she could tell her friends what she had been dreaming about.

The next day, Judy arrived at Grace's apartment. They sat at the table, Judy saying not a word, and letting Grace have the floor. "She spoke when she was ready to. In a voice filled with both joy and solemnity, Grace stated, 'I am so very much in love with the most wonderful man. I am going to marry...Prince Rainier of Monaco.'" Judy sat in wonderment for a few moments, then shrieked, *"No shit,*

Gracie!" They then spent the next minutes between hysterical laughter and trying to talk.

Like Lizanne had been, Judy was a bit skeptical at first. too. She knew Grace had only known the prince a short while, and hadn't spent much time with him. Grace put her at ease by explaining all the things she loved about Rainier and how, in the short time they had been together, they had shared their compatibilities about wanting children and family. Hearing that, Judy congratulated Grace and gave her blessing.

Letting the cat out of the bag to Judy was the easy part. Telling America was another thing altogether. Prince Rainier wanted his private life kept private. When approached with the idea of a large press conference announcing their engagement, he became apprehensive. Grace had already had a private dinner with her close friends, which included photographs, but even this small gathering was not an atmosphere the prince was comfortable in.

This was America, though. The capitalistic media wasn't going to let one of its most beautiful and famous women become engaged without their portrayal—and the resulting monetary gain. At a dinner at Grace's apartment, Grace, Rainier, Father Tucker, Jay, Judy, John Foreman (her television agent), and her lawyer, Henry Jaffe, met to go over the details. There were some tense moments as Rainier stuck to his guns about keeping things simple and private. Finally, after long negotiations among all of them and some additional help from Jack Kelly, a compromise was reached for a January 5th, 1956 announcement.

So on the fifth of January, after a private luncheon at the Philadelphia Country Club, a press conference announcing the engagement of Grace Kelly and Prince Rainier was held on Henry Avenue. Prince Rainier was a bit disturbed by the questions at the announcement, as well as by the repeat performance in New York the next night. But what was second nature to Grace, he managed to endure as well.

One other significant problem that became an immense disagreement was Rainier's request of a dowry from Jack Kelly, a European tradition. Rainier tried to soft-pedal his request by having Father Tucker approach Jack first. As Rainier had surely suspected, Jack Kelly didn't warm to the request. The proud Irishmen, who had built his fortune from nothing, was not pleased with handing over a significant amount of money for the privilege of marrying his daughter, and the conflict went back and forth a few times before it was finally resolved.

In the end, terms were agreed to, and no other serious problems got in Grace and Rainier's way. They were now officially engaged in what was to be the most publicized wedding ever…until 1981.

It meant everything to Diana Spencer to become a part of the monarchy that had dominated the world for centuries. Like a game of chess, her pieces made all the right moves. With her clever ingenuity, plus the help of her family and friends, checkmate was inevitable.

This is not to say that checkmate happened without some anxiety. As she waited for Charles to make his final decision, Diana's family, the queen mother, Prince Philip and the press all weighed heavily in the final stages leading up to Charles and Diana's engagement. This was certainly to be expected in the making of such a momentous decision. However, Camilla Parker-Bowles, whose relationship with the prince was to torment Diana relentlessly, held the trump card in the decision Charles would make—a secretive and intimate plan that doomed the other "wedding of the century" before it even took place.

As Andrew Morton reported, Charles's former girlfriend, Anna Wallace, and others were carefully probed by Camilla when she became aware that their relationship to Charles was more than casual. "She would have known, as Diana discovered too late, that Camilla's famous vetting of Charles's girlfriends was not so much to assess their potential as a royal bride but to see how much a threat they posed to her own relationship with Prince Charles."

Morton further relates that "Camilla evaluated all of Diana's characteristics, carefully screening her likes and dislikes. When she learned Diana had no interest in any of Charles's outdoor sports and games, she knew the hunting and riding she and Charles enjoyed so much, as well as the other parts of their relationship, could carry on. Camilla encouraged Charles's courtship of Diana."

The one dissenting vote in Diana's quest came from Queen Elizabeth herself. It was not a total rejection, but her conjecture of things she knew from experience: How was Diana going to adjust to royal life? Could she handle all the rigors and protocols royalty would bring to her life? Queen Elizabeth's concerns seemed valid; the never-ending pomp and circumstance called each to duty on a regular basis, with exhausting, boring and weary obligations that test the patience and willpower. According to Morton's account, "She had strong reservations about Diana."

The queen also recognized her young age as being a problem, along with Diana not following through on some of the goals she had set for herself. These concerns were going to come to the forefront quickly when Diana did become the Princess of Wales.

As the romance grew and the clock ticked, Charles' apprehension became more apparent. He knew if he made a mistake in selecting his bride, it would be something he would have to live with. Many of his friends had had unsuccessful marriages. Even with the divorce laws in England becoming more liberal, as they had in America, Charles' anxiety grew. Divorce would be out of the question for him, he was certain.

The media was related to one of the last episodes connected to securing Diana's engagement to Charles. In spite of their best efforts to keep their romance private, the media and paparazzi were always on the trail. The *Sunday Mirror* printed a story of Diana spending the night with Charles on the royal family's private train.

Before this, Charles' discretion had worked; for example, when he and Diana rendezvoused at Highgrove, the estate Charles had recently purchased. Highgrove gave them a sanctuary away from the stalking lenses. But their overnight proximity on the royal train couldn't be denied, and the story was run. The problem here was that it could hurt Diana's reputation as the potential chosen one. Like any other candidate, Diana's reputation had to be blemish-free.

Paradoxically, the incident played in her favor, as the both the royal family and Parliament came to her aid. As Andrew Morton stated, "For once Buckingham Palace came to her assistance." The queen herself asked for a retraction. The paper's editor, Robert Edwards, printed Charles's separate denial, but stuck to his guns on the validity of the story. The story didn't damage Diana's reputation; however, it opened the floodgate of media blitz publicizing that Diana was going to become the Princess of Wales.

Charles went off on a skiing holiday to Klosters, Switzerland to contemplate his future. During the trip, he finally decided to ask Diana to become his bride. According to Morton, Charles called Diana from Switzerland and told her "…he had something important to ask her when he returned."

In the middle of all the goings-on, her emotions reaching critical mass, Diana began to wonder a bit about Camilla. Camilla had befriended and advised Diana all through the final stages leading to the proposal. To Diana, Camilla had been a confidant who was looking out for her best interests…or so Diana thought.

As soon as he returned to London, Charles contacted Diana and, at his request, she went to Windsor Castle. Morton recounts that there, Charles told her how much he missed her "and then simply asked her to marry him."

Diana was so nervous she burst out laughing. A voice inside her was telling her something was wrong. She would never be the Queen of England. She pushed aside these negative thoughts, though, and accepted, confessing her absolute love for Charles.

Charles was very standoffish, however. At the first press conference to announce their engagement, he was asked if they were in love. Charles simply replied, "Whatever love means." Each time I see the footage, which is invariably shown on each anniversary of Diana's death, my awareness of Charles' lack of enthusiasm becomes more evident.

Upon returning to her flat, Diana excitedly gave the news to her flatmates. Jubilant all, they drove around London savoring the news. The following morning, Diana broke the news to her entire family. The queen made the formal announcement on February 24, 1981. This not only made the Charles and Diana's engagement official, but also started one of the most planned and extravagant events the world was ever to see.

After the proposal, Diana went off on a three-week holiday to Australia with her mother and stepfather. Here she was to experience the first taste of the distance Charles would often put between them—three weeks away from the girl he had just asked to marry him, and never once did he call her. Of that treatment, Diana was quoted as saying, "I pined for [Charles] but he never rang me up." This, as Diana was to admit later, should have been a wakeup call for her. All she received from Charles on that holiday were flowers, which he had told one of his staff to see to. Nothing of any personal nature came from Charles while Diana was in Australia.

One week after the announcement, Diana was to begin an emotional and psychological spiral that would lead her to suffer at the hands of the wickedness that plagues the human mind. The timid and innocent Diana was in way over her head. Totally unprepared for role that lay before her, she would bounce around like a coin in a clothes dryer. Her nerves were so frail that, one week after their engagement became official, the mere mention by Charles of having a couple of extra pounds on her waist sent her over the edge and into the compulsive disorder known as bulimia. The torment of this disorder would follow Diana like a possessed stalker for years and years. But although she wanted to, it was too late to turn back now—the overwhelming momentum was pushing her along like debris over a waterfall.

So now, the die was cast for the two idols who represented glamour itself. The plans, preparations, and never-ending details were methodically put into place by thousands and thousands of individuals, and the road was paved for the ride each would take to the kingdom of their dreams.

As Diana experienced in England after the announcement of her engagement to Prince Charles, Grace and Rainier's nerves were going to be tested by the overwhelming media blitz that was to invade the small principality of Monaco. Along with the happiness and elation, stress, tension, and outright aggravation were going to mix in the days leading up to the wedding.

London and England would handle the crowds and media better. Diana, though, was going to have her own set of problems and circumstances that would make the days prior to her wedding emotionally trying.

All else aside, there were practical matters to take care of—at least, practical from a royal perspective. The two future royal matriarchs were each given thorough gynecological exams to make sure they could bear children. This was—as it had been for centuries—the most important aspect they would fulfill, and the royal line of each respective monarchy must be assured a future heir.

Between her engagement and wedding, Grace Kelly still had to complete the filming of *High Society*. Prince Rainier, in contrast to Prince Charles, very much wanted to be near his fiancée. In demonstration, during the latter part of January 1956, he joined her at the set and observed the making of Grace's last film. But questions from the media about the future of Grace's film career after marriage followed them relentlessly. As to be surmised, the prince was always very vague with his answers. In an interview in the *Los Angeles Times* dated 1/22/56, Grace Kelly said she "might act again after a long vacation from it." The "vacation" would last more than two decades.

Grace was very focused on her immediate future. She knew that her film career was going directly to the backburner after *High Society*. How long it would remain there was anyone's guess, nor was she prioritizing it in any way at this point. She was looking forward to her new life, and being a wife and mother was her new precedent.

Grace's upcoming nuptials were an unexpected boon for her studio. In addition to her normal salary, MGM paid Grace a good bonus for her work in *High Society*. In exchange, they were given the rights to film the wedding.

It was time for Grace to say good-bye to Hollywood, and especially New York. She would be back now and again, but the single, free life she had cherished the past few years was ending. She spent the remaining time after the filming to pack and organize herself for the journey into her new life.

At Judy and Jay's Christmas party just before her engagement, where Leonard Bernstein, Marlon Brando, Marilyn Monroe and other notables sang Christmas carols into the wee hours of the morning, Judith gave a hint of what Grace's feelings must have been by saying, "We were all New Yorkers at a time when that was the most wonderful thing in the world to be."

Just before sailing for Monaco, Grace's New York friends gave her a final dinner at the famous, ultrachic "21." Of the event, Judith relates, "Jay tapped his fork on his plate and raised his glass. The instant Jay looked at Gracie, their eyes welled with tears. It was the same for the rest of us."

That last toast brought an end to an era of love, friendship, accomplishment and satisfaction for Grace. She had come to the world of entertainment and become one of its success stories. Now she was saying goodbye and embarking on a new life and journey that, for her, would become another major success.

On April 4th 1956, Grace Kelly left the country she had grown up in and embarked on the long voyage to Monaco. With her family, various friends, some of her bridesmaids and, of course, the media, the *USS Constitution* sailed from the Big Apple to take Grace and her entourage to Monaco. "The day we left," she told a friend, "our ship was surrounded by fog, and that's the way I felt, as if I were sailing off into the unknown."

The voyage was both elegant, relaxing, and a time for Grace to reflect on what had been and what was to be. It was a great vacation for all who had the privilege to be part of it. Peaceful moments interspersed themselves with festivity as the ship's bow cut the stoic waters of the Atlantic.

The media was bothersome at times before, during and after the voyage. Grace's engagement had naturally set off a frenzy in America that everyone got caught up in. As the day of the wedding drew nearer, fashion, film and print all showed their capitalistic fervor. The wedding of Grace Kelly was a major media overkill that was to follow Grace into her new life. Yet toward the end of the voyage, the mature star of stage and screen put her game-face on and became very serious and focused on what was to be.

Eight days after they sailed from New York Harbor, the *USS Constitution* dropped anchor in Monaco's harbor. Once again, Grace's dress reflected her mood. For what she knew would be a joyful and memorable—as well as awkward and somewhat difficult—day, she cloaked herself in a dark wool dress trimmed at the v-neck by a white collared scarf, the hemline falling about mid-calf, the left lapel accented by a corsage. Her wide-brimmed white hat and sunglasses concealed her inner emotions.

Prince Rainier boarded Monaco's royal yacht to bring his bride ashore. Grace and her parents boarded the yacht and, as soon as they came on shore, they were driven around the streets of Monaco to cheering crowds welcoming the world-renowned actress who would, in only a few days' time, become their princess.

The week before the wedding was filled with last-minute events and details that naturally kept everyone busy. It was now time for Grace and Rainier's families to finally meet. After reading the accounts, I'm sure this was a bewildering experience that Grace didn't expect. Prince Rainier's family got along like snakes and mongooses. Most of his family (with the exception of his father) was cold toward the Kellys. But Prince Pierre liked Grace, and was the sole exception in an annoying and abrasive group of royals. To add fuel to the fire, some of Grace's guests had jewelry stolen from them. The media, starved for a story by this time, pounced on the embarrassing dilemma. Rainier's mother, Mamou, who was the most unpleasant of Rainier's camp, had a chauffeur who was an ex-jewel thief. All fingers pointed to him immediately when the nearly sixty thousand dollars' worth of jewels were reported missing.

Rainier's parents had built-in animosity, having been divorced for years, and his father jumped to Rainier's side when he suspected his mother's chauffeur. This made for a complete scene right in front of both families. Of course, Grace found the entire altercation humiliating. According to one of her biographers, "Grace never liked a scene." But her likes and dislikes were of no consequence in the brouhaha that followed.

Rainier wanted the suspect, Rene Girier, to leave Monaco. His mother wouldn't hear of it though, and to display her displeasure, she left Monaco and never returned after the wedding. Even when Rainier and Grace traveled to visit her after their marriage with the children, she never relented, aptly demonstrating that, no matter how much wealth, power or influence a family may have, they are all still susceptible to the misery that they bring to themselves and others.

There were also some controversies with the media and press before the wedding took place. As Judith Quine told me in my interview with her, "This was the birth of what was to come. Monaco was not prepared, including staff and palace guards." There were over eleven hundred journalists when Grace and her guests first arrived. By the end of the week, they numbered two thousand, and reporters were lurking everywhere trying to get a story. Bribes and secret pictures were offered of various people involved in the events, no matter how minor. These boldly ranged from photographers invading Rita Gam's bathroom—photographers who, as Judith Quine told me, "Stationing themselves in the trees while the bridesmaids were getting pedicures,"—to one of the paparazzi prostrating himself in the road one day as Rainier was driving Grace and her parents around. When Rainier, who thought he had hit—and hurt—someone, got out to investigate, a swarm of photographers clicked their shutters. Rainier was very upset, and rightfully so.

Communications between the palace and the press had been consistently disorganized in the days leading to the wedding. The press was becoming frustrated and became even more so when Grace and Rainier emerged from a dinner and rushed in the rain to their car, managing to drive away without the photographers getting a chance to get any pictures. The media, which had been waiting in the rain for hours, became enraged. The police had to restrain them; some were even arrested. Finally, Rainier yielded to the pressure and held at least one formal photo opportunity each day. This, plus better organization of communications and press releases, helped all concerned.

Not all the wedding week was a cross between the Keystone Cops and Barnum and Bailey's Circus. There were many pleasurable and memorable moments also. Some of these included a Saturday evening dinner-dance hosted by Grace's family, an International Sporting Club gala, and a night at the Monaco Opera House. All these events were jovial, with excellent cocktails, cuisine, music, dancing, and memorable displays of up-to-the-minute fashion and style.

The strain of the week had taken its toll on Grace, though. After one of the never-ending dinner parties, which had gone till dawn, Grace confessed to the prince that she'd like to just run off with him and get married without all the hectic pressure. Of course this wasn't possible. They did, however, escape that very day, still in the wee hours of the morning, and drive into the hills of Monaco to be by themselves. This break in the chaotic atmosphere gave them a chance to catch their breath just before the wedding.

Diana's prenuptials carried their own unique stressors as plans and arrangements were made. While the frenzy and carnival-like atmosphere of Monaco had put Grace under pressure, the thing that put an immediate strain on Diana was the unaccustomed loss of freedom. According to one account, "Once the announcement of the engagement was made, Diana's world changed dramatically."

"Changed dramatically" is perhaps an understatement. In just a short time, everything she had known, everything she had been, and everything that mattered to her seemed to disappear. Her easy relationship with her friends and flatmates was ended abruptly; all became things of the past. A bodyguard was assigned to her, and he told the future princess right away, "I just want you to know this is your last night of freedom ever for the rest of your life, so make the most of it." It was just like a U.S. President-elect coming under Secret Service protection before taking the oath of office.

The loneliness and confinement were extremely taxing for Diana. Even more, the isolation and silence became boring in a very short period of time. She was used to joining in the giddy laughter and carrying-on of her girlfriends. Now her isolation from them was a complete reversal of the life she once enjoyed, even cherished.

To kill some of the time, Diana asked some of her old dance teachers to come in and work with her. Fortunately, her mother was also able to come in to help her in the transition. Oliver Everett, who became her private secretary, also filled in some of the gap by acclimating her to proper behavior and protocol. Everett helped Diana a great deal, and they had a good relationship in the period prior to her wedding.

Diana's natural sense of fashion ended up engendering a positive reaction to her public image. Yet before her engagement to Charles, her wardrobe was woefully poor. Diana conceded in her interviews with Andrew Morton that she only had one good outfit to her name prior to her engagement. To rectify the situation, Diana and her mother went on a shopping spree that was still miniscule compared to the wardrobe she would eventually own.

Like Monaco in 1956, there were many dinners, balls and engagements leading up to Diana and Charles' wedding day. Diana was an emotional wreck from all the loneliness and uncertainty of the situation, but never revealed it at all at any of the festivities. "Her head and heart were in turmoil but no-one would have guessed it," Morton wrote of one event, "when later that evening she and Charles entertained 800 of their friends and family at a ball inside Buckingham Palace."

England, and the world itself, was caught up in the celebration. Although from all indications this appeared to be a good and happy time for both Diana and Charles in their relationship, lurking secrets caused Diana great discomfort. To outward appearances, Charles made many compromises and concessions in an effort to make sure their marriage got off on the right foot. As one example, aware that Diana didn't like his relationships with Lady Tyron and especially Camilla Parker-Bowles, she made her feelings known to him, and he tried to mask the relationship with Camilla.

But Charles was amateurish in his efforts at deceit. Suspicious, Diana listened in on a conversation Charles had with Camilla. While taking a bath and using his handheld phone, he admitted to Camilla, "Whatever happens, I will always love you." When Diana confronted him, all hell broke loose.

When you have an entire bureaucracy looking after your every need, leaks are bound to appear. Someone on Charles' office staff made known to Diana that Charles had purchased a gold chain bracelet for Camilla. This purchase occurred just two weeks before their wedding. From the onset, Diana learned that trust was not to be a word in the vocabulary of their relationship.

Many more moments of despair were to invade and entrench what should have been a happy and triumphant time for Diana. The young princess-to-be had two more very traumatic experiences that were almost catastrophic. Remember, she was only twenty years old then, and very inexperienced at having such a tidal wave of fame and pressure bestowed on her. She was also trying to shed some pounds before her big day, which put even more stress on her fragile psyche. The purge-diet she chose to lose weight began to take its toll. When confronted at a polo match of Charles' by an onslaught of cameras, Diana lost her composure and escaped in tears. Charles had to console her, and the military police had to control the crowd in the mayhem.

The second event was even worse. Just days prior to the wedding, Diana hit the panic button with full force. At a palace cocktail party, apprehension grabbed hold of her, and she fled once more in tears. Fortunately, her sister Jane was there to help her, although this was by no means an easy task. The wedding dangled like the Sword of

Damocles for the next twenty-four hours. Wanting the wedding to ensue no matter what, the queen kept the press in the dark as to what had transpired.

If there was one thing Diana was, it was a loyal British subject, and in the end it was Diana's duty and loyalty that pulled her through. Had she been marrying royalty in another country, like Grace Kelly had, she might not have gone through with it. Yet tradition and responsibility, which had so scared her in the first place, in the end helped her reach the altar.

♛ ♛

Each bride and groom experiences stress, strain, and anxiety; wedding plans can stretch nerves like over-tuned guitar strings. Grace Kelly and Diana Spencer had the entire world watching in anticipation of the vivid images that would become legendary, yet each had to show an unimaginable level of strength.

Which one was stronger? Grace was older and had more experience to prepare her for all the hype those moments brought. But Diana must be given a great deal of credit also. She had to deal with situations she knew nothing about, situations that no amount of warning and instruction could possibly have prepared her for. There were many moments where she could have run up a white flag. Without the help of others, she probably would have. Instead, she persevered.

In the end, I believe it was a combination of women's intuition, true love, and responsibility that carried each of them over the last hurdle. The two hopeless romantics were committed. Like so many before them and so many after, they believed that the love and commitment they felt would conquer all. In some ways it did. But as they were to discover, genuine love and the search for happiness opens hearts to the uncertainties that life brings each day from the unknown chapters still to be written.

Chapter VI - I Do

Both Grace and Diana's wedding days had finally arrived. The final piece to the puzzles of their destinies was ready to be put into place. Fate, providence and history awaited each.

👑 👑

Finally, after all the traveling, planning, and what must have seemed like infinite parties and rehearsals, Grace Kelly's moment arrived. Fourteen days after she left America and her career behind, she took her first vows in the civil ceremony that was required by law in Monaco. With that, Grace Kelly officially joined the Grimaldi line. Howell Conant, who was busily taking pictures of each ceremony, commented, "It was all so impressive, and yet I had to wonder: was this Grace? It turned out that some of the same questions were going through her mind." In the photographs and film taken by MGM, Grace looked tired but composed for what she truly believed to be her destiny. After the civil ceremony, celebrations began with a garden reception and a fabulous fireworks display proclaiming the event.

The religious ceremony was held the next day. Thursday April 19, 1956: the sky was blue as the sun rose over Monaco's harbor, beckoning Grace and Rainier for their day. Grace and her bridesmaids were busily preparing themselves for the big day that lay ahead as every guest, no matter what their status, was shuttled from the harbor to Saint Nicholas' Cathedral. The church's hilltop isolation didn't sit too well with some, but that's the way it was.

The gown, a gift from MGM, flattered Grace just the way it was planned. Grace's main designer and close friend Helen Rose did an outstanding job displaying all of Grace's beauty with the gown. Materials included 125-year-old rose point lace, 100 yards of silk, 25 yards of silk taffeta and thousands of precisely stitched pearls. She looked stunning in the swanlike manner she had pictured herself. "Still, no sketch could possibly describe how unbelievably beautiful Grace looked when she joined us for picture taking," Judith Quine wrote later in her account, *The Bridesmaids*.

Grace was wearing a special perfume of her own design named *Fleurissimp*. The unique blend of floral scents and other ingredients in the formula were never revealed or distributed to the public during Grace's entire reign. *Fleurissimp* was hers, and hers alone.

When the bride was ready, Howell Conant set Grace, her bridesmaids, and flower girls into various poses for the formal portraits. Even though Grace was tying to concentrate on what was about to happen, she did not forget a final thank-you for the six women who meant so much to her. "Having all of you here today makes all the difference in the world," Judith remembers her saying.

The mass, adhering strictly to Catholic protocol, was very orderly as well as moving. Rainier wore a military uniform boldly emblazoned with medals and ribbons. Grace and Rainier exchanged the vows recited to them by the bishop of Monaco, Monsignor Gilles Barthe. As the solemn ceremony ended and Grace walked back up the aisle and out into her new kingdom, an inner peace seemed to envelop her entire being. Truly, her first life had ended and a new one had begun.

The road leading down to the harbor was filled with crowds of cheering well-wishers. Grace stopped at the Saint Devote Chapel long enough to lay her bouquet on the altar and pray to the young girl who had given her life in faith during the persecution of early Christians of the Roman Empire. Here, where the martyred patron saint of Monaco had been laid to rest hundreds of years before, the new princess of Monaco would return regularly, especially during the annual national celebration held each January. The spiritual faith of Christ had indeed filled her soul, and all the training and discipline she had received was now flowing through her veins. The journey and search was complete now; the *moiré* she had so wanted had been bestowed.

Diana and Charles's day was even more spectacular. The British Empire and the entire world were consumed by the event. Subjects, media, royalty, and heads of state were all totally focused on the pageantry and splendor that was about to unfold. All through the previous night of July 29, 1981, the streets had been lined with spectators. As the clocked ticked, the electricity grew with more voltage as each moment passed.

Diana Spencer started her wedding day at 6:30 AM. Like Grace Kelly (and I'm sure most other brides), she hardly slept the previous night. Now in the full clutches of bulimia, she had consumed a very large meal the night before her wedding, and then promptly purged it. Her mood would swing in several directions throughout the day, including at Clarence House, where she was dressed and made up for the wedding.

However, in spite of all the anxiety, pressure, and tension, Diana felt relatively calm as the day began. "Listening to the crowds outside," Andrew Morton relates, "she felt a deathly composure combined with great anticipation at the event which lay ahead." Her young body, pumped with adrenaline, would carry her quite sufficiently.

After the crowd of laypeople had prepared her hair, makeup and dress, Diana's anxiety took over. She broke down in tears once more and had to be restored and calmed by her sister Jane. "All I want to do is marry Charles," she was quoted as saying. "I can't face all this...look at everyone...I can't go through with it."

This discomposure was to be short-lived, however. After composing herself and having her makeup touched up, she was escorted from Clarence House to the glass horse-drawn coach for the ride to St. Paul's Cathedral. Although she was stirring inside like a blender, the world saw a beautiful young woman emerge; even with all the apprehension, Diana made a splendid bride.

The moment had arrived. Polished and gleaming, the abundance of glass surrounding the coach gave the world a birds' eye view of Diana all along the route, with horses and guards precisely cantering in procession before, beside, and behind her.

The choice of St. Paul's Cathedral drew applause and admiration in additional celebration of the noble event. St. Paul's was named for the apostle who had brought the word of Christ to the Gentile world, thus eventually spreading Christianity to Western Europe and the Americas. Here, in the same church Diana and Charles would be wed, the Church of England was formed because Henry VIII had wanted a divorce in the sixteenth century and the Roman Catholic doctrine would not allow it. Ironically, this marriage would suffer the same fate.

The coach pulled up to the cheering crowds welcoming Diana to the historic church, which was rebuilt in the late seventeenth century by Christopher Wren after several devastating fires. Citizens of London, known as St. Paul's Watch, had guarded and protected the cathedral at all costs during the Battle of Britain in 1940. Outside the cathedral flags, carpets, banners and flowers brought the sooty facade back to life from its centuries of war and wear. As Diana disembarked from the coach and climbed the stairs, the huge, wooden, raised panel-doors opened as if to her command.

Earl Spencer, who as Diana's father had the privilege of giving his daughter's hand to Prince Charles, was still recovering from a stroke he had suffered, and was not yet good on his feet. Even with the once-vibrant gait now withered by disease, the country gentlemen still had plenty of love and determination in his heart to give his youngest daughter away for "country and Queen."

Unhurriedly and steadily, Diana leaned her father on her strong, youthful arm. With the music resonating, she and her father walked down the aisle past each set of massive pillars, then down the Nave, passing under the chandelier that hangs below the 365-foot dome. Their feet crossed the etched stone floor which pays tribute to the brave men and women of England who had given their lives in World War II. The distinguished guests and dignitaries watched in awe as the long train of Diana's dress slid smoothly with their cadence as through the chancel Diana and her father came to where her prince was waiting.

Years later, Diana would admit to Andrew Morton that thoughts of Camilla hovered in her mind as she advanced down the aisle. Finally though, Diana's mind eased. "As she walked down the aisle, her heart brimmed over with love and adoration for Charles. When she looked at him through her veil, her fears vanished and she thought that she was the luckiest girl in the world." So as Diana neared the end of the majestic aisle, and with Prince Charles' unknowing assistance, her thoughts finally focused on the moment.

With music resonating in every corner of the architectural masterpiece, Lady Diana Spencer's dreams of a historic destiny became reality. Her apprehensions and worries left and were replaced with a radiant feeling that everything was going to be fine.

Charles looked undeniably distinguished as well, waiting patiently for his bride to proceed down the aisle with her father and looking resplendent in a commander's uniform from Her Majesty's Royal Navy.

Finally, the earl gave his youngest daughter a farewell kiss as the couple almost the entire world was focused on stepped up to the High Altar, where the Archbishop of Canterbury awaited them to begin the ceremony, complete with full orchestra and choir. The couple's vows were exchanged in clear, eloquent tones. With a simple "I do," Diana Spencer became Princess of Wales. When they turned to walk back down the aisle as husband and wife, the three stained-glass windows behind the altar showed with profound imagery what lay ahead for Diana—the primary colored-prism images showed the service, suffering, and sacrifice of Christ, which would become so much a part of Diana until her death.

The wedding was the pinnacle in Charles and Diana's relationship, and their wedding day was suitably filled with joy and celebration. Crowds cheered ecstatically as the happy couple rode back to Buckingham Palace, the swelled masses lining the entire route wishing them well.

As Diana and Charles waved to the crowd with excitement and exhilaration, the open coach proceeded down the Mall running adjacent to St. James Park, around the circular rotary where the enormous stature of Queen Victoria greets all whose journey takes them to the palace gates. Moments later, in triumph, Charles, Diana and the entire royal family gathered on the balcony of Buckingham Palace as thousands cheered the enchanted couple.

👑 👑

So now the two princesses were royalty, and their quests for their Holy Grails were complete. New worlds, which neither of them knew very much about, would unfold shortly. The actress from America and the aristocrat from England were to embark on journeys that would encompass the attention of the world, and the futures before them would be filled with triumphs and trials that would make each of them a fascinating part of the twentieth century, and perhaps the millennium.

After their receptions, Grace and Rainier's in the palace garden and Diana and Charles's traditional royal wedding breakfast at Buckingham palace, the two princesses and their husbands embarked on similar honeymoons. Boarding the royal yachts of their respective countries, they set off for fun and escapades in the aqua-blue waters of the Mediterranean.

Grace and Rainier bid farewell to their seven hundred guests and descended to the *Deo Juvente II*, Monaco's royal yacht. The exhaustion they must have felt was finally going to get a welcome abatement after each publicly expressed a genuine appreciation for all that had made the moments of the previous week possible. As the yacht left the harbor, the happy couple waved goodbye to all from the bridge of the yacht. Finally, they were alone to enjoy their honeymoon.

The Mediterranean was a bit rough during the Grimaldis' voyage, and Grace experienced some seasickness from time to time. Nonetheless, many of the ports along the way were filled with sunny days and private beaches for the newlyweds to enjoy.

The honeymoon, like everything else in Diana and Charles relationship, had its ups and downs. After spending two days at Broadland, the couple flew to Gibraltar and boarded the royal yacht *Britannia* to cruise the Mediterranean and Aegean seas. They happily frolicked and basked in the sun in a carefree manner. The many ports of call, including Sicily and Greece, brought both amusement and fun.

While in their new-married glow, they entertained and visited some world-renowned people, such as Egypt's President Sadat. While getting dressed for this formal dinner, Charles saw the fiery temper of his bride. "[Another time] on our honeymoon," Diana related, "we have our white-tie dinner for [Egyptian] President Sadat. Cufflinks arrive on [Charles'] wrists - two C's entwined like Chanel C's. 'Camilla gave you those, didn't she?' [I said.] And boy, did we have a row."

As history relates, there were many more to come.

Their honeymoon was also where Diana began to discover just how different she and Charles were. Diana wanted many more private moments on their honeymoon than she received, but the vessel's full crew, coupled with the constant formal dinners, gave them very few intimate moments.

Charles had a completely different idea of what a honeymoon should be. He didn't mind all the people scurrying about at all—this was his way of life. Also, he wove an intellectual theme into the honeymoon that Diana knew nothing about. Charles, an extremely literate person, brought books by Sir Laurens van der Post, a South African philosopher and also Charles' good friend. Several readings and discussions of these works between Charles and Diana were done at various times during their honeymoon, even during some of their meals. These were as interesting to Diana as watching paint dry. It was not all dull and boring, however; there were ports of call, with the expected shops and sightseeing that were more Diana's speed.

Diana's control was slipping away with each day, though. The bulimia was getting worse. As Andrew Morton wrote, "Their honeymoon gave no respite. In fact it became much worse as Diana would make herself sick four, sometimes five times a day."

Grace Kelly and Diana Spencer now had prestige and riches very few ever know in their lives, along with servants and other staff to fill any material whim and desire they might have. When their honeymoons ended, though, each would be given a reality check about their new surroundings and lifestyle, and be challenged by formidable tasks that would test their wills and characters, pushing each of them to the brink. Their providences contained ingredients that showed each of them what they were made of, a timetable of trials and triumphs that would forever document their place in history.

Chapter VII - Reality

The profound similarities between the two princesses presented themselves immediately as they entered their new lives. This is where the real mirroring of each of their lives began to reflect one another.

The adjustments and changes in their new worlds were filled with roles and responsibilities neither was prepared for, nor could have been fully prepared for. Also, as Judith Quine stated during a recent interview, "Both Grace and Diana had to deal with their loss of freedom." They were to learn quickly that the image of living happily ever after was merely a fantasy. Not that misery lurked around every corner; there were periods of happiness and joy. But this is where each of them showed a resiliency to adapt and overcome trials. The true personas behind their undeniable beauty dug down to the inner sanctuaries of each soul, thus exhibiting the legacies all the world would remember.

After returning from her honeymoon, the newly married Princess Grace of Monaco had to be acclimated to her new world. Even though she was more mature and worldly than Princess Diana, the transition was extremely difficult the first year. Challenges awaited her as soon as she returned from her honeymoon.

Monaco was and still is a playground and vacation resort for the rich and famous. Its main industries are gambling, tourism and entertainment. In 1861, while American men and boys were killing each other on the fields of Manassas, France annexed most of Monaco and left the principality with only its harbor and the few surrounding hills. Prince Charles III adopted what was left of the principality, and began the casino business that assured Monaco's existence into the present day. Its carnival-like atmosphere brought monarchs and dignitaries from all over Eastern and Western Europe.

Controversy has surrounded Monaco since World War II. Many Nazi and S.S. officers of the Third Reich took advantage of Monaco's facilities during the occupation of France. This did not sit well with America's State Department. To his credit, Rainier joined the free French Forces during World War II. After Germany's surrender, he worked in French intelligence. According to one of Grace's biographers, "In this capacity he saw seventeen months of service and was awarded the medals that he wore so proudly on his wedding day." His efforts were rewarded with the *Croix de Guerre*, the equivalent of America's Bronze Star.

Rainier was intelligent, crafty, and shrewd. Also, he was extremely loyal and focused when he became ruler of Monaco in 1949. With his loyalty to the Allies during the last part of World War II, fences were mended. Grace, however, would become one of the key components to Monaco's revitalization. Her presence brought a flood of American tourism to the principality, though the beginning of her tenure in Monaco was a tedious one.

The transition into Grace's new life and residence was very difficult. She knew the role she wanted to play in her duties, but felt somewhat stifled. Yet the discipline of her mother's examples on Henry Avenue, plus her maturity, displayed the purpose she desired. She was better prepared than Diana for her role as wife and mother because of the role-modeling she had received from her family, and her religious upbringing. In our interview, Judith Quine stated that the period in which Grace became princess should be considered. "Grace was more conscious of her sense of duty, again this being a characteristic of her era."

That awareness wasn't enough, though, for some of the obstacles she immediately faced.

Parenting was going to be an instinctive evolvement for both Grace and Diana; they were both naturals in the nurturing and love they gave their children. Even so, their relationships with their husbands were going to be a completely different matter. Those relationships, along with the lifestyle changes for Grace and Diana, were going to bring burdens they never considered.

Grace was a foreigner in a foreign land, so the citizens of Monaco were at first a bit cold and unresponsive to the American who had invaded their territory. Any minor change she tried to make was met with resistance by the palace staff. According to the book *The Royal House of Monaco*, "Palace officials drilled her daily about what she could and couldn't do as princess." It seemed that the protocol powers-that-be in Monaco were very austere in how they wanted traditions and procedures followed.

Rainier and Grace were also making their own adjustments to each other. Their courtship was brief, to say the least, and Grace was in Rainier's domain now. The prince's temper, which several authors have written about, could ignite at a moment's notice. Rainier's secretary, Madge Tivey-Faucon, related many scuffles. This sometimes caused embarrassment for Grace. "How many times I have seen the princess coming out of her room sniffling, red eyed," Tivey-Faucon said. "'I have a cold,'" she would tell me, to hide her embarrassment."

Both princesses had a hard time establishing a common ground with their husbands. With both Rainier and Charles, their upbringing was reflected in their personality traits. The two men were used to being served, and having their own way. Privileged and catered from childhood, they were used to their power and authority, and had no hesitation about asserting themselves. Also, this was Europe, where wives were expected to fill their roles in European tradition. As written in *The Royal House of Monaco*, "A European husband is definitely head of the household."

Princess Grace adjusted to and played to the tradition more easily than Diana. There were several of reasons for this: Grace's nonconfrontational personality, her self-discipline, and her acceptance of the atmosphere she had chosen projected the appropriate image. Most important, though, for the prince and princess of Monaco, was the love they had for each other, which went only one way in the case of Charles and Diana. At times, Rainier's overbearing nature and the loss of her former life brought hurt, heartache, boredom and melancholy. However, these were sacrifices Grace was willing to make, and the sanctity of her marriage sacrament was unwavering because of her faith.

After the birth of their first child, Caroline, a trust and bond began forming between Grace and all of Monaco. It was a slow process, but was the opening she had worked for and deserved. For example, the eight-hundred-year-old royal residence was in desperate need of renovation. Grace rolled up her sleeves and set to work modernizing the gloomy, disheveled castle, bringing in contractors and decorators from all corners of Europe to effect the transformation. Even Rainier admitted the castle was long overdue for a transformation, which Grace accomplished with excellent results.

Princess Grace's new role had an immediate positive effect on Monaco's economy. This provided the much-needed funding for the work the principality needed, and tourism flourished there as never before. Grace's impact and celebrity status gave the principality an even greater push as a desirable status symbol.

Though there was a downside because of the principality's small size, as with their wedding, with the crowds came the media. The overwhelming influx of tourism and media interest sandwiched Rainier and all the other citizens into frequent mob scenes, something few of Monaco's citizens were accustomed to. While this was a burden they would have to tolerate, it was a frustration Rainier was never going to get used to.

With everything taken into consideration, Grace was just the shot in the arm Monaco needed. As is so well stated in *The Royal House of Monaco*, "They were coming to Monaco like Arabs go to Mecca."

Without Grace, Monaco would never have become the resort playground it did become under her influence. As far as the Princess of Wales was to experience, the adjustments, crowds, media and problems were going to be even more overwhelming.

Reservations and apprehensions entered the picture for Charles and Diana even before the honeymoon ended. This was due to one central fact: Charles' love was never committed on a personal or romantic level. They were both naïve in their expectations, though. Charles had hoped for a part-time wife and marriage that he could call upon when the need arose. Diana wanted the burning, passionate loving relationship she had dreamed of. With Charles' lack of commitment, that was not to be, and the smooth road each sought quickly became a pavement of bumps and potholes that neither asphalt nor concrete could repair.

With Charles being a world-renowned dignitary, he and Diana were required to consort with other celebrities and world leaders during their honeymoon. President Sadat of Egypt was the first. Diana was very flighty and giddy in her behavior during his visit, failing to act with the reserve Charles had expected. This was what Charles was used to, and was the way he had been brought up, and he expected a mature and more experienced demeanor to pervade the princess' personality. "The honeymoon period," said a connection of the royal family and possessor of one of the greatest titles in the land "did not last past the honeymoon."

Not being a confrontational person, Charles delegated this responsibility to Diana's private secretary, Oliver Everett. This was to lead to the first of many head-butts for the newlyweds.

The fault of Diana and Charles's early marital problems did tip the scale in Charles' direction, although Diana was not completely innocent by any means. Diana was barely out of her teens, and had not been raised by the strict standards and protocol Charles had. Her immaturity, though prevalent, could have been looked upon with understanding. On the other hand, Diana did not help herself. She knew the responsibilities of her new life were going to be astronomical and, in the beginning at least, she wasn't willing to do the required work to achieve the needed results. She detested studying history, or anything that had to do with protocol or politics. By neglecting these necessities, she put herself at a disadvantage that would make her vulnerable in many situations. In the face of her new duties, this all surfaced quite abruptly.

This was not the only obstacle standing in the way of success for this infant marriage. Diana did not like the country life, and grew bored with it quickly. During their courtship, she had deceived Charles into thinking that she was comfortable in the country. Nothing could have been further from the truth. The world-renowned union the world had been captivated by was quickly building walls that even the most powerful explosives could not penetrate. The future king and queen came to discover very quickly that they were thoroughly incompatible.

Diana and Charles had both made grave mistakes in their assessment of each other. Diana was a young, vibrant woman who loved the fast-paced glamour of the city. Shopping, music and dancing in the clubs and pubs were the pleasures she desired. Also, the burning furnace of romance she fantasized about was quickly being extinguished by their irreconcilable differences, and the shadow of Camilla Parker-Bowles.

Charles, on the other hand, was as much the country gentleman as Diana's own father. Even though his duties brought him to all points of the globe, from urban to rural, he cherished his leisure time in the country. Here riding, playing polo, hunting, fishing and gardening were his passions. The two personas could not have contradicted each other more.

Another ingredient that drove the wedge between them even more firmly was stubbornness. Compromise was not a word that either of them had in their vocabulary—Diana because of immaturity, and Charles because of his upbringing. Neither one of them had any thought of meeting their new partner halfway. It was as if they were sitting on opposite ends of a long table with neither willing to take one seat towards each other.

Could anyone or anything have helped? Perhaps, but no one and nothing seemed to ever be offered. All their family and friends could seem to do was either ignore the situation, or make it worse. All parties dug in quickly for the many battles in the war that would go on for more than a decade. This was a nonnegotiable situation that was going to play itself out with torment, anger, and heartbreak in the years to come.

This even reflected in the newlyweds' residences. When Charles bought Highgrove, he did so with his tastes and interests in mind: the gardens, nearby polo fields, his sister's home and direct neighbor, Camilla Parker-Bowles, whose sharp thorns quickly poked in Diana's side from the time of her marriage. Charles did give Diana full reign over the interior decorating, which like Grace in Monaco, she did a splendid job with. Though immature in other respects, when it came to taste in fashion or decor, Diana was wise beyond her years.

She didn't like Highgrove, though. It was too small a house for her liking. Also, it was too far away from the things she adored. Kensington Palace, with its grand space and increased potential, was her style. Here she could live and lounge in the manner she saw herself in as the future queen of England. The large rooms at Kensington Palace ignited the energy she desired when entertaining the friends her young spirit longed for. She could also see her sister Jane at Kensington whenever she chose, since Jane resided there. Again, this was to become a constant tug of war between Diana and Charles.

The two princesses were now established in their new environments. For better or worse, which would play itself out for each, this was now the reality they would face. Each had their new homes, and duties before them. The first and foremost of those was being mothers, and each fulfilled that one immediately.

Grace and Diana, long before their "I do's," were each examined to make sure they were able to bear children without complication. The doctors' prognosis that each of them was able to conceive without difficulty was correct. Each princess became pregnant shortly after her marriage.

The confirmation that Princess Grace was pregnant came in May of 1956. Some of the seasickness she experienced during her honeymoon was probably a combination of rough seas and pregnancy. Grace, Rainier, and everyone else were ecstatic. Grace immediately wrote Judy Kanter (Quine) and the other bridesmaids to spread the good news: "Darling Judybird, We're preggos!"

Wanting to have the best of everything for their arriving child, Grace and Rainier decided to go back to America for a shopping spree. The couple, who knew that American manufacturing would have latest equipment well before Europe, returned to the "Big Apple" to pick up every new appliance or device that could modernize the palace.

During the stay, they naturally visited many of Grace's family and friends. It was the peak of autumn then, when the Northeastern United States turns into a prism of colored foliage in all manner of vibrant pigments, and the cooling north winds and Indian summer days bring school bells and football games in an excitement known only in the Continental United States.

The new princess had a few moments of homesickness as her mind drifted to the carefree days of youth. As Judith Quine relates, "'I'm going to miss autumn in New York,' she told her friends, and then realized she had just let us know—for the first time—that not everything in her life was perfect."

In truth, the transition *had* been extremely difficult for Grace. Her new world was completely different from the suburbia of Henry Avenue, or the hustle and bustle of Broadway and Hollywood. However, Grace Kelly was no quitter. Good and bad days lay ahead for her, and she was up to the task of facing them. Her sad feelings passed, and she returned to the life she had chosen.

On January 23, 1957, a girl named Caroline was born to the Prince and Princess of Monaco. Because of the publicity it would surely draw, Grace and Rainier decided not to have the birth at a hospital. The library at the palace was converted into a delivery room to keep the microphones and cameras away during the final critical hours. The royal couple and their families, as well as Monaco's citizens had great joy and celebration: Fireworks and a festive atmosphere carried throughout the tiny kingdom and expanded across Western Europe, America and the world itself.

Grace Kelly, the devout Catholic, had now totally fulfilled the sacrament that meant so much to her. Since her days of folded hands and white gloves at Ravenhill, she had completed the teachings of the Church she was so dedicated to. She now no longer had to worry about having marriage and motherhood pass her by. One of the most beautiful and exquisite women God ever created now felt complete.

👑 👑

Like so many other things in the two princesses' lives that mirrored each other, the events leading up to the birth of their first children were no different. Like Grace had, Diana also became pregnant during the last part of her honeymoon. Yet unlike Grace and Rainier's experience, there were some reservations about the news. Charles had wanted to wait about three years, or until the marriage was on a firm footing. However, the future King of England found out shortly after his wedding that fatherhood was not far away.

As it turned out, this was probably the greatest blessing Charles and Diana had in their entire marriage. After getting over the initial shock, Charles became totally absorbed by the impending future. He read and studied diligently in preparation for parenting. This period gave Diana and Charles some of their happiest times. Unfortunately, these were also some of their darkest times.

Even though Diana became pregnant easily and had no trouble carrying the baby to term, her emotional and psychological problems had almost disastrous results. This did not take long. By Christmas, after only five months of marriage and at three months' pregnant, Diana's problems and misery built up such pressure that desperate measures were all she had left. By January she was threatening suicide. Charles, as green as a boot-camp recruit in dealing with this, didn't take her threats seriously; he alternately ignored Diana's distress, or would tell her to get hold of herself and grow up.

This is one of the saddest things about depression. For those who have never suffered a serious attack of clinical depression, the unknown pain and misery is often misunderstood. The stifling, imprisoning bouts that cripple individuals send them through torturous periods that leave energy levels on "empty" and thought processes in a thick fog. The depression can become so punishing that any and all means of escape are tried, even if the end of life is the only peace. In Diana's case, she needed to get someone's attention, or as she put it, someone to answer "My cries for help."

During one of those moments, Diana pleaded with Charles for help. Again, thinking she was crying wolf, he ignored her. After he had left, Diana followed through on her threat. As Andrew Morton described the incident, "Standing on top of the wooden staircase she hurled herself to the ground, landing in a heap at the bottom." The shock sent the queen mother, the first one to arrive on the scene, into a complete state of panic as she shook with fear.

Diana, Charles, and all others connected with their turbulent lives were lucky. Upon the arrival of her doctors, an examination found she had only suffered some bruises. Further examinations showed the fetus was not damaged. A large caliber bullet had been dodged.

Even with an incident like this, one that could have had grave consequences, no lessons were learned. Charles still avoided the realization that his wife was a very sick young woman. This was only Diana's first attempt to harm herself. In the following weeks, she injured herself in other ways. These ranged from throwing herself into a glass cabinet, slashing her wrists, and cutting herself with a penknife. When Diana's sister Jane observed her wounds, she was appalled. The Princess of Wales' self-mutilation—physical evidence of her suffering—was a direct link to all the other traumas that surfaced.

Years later, in 1995, Diana's status would bring this psychological disease to the forefront. After her death, *Time* Magazine published a story in their Behavior section on the plights and quandaries of the disorder. Diana had told the BBC in one her many interviews, "You have so much pain inside yourself." The description Diana gave was like so many others' cries for help, and the direct link to her eating disorder made her a pioneer in recognition of the suffering millions of women have endured.

Diana did receive some psychotherapy from a number of psychiatrists and psychologists. Various methods, medications, and techniques were tried, but with limited success. This parallels the experiences of many others. The predominant problem with mental illness is that it is as far removed from an exact science as anything in the medical world. The normal nature of most diseases, whether curable, treatable or fatal, provides some direction to follow. Yet there are a number of diseases that baffle both patient and physician with respect to treatment; none, though, have as many gray areas as depression.

Different mental health professionals can all reach different conclusions and prescribe different medications. This is how it seemed to be for Diana also. Although some doctors helped a bit, she suffered through the same trial-and-error stagnation of mental illness for years. Although she did make some definite strides, her personal life was filled with too much despair, loss, and disappointment to ever break out completely. Even with all the help that was available to her, the number of problems she had was overwhelming. The web of problems for Diana that began just before her marriage spun more and more during the first few years, choking her emotions to asphyxiation. Each time she was able to flail enough to release some of her bondage, more troubles would arise and sever any therapeutic oxygen.

Diana's world for the most part was out of control, and there was further suffering that had to be endured. As oppressive as it was, it shaped a character that became mature, intelligent, savvy, shrewd and most of all compassionate. When she hit bottom, she did not give up—she got up and found the path back out, slowly but surely climbing to a destiny that would elevate Diana to humanitarian heights never seen before in Britain's royal family.

Between Diana's bulimia, anxiety, depression and pregnancy, she still had to perform her duties. The United Kingdom and the world itself had fallen in love with her. This again was a no-compromise situation as far as Charles was concerned. No matter how she felt, Charles would hear nothing of her deviating from their schedule. This, too, had a good and bad side. As miserable as she was, the engagements she had to get through passed the time and focused her mind on the events themselves, thereby taking her mind off her other problems, and gaining the valuable experience she needed to rise to the heights of popularity no one had seen before. "At the same time," Morton relates in his biography, "her deep sense of duty and obligation impelled her to keep up public appearances for the sake of the public."

Charles was the definition of responsibility when it came to his work and duties. In her own way, so was Diana. The shy, coy girl, who was thrown from ordinary subject to the highest form of prominence, always came through when the curtain rose. Her public persona never wavered from adversity when out in public. The inner explosions were temporarily tucked away so she could pass along the warm smile and gentle touch that made ordinary individuals feel special. This precious, God-given gift was matched by few women in history.

Between Diana's conflict and sadness, there were some good times. The coming of their first child helped somewhat to bond their inept relationship. Suddenly, the awkward atmosphere was enriched with flowing conversation that brought the two of them as close as they ever were.

The media, press, and tabloids were given much easier access to do their jobs with Princess Diana's pregnancy than they had with Princess Grace's. Diana chose a hospital delivery, making photo opportunities much easier for the cameras that captured the comings and goings of all concerned. Diana was given the entire top floor of the hospital for the historic event. Princess Grace had delivered naturally, with no anesthesia, but Diana was not one for pain. She instead chose the easier road of a spinal injection.

Diana delivered a healthy baby boy two weeks early, at 9:03 PM on June 6, 1982 at St. Mary's Hospital. The baby's weight was seven pounds, ten ounces. He was named William. Diana's mother, Frances Shand-Kydd, was the first grandmother to pay homage the following day. The queen followed a while later. Upon seeing her new grandson, Queen Elizabeth seemed relieved as she commented, "Thank goodness he hasn't got ears like his father."

Diana phoned several friends to relay the joyous news. Wanting to leave the hospital as soon as possible, Diana asked the doctor if she could leave that day. Everything had gone fine, so the doctor granted her permission to leave.

Back at Kensington Palace, everything was in place for the homecoming. Nursery, bathrooms, and nanny quarters were all ready to handle the young couple and their newborn. Barbara Barnes, who was well qualified and had come highly recommended by Princess Margaret, became the infant prince's nanny.

England, as well as the entire world, by celebrating the birth of the new prince, had a refreshing break from the torment some subjects were dealing with during the Falkland Islands Campaign. With lives lost and nerves on edge, the birth temporarily replaced the headlines that had brought anguish to Great Britain.

Diana had her own party at Kensington to celebrate William's birth. The big event, though, came on August 4, 1982—both Queen Elizabeth's and the queen mother's birthdays. This day was also chosen for the new prince's baptism. So with great pomp and circumstance, William Arthur Phillip Louis was baptized and took his rightful place of second in line to the kingdom of Great Britain.

👑 👑

For both young women, the setting was complete. They had now put the final piece of each of their puzzles together. Crowned royalty, married, and now mothers, the dreams of each had become reality. The future before them, though, was to test each character severely. Each would experience many triumphs, but trials lay ahead as well.

Things had changed drastically from the lives they had known. Diana quickly learned that the man she was totally in love with pledged most of his heart to another. Grace, who had felt the total inferno of romance and intimacy in her earlier relationships, would have that in parts of her marriage, but at other times, she would see the thermostat with her husband fluctuate. They had each given up the freedom so cherished by most individuals. Hemmed into an environment that, although luxurious, binds its inhabitants with constricting isolation, they would each grow, age, mature and experience lives few know. Praise, respect, and adoration would be showered on them in their public lives, comforting and humbling their egos. At other times, the media, press and those wanting their pound of flesh would bring a cold, hard driving deluge pelting, stinging and chilling them to the bone.

As the personal aspects of their reigns evolved, Princess Grace would hold her family together. Even though problems would arise, there was enough love given to her and enough love she had to give to last until her death. In contrast, Princess Diana was on a one-way street with all the traffic against her. Without true love, her unhappiness was the primary result of not being number one in her husband's heart. From her wedding until her death, Diana's heart gave love many times, but only received it briefly.

Both women knew they were special, and were always thankful for what God had given them. However, human they were. Their natural feelings of love, intimacy, and self-doubt could not be supplanted by anything material, and their parapets couldn't shield them from the arrows that would wound their spirits many time. Yet their hearts, though hurt, became their release valve, demonstrated in the love and compassion they showed others. By giving back much more than they received, their faith and survival skills worked, coped, and triumphed.

Chapter VIII - Parenthood Priorities and Problems

The two royal couples were now in an aspect of their lives where each would excel: parenting. Though there is no such thing as a perfect parent or parents, the four royals were dedicated and capable. Mistakes were made as in all families; however, each cared, nurtured and loved their children as much as any other devoted parents. Far more important that the material world each child was born into was the affection, tenderness, and compassion present. Silver spoons can never replace these crucial ingredients in a child's world. Child abuse and neglect, so prevalent by the end of the last millennium and carried into this one, was and is the darkest disgrace of society's shame.

But Diana and Grace's children were fortunate. True wisdom well beyond her years was paramount in each young mother. Each mother emphasized character as an essential and mandatory component as far as her children were concerned. Also, each princess had decided from the beginning that their public lives were never going to be put ahead of their motherhood. In *Grace: an Intimate Portrait*, it was written, "Shortly after Caroline was born in 1957, Grace declared to a reporter that she would 'not let public life or anything else push me out of my job as a mother.'"

♕ ♕

Fourteen months after Caroline's birth, Princess Grace gave birth to a son. Prince Albert was born on March 14, 1958. Naturally, everyone involved was ecstatic. Now there was truly an heir to the throne of Monaco.

Both the Prince and Princess of Monaco had unbiased desires to make sure their children grew up with love, compassion and understanding. According to Judith Quine, Rainier's ambition for this was as strong as Grace's: "The strongest characteristic of their compatibility was their commitment to family." The prince's parents had divorced during his childhood, and he did not have many fond memories of his growing-up years, so he wanted to make certain his children were raised with the safety and stability of a complete and nuclear family.

Grace also had her own philosophies about family, and she wanted to bestow them on her children. The strict, stern upbringing she had received left a blueprint for change in her mind; in particular, she wanted her children to be allowed more openness and expression in their endeavors. "She also liked to encourage Caroline's relationships with other children," Judith Quine said in our interview.

Together, Grace and Rainier imparted a warm and loving atmosphere for their children. To that end, Prince Rainier wanted a special place for Grace, the children, and himself to get away from the monarchy's sometimes overbearing protocol. He bought a sixty-acre retreat high above the hills of Monaco called Roc Agel. Here they could relax and be themselves. Grace found that she could unwind there and be more American: Casual clothes, barbecues, and playing with the children gave them the escape they needed, and they tilled and planted gardens together, brought a variety of animals, and developed various hobbies that interested them. Very seldom did they have overnight guests—this was their sanctuary, and they wanted to keep it that way.

These were the happy, joyous times the American actress had always dreamed of. When the children were growing up, Grace would organize an "American week" each summer. This would bring the culture of the States to Monaco in the form of cookouts and softball games. When the children were small, they also looked forward to their weekly visit from Aunt Leonore. They were told that she lived in one of the remote rooms of the castle. In reality, this was actually Rainier himself, who would put on a full garb to entertain the children, a 1960s version of Mrs. Doubtfire.

The Christmas season became a center of celebration for the Grimaldis. Advent's waiting time became a vestibule of preparation in which Princess Grace poured out her service for mankind: not only for her family, but for the citizens of Monaco as well. Christ's place in all of the Grimaldis' Christmas celebrations was firmly predicated in the birth of the Savior. In Howell Conant's book, *Grace: An Intimate Portrait*, "She [Grace] and the family celebrated a private midnight mass in the palace chapel each year."

With her stage and cultural background, Princess Grace bestowed her literary and acting talent on her children. Nightly readings and storytelling became a ritual even the children's nanny looked forward to. This was one of the gifts and qualities God had bequeathed to the young mother, one she took full advantage of. Grace had done much research on childrearing and became a student of Dr. Benjamin Spock, the guru of his era on parenting. According to Robert Lacy, one of her biographers, "Grace studied her Spock as if it were the Bible."

Grace thought she was strict; however, the modern techniques she employed left rigid and disciplined philosophies on the backburner. Often the children would accompany her to fashion shows and art galleries. The children's behavior became mischievous from time to time, a normal response for any toddler when boredom appears. With Princess Grace being the mother and primary caregiver, the children were nurtured more with American customs than European. Predictably, Princess Grace's friends' feelings varied by their continent: her American friends approved, and her European friends did not.

Besides Grace's strict Catholic values, politically she was on the conservative side. In the end, though, the hopeless romantic and compassionate personality was what showed, and her heart always had a place for the troubled individual, whom she was always willing to listen to. The loyalty to family and friends was one of her greatest virtues. Even when Caroline would fuss and cry when engagements took Grace away from her first child, Grace's motherly instincts comforted her. She never became angry or upset with her daughter.

A third and final child came to the Prince and Princess of Monaco on February 1, 1965. She was a girl, and they named her Stephanie. Grace had suffered two miscarriages prior to Stephanie's birth, so the joy of giving birth to what was to be her last child illuminated the princess. Being the devout Catholic she was, it is certain she would have had more children had she been able to; however, she suffered many complications. Finally, in 1967, on vacation at the World's Fair in Montreal, Princess Grace became gravely ill. Not only was she found to be having a miscarriage (her third), but the doctors also determined the baby had been dead inside her for about a month. The doctors then gave Grace and Rainier the sad news that her childbearing days were over. So the three healthy children she did have were to become the center of her universe.

Like so many times before and after, the bond between Grace and Judith Quine aided each other during this loss. After leaving the hospital in Montreal, Grace and the children went to Ocean City and then on to California, where Judith lived. Judith Quine had recently separated from her second husband, actor Tony Franciosa. In the quite tranquility of the poolside, they had another therapeutic talk.

It had been eleven years since the wedding in Monaco, but both Grace and Judith were candid in the changes that had taken place over the years. According to Judith, that day their conversation centered on the failure of two marriages for Judith, and Grace's full commitment to the sacrament she would not break. "I know you don't believe in divorce," Judith said to Grace, "that it runs contrary to your religion, and that you would not, no matter what the circumstances, allow your marriage to fail."

"'You're right,' Grace said, nodding."

The critical issue Judith was pointing out to her most intimate friend was the emotional loneliness she felt, whether married or not, and a detachment causing her to feel lost and isolated from the familiar, loving security we all desire. Judith shared with Grace her hope that, when she found love again, she would find the gift of two-way intimacy with a man.

For Grace's marriage, there were no alternatives. She told Judith, "Some of us sign for a run-of-the-play contract no options."

There was a difference for Grace, though, which was her faith. Even in the rough periods of her life and marriage, when God seemed far away, she knew He was beside her. Though the trials she experienced tried to pull her towards those hopeless feelings of being all alone, she always had Christ's love with her, a love that was renewed with the her consistent practice of receiving Christ's body and blood in the Eucharist each time she attended mass.

These two best friends, who became as close as any siblings, knew they had to lead their own lives; but the care and protection they brought each other would always maintain the cohesion, even when they were thousands of miles apart. "I rose from my chaise, moved to hers, and we hugged each other so hard that I could hear her heart beating," Judith wrote in her book *The Bridesmaids*.

The joys and sorrows of parenting became the lifeline that held Grace steadily throughout the remaining years of her life. In his book about her life, Howell Conant wrote, "For Grace, this was a magical time. Asked if winning an Oscar (for *The Country Girl*) was the most exciting thing that had ever happened to her, she said, 'No, it was the day when Caroline, for the first time, began to walk. She took seven small steps by herself, one after the other, before reaching me and throwing herself into my arms.'"

Like all children, Caroline, Albert and Stephanie had their fair share of antics, escapades and annoyances during their childhoods. Some of these included Caroline's cutting up her favorite book because Albert had touched it. Another was when Judy Quine's ten-year-old daughter and Caroline were found trying to lower Stephanie's head into a poolside toilet bowl. (With my being eight years younger than my brother, I, too, had made a few resounding echoed syllables, as my cranium met the same fate.)

Yet what the Grimaldi children did while they were young was fairly harmless, and at times their frolics even brought on a good amount of laughter. As the girls grew into their mid-teens, though, things began to happen that weren't a bit funny; a period began that put both Grace and Rainier through episodes that would challenge people of any stature.

Caroline had completed her education at St. Mary's Catholic School. However, the Catholic education she received had different results than that of her mother's. As is related in *The Royal House of Monaco* "...Caroline, thrilled to be free from the strict school environment, suddenly rebelled, directly challenging her mother's conservative standards." The end result: she needed to study further in Paris. The then-sixteen-year-old asked Grace and Rainier if she could live with a girlfriend while attending school. At first Grace, as she should have, gave a resounding no, reasoning that Caroline was far too young. Finally, Grace relented and sent Caroline by herself to live with friends of theirs, the Ciorettos. From almost the day she arrived, the paparazzi hunted Caroline endlessly. When the endless stalking didn't abate, Grace had no choice but to go to Paris and help her firstborn. This did not stop the media, but at least Grace was there to help Caroline deal with the onslaught. Yet the paparazzi's fury would only escalate from these moments to Grace's tragic death and beyond.

Another way Grace did not live up to her ideals was her cavalier disciplining of Stephanie. Both Grace and Rainier were much more

81

tolerant and permissive of their youngest child than they had been with Caroline. Stephanie, a very manipulative child, took advantage of their largesse and played her parents round and round like a carousel. When Stephanie was just a baby, Grace commented that: "My baby Stephanie is going to be the most interesting of my children. You wait and see."

This was to become an understatement that would send Grace and Rainier on multiple scenes of aggravation and heartache, the worst of which to be played out after Grace's death.

Diana, like Grace, was a natural at motherhood. Both Diana and Grace were hands-on parents, pure and simple. Even more, Diana had worked with children throughout her adolescence and teen years, and had no trouble nurturing her own. Charles had done his homework also. He read and studied all the latest books on parenting, and was very devoted and forthright in his quest to be a good father. In the beginning of William's life, this bond quelled some of the friction between the couple. The thrill of motherhood even set her bulimia into a short remission.

The Prince and Princess of Wales had a second and final child come into their life on September 15, 1984. His name was Henry Charles Albert David. The entire world would know him as Harry, though. The second pregnancy went very well. The Princess, still in the clutches of bulimia, did not gain very much weight at all; and with their mother's problem, it was a blessing that the two boys were each born normal and healthy. Like William, Harry was also born at St. Mary's. Charles and Diana did the nurturing aspect of early development as well with their second son as their first. Diana was extremely understanding and caring in her introduction of William to his new brother.

However, the prince and princess had somewhat different philosophies about the upbringing of children. Although both of them were extremely dedicated to their role of parenting, clashes about childrearing emerged with the many other problems that always faced these two completely different individuals. Andrew Morton noted, "She believes that it is essential that her children grow up in the outside world and not hidden away in the artificial environment of a royal palace."

Princess Diana respected her royalty, but wasn't awed by it. In contrast, Charles was completely dedicated to it. Even though William's birth made him cut back somewhat, he still had a stoic sense of duty. This is not surprising: after all, this is how he had been raised. Duty and responsibility were the number one priorities that his parents, lay staff, and teachers had ingrained in him from childhood. Diana had different views, and had no problem pointing them out. Although seemingly coy in mixed company, she could convey her feeling quite clearly to people she knew, especially Charles. When it came to assertiveness, Diana was far away from keeping her feelings and opinions hidden—a distinct difference between Diana and Grace.

Diana put motherhood well ahead of any sense of duty she had, especially in William's first couple of years. Also, to go along with the bulimia, Diana suffered postpartum depression after William's birth, which just added to the growing list of problems. The never-ending tug-of-war over the amount of time Charles spent with them became a problem for both Charles and his staff. This was not the tiny principality that Monaco was; engagements, speeches, dedications and various other events demanded a never-ending agenda from the future king. Diana would hear none of it, though. When Charles told her time after time what was expected of the two of them in their roles, she complained relentlessly.

The more relaxed, even carefree environment Diana had grown up in was history. She rebelled, though, by continuing to feel the priorities of her title weren't all-encompassing. As far as any decisions about "the boys" were concerned, nothing got past Diana. When it came time to make a decision on their education, Diana's philosophy won out. Charles had wanted the boys to be reared in the same manner he had been. This would have involved the constant presence of nannies and governesses, not the parents. As a boy, Charles only saw his parents once a day, and they were never his first human contact of the day. Usually midday was the only time spent with his parents at all.

There was no way Diana was going to follow this tradition. Diana wanted the boys to be exposed to the social aspects and camaraderie of being with other children. Like Grace, she wanted them to experience as much normalcy as possible in their abnormal world. So when the time arrived to make decisions on the boys' formal education, Diana made sure she took the lead. For his preschool education, Diana started William at Mrs. Mynor's School in the Notting Hill Gates section of London. The school, only a short drive from home, had average children whom Diana wanted William to socialize with. When William proved to be quite a handful, especially on the playground, Diana was stern with him when she was told of his behavior. She was very supportive of her son's teachers, and made him toe the line herself when needed. From there, William went on to Wetherby Pre-prep and then Ludgrove Preparatory School.

The schools Diana chose for the boys over the years proved to be the right choices. Harry followed his older brother to Mrs. Mynor's, and eventually on to the same secondary prep school, Eaton. Both princes received marvelous educations as a consequence.

Yet, as went with the territory, the paparazzi were always lurking. Unless Diana kept the boys completely isolated, which would have been completely contradictory to Diana's philosophy, the media attention would become a part of William and Harry's world also. And so she allowed it to a degree.

This was one of the best decisions Diana made as a parent. Exposing the boys to as much of the surrounding world as possible, they were prepared for and adjusted to what the future would be. Even as teenagers, they already realized this gift of preparedness they received from their mother was vital to their happiness and success.

This is not to say that theirs was in any way a happy household. The hell Diana and Charles put each other through for the first part of their marriage took staff along for the ride as well. The three that were involved most in these encounters were their two private secretaries and the children's nanny. Oliver Everett, Edward Adeane, and Barbara Barnes endured many frustrating and anxious moments that both interfered with their jobs and caused them unjust blame. Almost everyone during their careers becomes a member of this club at least once, and this was certainly the case of working for the prince and princess. As one example: after William's birth, Diana would arrange her schedule so she could be with him during the most important times, which included meals and bedtime each day. This became very frustrating for all, especially Oliver Everett, the one on whom the burden fell to try to keep Diana on task. Conflicts would result from Diana's canceled appointments, usually scheduled months in advance.

Sadly, the once-gregarious relationship Everett and Diana had together eroded as Charles and Diana's problems mounted. Of the three staff, Oliver Everett got the biggest royal screwing, as Lady Colin Campbell related in her book *Diana In Private.* In the book, Lady Campbell wrote, "She turned against him, for no apparent reason."

But of course there were reasons, partly due to Diana's own misery and her controlling personality. Even with that understanding, Oliver Everett was in a no-win situation from the beginning. He had left a promising career in the British Foreign Office to become Diana's private secretary, and was led to believe that he would be Diana's private secretary indefinitely. When the friction between Everett and Diana grew beyond repair and he was dismissed, the Foreign Office wouldn't take him back, so he was relegated to a go-nowhere job in the library at Windsor Castle. Since he had hired him, Charles felt extremely guilty about this, but there was no remedy.

Barbara Barnes was the second victim to be undermined and finally dismissed by the immature, jealous, and self-centered princess. Diana, through the first few years in her new life, suffered very low self-esteem: Anything that a person satisfied with their surroundings or existence would simply shrug off made her spiral downward even further. In the case of Barbara Barnes, Diana's jealousy simply got the best of her. Barbara Barnes' skills as a nanny were aboveboard—so much so, William preferred her to his own mother. After Harry was born, Diana's insecurities built up to a point she could no longer tolerate. Harry's personality reflected more of Diana's in that the bond between Harry and Diana felt more natural to her because of his carefree nature, which reminded her of herself as a child. Diana wasn't going to allow anyone, especially a nanny, interfere with any phobias she felt about her youngest son.

Finally in 1987, the situation came to a head. After a birthday party that both the Princess and Barbara Barnes attended, the press reports gave them equal billing. This sent Diana over the edge, and she confronted the nanny. By Lady Campbell's account, "She [Diana] was furious." No matter how insecure Diana may have felt, she certainly told Barnes in no uncertain terms that she was "done" when Diana returned from vacation.

William was to begin school at that same time, and Diana thought that would distract any bad publicity from the announcement. She was wrong, though. The media noticed the departure right away, and criticized Diana for it. This put another kink in Diana's armor. Diana replaced Barbara Barnes with Ruth Wallace, someone who was well qualified and, more important, someone Diana could live with. Nonetheless, Barbara Barnes' career went on without any real turmoil. Good nannies, especially someone with her qualifications, are always in great demand in today's two-family-income societies.

Edward Adeane, Charles' personal assistant, was the third major staff member to receive the ax from the prince and princess's unending discords. In Adeane's case, it was never being able to get used to Charles' family life. Things were different now. Even if Charles and Diana had fit together like a new tailored suit, the changes in Charles' life were something Adeane would have had a difficult time getting used to. Charles wasn't single any longer. Not that he and the prince had a perfect working relationship before the marriage—Edward Adeane wanted everything done to perfection, and although Charles talked a good game about dotting every "i" and crossing every "t," he seldom followed through. When the princess came along, the problems eventually became too much. So finally Edward Adeane left, making 1984 the "purge year" for Charles and Diana's staff.

On a personal and professional level, motherhood and parenting were as important and successful for each princess as any of their other achievements. Like most women, their children were their first priority. No matter what life threw at them, the love they gave to their children was unquestioned, unparalleled, and most of all, unconditional. Each of them would have walked through fire at a moment's notice for their offspring. The love they gave to so many was accentuated for these three boys and two girls. Their hearts, which devoted so much to others, beat with an endurance that always circulated their precious devotion to their children. Many happy, fun loving moments brought smiles, laughter and closeness. They each put in the time, commitment, and work necessary to reap the rewards of love given back to them by and through their children. Whether grilling hamburgers on a barbecue or riding a log flume at an amusement park, they poured love on their children like a waterfall.

Yet both princesses felt both joy and sorrow in their roles as mothers and parents. At the beginning of motherhood Grace had the much easier set of circumstances. Diana's problems, already great, only grew larger and more complex as time went on. However, as time passed and Grace's girls grew from children to teenagers, she faced situations that came in close proximity to Diana's, especially the aspects of the "face-rape" which Diana described so much in her torment from the media.

Like so many other women, Grace and Diana's natural nurturing characteristics were deeply and profoundly rooted. The spontaneous reflex of love and compassion they gave to their children were at the very core of their existence. This became especially evident when their children were older. Cruelly, though, fate would pounce upon them and snatch each away from those who needed and loved them most.

Chapter IX - Looks and Fashion

Vibrant energy surrounds the streets and sidewalks. With fervent anticipation, crowds of photographers focus lenses with bull's-eye precision. Their index fingers twitch and quiver in anticipation for the shots they want.

Smooth, sensual ankles top expensive footwear that matches the wearers' elegant gowns. The emergence of perfectly styled heads display radiant beauty, and begins a rapid-fire volley flashing and illuminating the entire area. Shimmers of light continue, filling the darkness and capturing the latest fashion statement.

Glimmering in splendor, dazzling smiles and waves precede the path taken by each princess upon reaching her destination. Shouted greetings and welcomes, which have become commonplace to these guests of honor, accompany the fanfare accorded the glamorous, stunning live portrait of each princess.

Scenarios such as these were frequently played out during the lives of Grace Kelly and Diana Spencer. Not only did their many pursuers want to gaze at these two icons' physical beauty, but also admire their chic style. The combination of art and science encompassed elegance at each public appearance, which became stages for all to envy. The admiration and desire of all those seeking their esteem were painted with an intrinsic brush that displayed portraits of worship.

Each princess had an array of designers. Some produced more of their fashions than others. With their popularity, top people in their field competed for Grace and Diana's homage and clientele. In all, the elite of fashion, photography, make-up and hairdressing produced looks for the two princesses that drew admiration the world over.

Grace Kelly's fashion statements began early in her career, well before she became a princess. In the late 1940s, her perfect, slender figure landed her numerous modeling jobs ranging from advertising household products to cigarettes. Low-heeled shoes and wool tweed suits gave the beautiful young lady a sophisticated look. Her hair was pulled back with a fishnet veil over the stunning nose, eyes and cheekbones. Her cover-girl image on various magazines showed the fresh, clean look she became known for.

There is no question that she could have made a career for herself just modeling. The long thin frame was truly made for anything the fashion world wanted to show off. Her tiny waist, which looked as if it could easily fit inside a child's swimming inner tube, accentuated her slim hips and legs. But like many young women, she felt she was too flat-chested. During her teen years she tried various methods to make herself better endowed, without success. Implants were still some thirty years away. In reality, though, Grace had the figure many young girls dream of having upon passing puberty.

As her film career blossomed in the early fifties, so did her vogue. The world of fashion is a perk all starlets are given as they climb the ladder of success. Grace was no different. The hand-me-down frugalness of Ma Kelly rubbed off on Grace somewhat. This trait made her a bit of a packrat. She kept everything she bought, never discarding anything, even when it went out of style. When out in public Grace was meticulous about her dress, though her casual dress was somewhat frumpy. With her glasses on and in her "practical dress"—as she would refer to slacks, blouses and canvas slip-on sneakers—was a completely different appearance for the woman who sent gasps throughout rooms and audiences in many of her entrances.

Oleg Cassini observed this during the early stages of his courtship with Grace. Cassini had met Grace right before her Hitchcock films vaulted her to true stardom. He suggested that she arrive at the studio glamorous, thereby becoming her part. At the time she was filming *The Country Girl*, the most non-glamorous role she ever played. Grace, who felt that she'd be depicted as just a glamour girl, said, "But I want to be taken seriously."

Cassini was a true professional, however, and knew how much potential her image had in the world of fashion. "You are becoming a major star," he told her, "and should be a leader in fashion also."

In reality, it was Alfred Hitchcock, Oleg Cassini and Edith Head were the trio that made Grace the star and fashion icon she became. Cassini's designs and mentoring coincided perfectly with Hitchcock and Edith Head in bringing Grace's fashion to the top. All three were perfectionists, totally dedicated to their profession.

Once, Cassini asked famous fashion photographer Milton Green to do a layout of Grace in some of Cassini's fashions. The result was cover girl exposure. "I thought of her as a pale, delicate English Rose," Cassini wrote in his book, *In My Own Fashion.* "The gown had a simple top and a complicated, petal-like skirt; it was made of heavy taffeta, an almost antique, soft pink, carefully selected to compliment her skin tones." This photo shoot began the "Grace Kelly Look" she became famous for.

Alfred Hitchcock also showed the world how stunning Grace could look. The roles she played in his films, especially *Rear Window* and *To Catch A Thief,* called for elegant and exquisite wardrobes. Designer Edith Head was hired by Alfred Hitchcock to transform Grace into the radiant beauty he wanted, "Like an untouchable piece of Dresden china."

Each dress or costume Edith Head designed was planned down to the last detail and color by Hitchcock. "There was a reason for every color, every style, and he was absolutely certain about everything he settled on," Head was quoted as saying about his involvement. This was a designer's dream for Edith Head, who had a generous budget at her disposal. With those funds, she and Hitchcock transformed Grace into one of Hollywood's greatest looks ever.

By the time Edith Head worked with Grace, she was already a veteran and one of the top designers in Hollywood. Having begun with Paramount Studios back in the 1930s, she had already worked with famous stars like Dorothy Lamour and Mae West. After designing Audrey Hepburn's stunning outfits for *Roman Holiday* and *Sabrina*, she began a working relationship with Hitchcock. Her first star with the "Master of Suspense" was Ingrid Bergman. Next came Grace, who she dubbed her greatest star.

Head painstakingly worked hour after hour, sketching, fitting, hemming and sewing all the fabrics that gave Grace the alluring fashions for *Rear Window* and *To Catch a Thief.* So impressive were the results that *A & E's Biography* used one of Grace's tantalizing entrances in *To Catch A Thief* to show Head's work—the scene of her first date with Cary Grant when she emerges from the elevator, dressed in a stunning black and white day dress, complete with a wide-brimmed hat to match. The hat, worn on the crown of her head, gave full view of the confident face that compelled the viewer to stare at it for its sheer beauty. The scene-setting by Hitchcock, along with the design of Edith Head, made Grace's vogue unforgettable.

Many of the gowns and dresses Grace wore in *The Swan* were a preliminary to the European monarch look she would exhibit during her reign. Although *The Swan* was by no means a box office bonanza, Grace looked radiant in all the Victorian designs in that film. Cloth, material and thread were woven in custom-designed patterns that accentuated the class and quality of future stature. The various fabrics contoured perfectly with Grace's slim figure, illustrating the essence of her beauty.

Make-up artist Harry Ray said Grace had the most beautiful skin he had ever seen. So perfect was its color and texture that she hardly needed any make-up. "I have never met anyone with skin as lovely as Grace's," he added in tribute. While other starlets would take hours to prepare for the cameras, Grace was ready in no time.

In 1955, Grace was named as one of the "best tailored women in America." With her reaching an apex so quickly on stage and screen, the "Grace Kelly Look" became all the rage. Women all over America wanted to groom themselves in Grace's style. These included the tweeds, sweaters and gently flared skirts in simple or solid patterns, low-heeled shoes, and just a touch of make-up. Also in 1955, Grace received the Neiman Marcus Award for consistently high standards and fashion. Oleg Cassini was the master fashion designer behind these honors.

When Grace won the Academy Award, another Edith Head design was exhibited to her fans and the public—a long aquamarine spaghetti-strapped sheath. Naturally, the famous white wrist-to-elbow gloves complemented the stunning outfit. Wearing this outfit, and with a shy smile and modest pose, Grace surrendered to tears from the overwhelming emotions of winning the prestigious award.

While Edith Head dressed her as a movie star, MGM was the one footing the wedding bills, and with Head working for Paramount, she had to bow out. While disappointed that she wouldn't be able to design Grace's wedding gown, Head did design the light gray silk suit with a small hat that Grace wore as she bid farewell to her family and friends and she left on her honeymoon.

When she became engaged, fashion authority Elenor Lambert put Grace's wedding trousseau together. The majority of Grace's trousseau was purchased on Madison and Seventh Avenues in New York City; there was only one gown from Paris included. Along with Lambert, many others of Grace's favorite designers also took part in the project. These included Ben Zuckerman, who helped with the main wardrobe. There were also gowns by Ceil Chapman, cocktail dresses by Samuel Winston, and day dresses by Mollie Paris. The trousseau included some stunning blue tunic suits, black and white tweed coats, hats, handbags and shoes. Mr. Fred provided the hats that put the finishing touches on each outfit. The trousseau of the future princess also included a lingerie ensemble. Juel Park of Beverly Hills coordinated designs of white and pink silk chiffon. The total for the entire trousseau came to $25,000. This was pricey for its time, if still not what some other women of the world spent during that decade.

Grace also purchased some stunning furs. These included a Canadian sable coat for $7,200, and a mink jacket for $4,800. This is when the fur industry was at its height. In fact, men like my own father toiled in New York's garment district, turning out creations for the women of the fifties. From Madison Avenue to Broadway and beyond, the look of fur was evident throughout fashionable cities that experienced a cold winter climate.

Of course included in with all these talented people was Helen Rose, whose magical hands captured Grace so stunningly in her wedding gown. Helen Rose and Grace had grown so close over the years that Helen Rose herself gave Grace one of her bridal showers. The stunning wedding gown created by Helen Rose, which made Grace one of the most beautiful brides ever, did not remain in Monaco. It was given to the Philadelphia Museum of Art in 1956, where it remains. Coincidentally, the famous steps leading into this museum are the ones Sylvester Stallone ran up in the first *Rocky* movie.

Grace's retirement from stardom brought an end to her working relationship with Edith Head. The Oscar Award-winning designer had many more beautiful stars to design for though, among them Natalie Wood and Shirley McLaine. Her career would continue for more than two decades when she died, less than a year before Grace, in 1981.

All the preparations of the various designers, their staffs and Grace herself paid dividends during the entire time encompassing the wedding. Newspapers and magazines featured pictures and articles daily from the time the *Constitution* left for Monaco. For the captain's dinner during the cruise to Monaco, Grace looked stunning in a golden beige dress made of silk organdy. A fox stole accented the gold-black print and high collar with shoes to match.

Grace's dress for the civil ceremony was much like her demeanor that day, very focused and businesslike. She chose a rose lace dress with embroidered florals. A full skirt and short jacket gave rise to the high neck, topped off with a Juliet cap and shoes to match.

Although Grace's marriage signaled the end of the limelight of Hollywood and all the glitter she had shown, the beautiful young princess still had many fashion statements to make. When she became Princess of Monaco, Her Serene Highness had an immediate impact on European fashion. Paris wasn't going to take a backseat in her fashion any longer, and the gown Princess Grace wore to her first official engagement at the Monaco Opera House was from Paris. It was designed by Lanvin-Castillo, who also made the Princess' favorite perfume, Arpege. After she returned from her honeymoon in July of 1956, Lanvin-Castillo had a private fashion show for Princess Grace, where she was shown some top-secret styles. Various choirboy skullcaps and veils, which would become fashion items, were displayed for Grace. An evolvement began instantly. All along the Riviera, casual and play clothes became a reflection of Grace, evidenced by the mass-produced wear sold in the quaint shops lining the sea.

After her marriage, many gala affairs and engagements filled the princess' social calendar, the most prestigious of which was the annual Red Cross Ball held every August. Famous friends and dignitaries descended on Monaco in extravagant ensembles, showing the lavish abundance of the rich and famous. The Princess was always on top of her game during this event, for which she was responsible, and her costumes were always among the most spectacular of the ball. One year, she had to be taken to the ball by van because her headpiece wouldn't fit inside a car.

In January of 1960, Princess Grace was named one of the best-dressed women in the world. Along with others such as Jackie Kennedy, the fashion world had several women to photograph and write about. In 1962, fashion designer Guy Laroche took sketches of some of Princess Grace's dresses for the wedding of Princess Sophie of Greece. He was intrigued by Grace's wearing black and pale colors, along with the somber lines, bateau necklines and fitted sheaths that were popular then.

As she aged, Grace's dress became more conservative. She chose simple, solid one-piece dresses with hemlines cut just above the knee. Various pleated skirts, sweaters and tops were a comfortable style for all Grace's charity work, along with tweed and wool suits for more formal daytime engagements.

In her travels representing Monaco with Rainier, Princess Grace's wardrobe reflected the countries and cultures thematically, much the same way as Princess Diana's would later. On their tenth anniversary, Grace and Rainier traveled to a folk festival in Seville, Spain. Here, Grace was crowned queen of the festival. Her garb included the traditional mantilla, which draped almost to the hemline of her dress. Later at a bullfight, Grace wore a long, flowing white flamingo dress, the beautifully ruffled lace and silk draping to the ankles. The long earrings and flowers in her hair accentuated the princess' stunning smile.

In some casual moments on vacation, Howell Conant captured Grace in family moments, going about chores much like any other woman whether she was going to the market, preparing dinner or doing things with the children at Roc Agel. Here, too, Princess Grace's casual wear reflected her personality. She wore solid day dresses, blouses and slacks, her hair up with kerchiefs gently draping the neck and shoulder, and light jackets, scarves, and saddle shoes for frolicking around the favorite retreat.

From 1956, around the time of Grace and Rainier's marriage, to 1981, Howell Conant took all the Grimaldi family portraits over the years, and they are an exquisite and poignant collection. Princess Grace's dress in the family portraits further reinforces her style and class. In them, various fashions of each era display Grace and her family proudly.

In the fall of 1997, the magazine *In Style* ran an article on Hollywood's five greatest looks. The story, by Carol Kramer and Hal Rubenstein, presented an intriguing description of how each woman carried herself, and this was attributed to each woman's own self-image. It cast the account of Grace Kelly and Audrey Hepburn facing each other at the 1956 Oscars as, "Their auras are perfect." In addition, both had the ability to make an entrance. "Glamour doesn't have to be fussy or costumey, or foolish," Vera Wang said in the fall, 1997 issue of *Style* Magazine. This was certainly true in Grace's case. There was no doubt about Grace being one of the most glamorous women of all time, when glamour meant "a woman looking her very best—like a star."

More than forty years later, Grace's look of the fifties still brings memories to the fashion world. One of the "looks" for 1999 was a sweater-skirt combination called *Retro Combo* by L. A. fashion stylist Tod Hallman. The look presented a cross between Grace Kell and Cinderella. As the century and millennium were drawing to a close in June of 1999, *Time* magazine included Grace as one of the twenty most beautiful stars of the twentieth century, saying, "Her looks were perfection." The fashions that she wore so elegantly, combined with the way she presented herself, made the star and princess one of the most breathtaking women the world will ever know.

For a country girl who never wanted to dress up for any occasion during her childhood, the Princess of Wales became the virtuoso of fashion and design. By doing so, she brought the ancient monarchies into the modern world. Barring none, Diana Spencer was the most sought-after person in all history. Many traits contributed to the perfect recipe that constituted her astounding popularity: Along with position, personality, controversy, caring and compassion, fashion was also a key ingredient.

In addition to her professional training, Diana was a natural at fashion and glamour. She had a well-proportioned 35-28-35-inch figure to complement her tall, five-foot-ten-inch frame, making her look good in any outfit. Swimming, her main form of exercise, helped to keep her lean, well-defined look. Like great tennis players such as Chris Evert who had great court sense during her tennis career, Diana's natural style for fashion as well as her compassion was born with her, too. All these attributes drew people to her like a magnet.

In November of 1997, *Harper's Bazaar* featured an article by fashion editor Liz Tilberis, who had met Diana just after she had gotten engaged to Prince Charles. Liz commented, "Lots of us would love to take credit for her transformation from conservatively dressed kindergarten teacher to fashion icon. But the truth is, she worked it all out for herself." This was true; Diana was as much of a natural at fashion as Florence Nightingale was at nursing.

So fashion and style became a multiple passion for the Princess of Wales. Through this talent she achieved attention, admiration, envy and recognition. This became even more apparent after Harry was born, when a steady transformation took hold of Diana. She began to take stock of herself and began to mature. The trials she had endured, which she had at least a partial responsibility for, finally began to bring out her strengths. By working and improving her talents, Diana's wounded self-esteem improved, and her real womanhood emerged. Fashion was the trademark characteristic that vaulted Diana well beyond any royal the British Empire had ever seen. Even more than her royal marriage, she began to display an exterior that the entire world was to cherish.

Experience and the sixth sense she had for fashion brought out a photogenic side that appealed to every camera. In *Diana: A Princess and Her Troubled Marriage*, author Nicolas Davis wrote: "The photographs taken before and just after her marriage contrast dramatically with those after William was born. She had been transformed from a pretty, round-faced young girl into an angular, sophisticated fashion plate."

Unexpectedly, Charles and Rainier both became a bit jealous of the attention their wives received. With Charles the jealousy was more prevalent. Even so, when it comes to the feminine allure, all husbands take a backseat. Even the charismatic Jack Kennedy was no match for Jackie with her double attractions of both fashion sense and a sophisticated charm. In the case of Charles and Rainier, it was like Picabo Street skiing against a weekend novice.

When single, Diana had worn the look of most women of her status, sort of an American or British "prep" look that consisted of blouses, sweaters, and dark blue skirts. This was a fitting look for a nanny or teacher, but not for the Princess of Wales. Her style was in need of a change…a daunting task, especially under the media's microscopic view.

Diana did have some help in her transformation. When she became engaged, her sister and mother got her off to a good start. Diana's sister, Jane Fellows, was working at *Vogue Magazine* as an assistant editor. According to Nicholas Davies, "When Jane approached the London editors of *Vogue* and suggested they help her sister, they enthusiastically agreed." Diana started spending time at the magazine, and soon had staff helping her mold her image. Trying various items, she discovered a blouse to her liking that had been designed by a young, unknown couple; their joint name was Emanuel. This couple became one of her early guides, giving her tips on dress, confidence and carrying herself as her title deserved. Another key person in Diana's world of wardrobe was Anna Harvey, who ended up overseeing all her early wardrobes.

Diana's instinctive fashion ability made all the clothes she wore become all the rage, and drew the attention of the world's media. In public, she had to wear British fashion designers. The main British designer she used was Catherine Walker. After Diana turned thirty, Walker became her main designer because her tailored designs fit the princess' maturing, businesslike style. "Off duty," however, she could choose from any of the world-renowned designers eager for her to display their work. St. Laurent and Armani designs became regular parts of her wardrobe.

Diana was appreciative of her designers' talent and efforts, and always remembered to give them thanks and praise. Yet this became a win-win situation for both princess and designer. You couldn't get better advertisements for your line than by having the most popular woman in the world wear the choicest selections from it. With all the problems Diana endured, her fashion statements were beyond even Jackie Kennedy's in the early 1960s. Like any other celebrity, she loved the fame and attention given to her as a result.

Being able to choose her clothing occasionally required some ingenuity. At first she was able to attend various public fashion shows. When her popularity exploded, though, she opted for private showings to dispel some of the frenzy that was always with her. At times she would pop unannounced into various shops, her private detective in tow. Sometimes this spontaneity worked out quite well for her, and she was able to look and browse without being disturbed.

Other times, she would arrange to visit stores before they opened or after they closed.

This change was, of course, necessary. Being who she was, Diana was always evaluated whenever she went out in public. People and the media were forever looking her over to see how she was dressed and scrutinizing her mood, including any communications she made with anyone. This had to be extremely trying. For the most part, though, she carried each of these exhibitions off very well, with few errors.

Negative press was a different story altogether. Although she didn't like studying history or protocol, she would review the papers each day to see what had been written about her. In her early years as princess, the media's criticism bothered her. When she matured, though, she learned to roll with the punches. During the recession of the late 80s, the media reported criticism for her spending too much on her wardrobe. She was able to halt the criticism by wearing a dress she had worn previously. However, this made all the pictures taken of her less valuable to the paparazzi.

Diana simply loved fashion, and it became the favorite part of her professional life. All Diana's clothes were organized with great care, far more than average, since whatever she wore had a direct effect on Britain's fashion industry. After she had worn an outfit, it was cleaned…then labeled and dated, just as any potentially important historical artifact is handled.

While not her first or favorite priority, jewelry was an important aspect of Diana's wardrobe, and she had a good collection that grew over the years since her marriage. Various heads of state gave her some very good pieces. Her mother-in-law, the queen, owned one of the most stunning collections in the world, and would let Diana borrow anything she needed. So jewelry became another part of the fashion statement she made wherever she went.

At home, which eventually became one of her only sanctuaries from the unbounded media, she could be casual. In this respect, she was very much like Grace—comfortable blue jeans and sweaters was the garb in which she could watch television or play with the boys. In the winter she wore men's pajamas; on London's cold, wet and nasty nights, she liked the warmth and comfort of them.

Her inborn fashion sense always came in handy when "themes" became her preferred way to present herself at certain events. Sailor hats and army jackets were well appreciated by all the military personnel she visited. Also, many foreign leaders and dignitaries were greeted with something that reflected a unique aspect of their country.

This type of fashionable notoriety made her even more enchanting to the press. Like anyone of her status, Diana tried to keep her private and public life separate, even though for someone like her, complete separation was impossible. The princess' cunning and skill enabled her to hoodwink the paparazzi most of the time. When things were in her favor and she was in control, they got their shots...but on her terms, not theirs. She would lose that control eventually, when sheer numbers of paparazzi that chased and hunted her wherever she went became unmanageable.

In the array of planned photo shoots Diana posed for over the years, she was a valuable asset in the editing many times. Photographer Patrick Demarchelier took a fabulous layout of Diana and her boys at Highgrove. After all the film was developed, Diana sat down with Demarchelier and they carefully went through the prints together, Diana as always making sure each one to be published was appropriate. Yet except for the constant hounding of the cameras, she was able to maintain some degree of separation.

Shortly before her death on August 31, 1997, Diana posed for a portfolio of some of the dresses and gowns she auctioned off for charity at Christie's. The pictures in the July 1997 issue of *Vanity Fair* were stunning. They exhibited the ascending Diana, the beautiful young women who had survived so many battles and wars. Here, a new, vibrant, happy individual, despite the pressures, anxieties and stress, had attained a more peaceful and simple life.

Most of the wardrobe items exhibited in the magazine were Catherine Walker creations. These included formal evening and dinner dresses of various styles, silk crepe and velvet revealing Diana's sensual shoulders with just a trace of cleavage. The stunning smile and perfect teeth joyfully conveyed the pleasure the princess truly felt during the shoot: Her head was thrown back or to the side, unmistakably displaying the trademark hairstyle, parted to the side and tucked behind the ears.

Buoyed and motivated by the shoot, Diana playfully requested that 'photographer Mario Testino teach her the catwalk. As he related to *Vanity Fair* magazine, "Not long after lunch, she wanted to learn the catwalk. Imagine, the most celebrated woman of our time: glamorous princess, champion fund-raiser, benefactor to the poor, mother of England's future king-learning to strut like a runway queen!"

Who could blame her, though? If there was one thing Diana Spencer and Grace Kelly were, they were one hundred percent women, from the compassionate and caring mothering side to the sultry, flirtatious sexy personas that drew the world to them.

The Christie's Auction for Charity, prompted by an idea given to her by her son, Prince William, was held in London and New York on June 2nd and 25th.,1997 respectively. Maureen A. Rorech of Tampa, Florida became an anonymous buyer of fourteen of the seventy-nine dresses Diana donated for charity. After Diana's death, Rorech personally carried on Diana's work with the theme "Dresses Save Lives." As a mother of three sons, Mrs. Rorech, like so many others, came to feel such respect for Diana she decided to use the power of the dresses to continue the work Diana would have if she had lived. The goal of this worthy project is to raise one hundred million dollars for AIDS, cancer and children's charities globally.

This project ultimately led to giving me my first real dimension of and material contact with Diana or Grace. On a dull, gray, rainy day in late December 1998, my wife and I went to view the display at the American Textile History Museum in Lowell, Massachusetts. Here in the city where I teach, I was fascinated by the elegance and beauty of Diana's wardrobe. The exhibit was gracefully displayed in a winding procession. Glass casings protected the precious cargo, as expanded pictures of the princess in her various roles gave each onlooker a feeling for Diana's life.

The twenty dresses came from four designers: the majority from Catherine Walker, along with others by Victor Edelstein, Zandra Rhodes and Bruce Oldfield. The dresses present a variety of styles, and aptly demonstrate Diana's flair: dinner and evening dresses accentuated with velvet and silk chiffon; bustles, V-necks and pleats accent rich, bright colors of the various functions where they were worn; two thematic evening dresses of nautical and Scottish design emphasized the princess' awareness and sensitivity to each even she attended. Some stunning cocktail dresses, which were worn to the auction itself, feature tediously hand sewn embroidery. Each dress represented a variety of engagements, from film premieres and performances to state dinners, including the notorious ink-blue silk velvet dinner dress the princess wore when she danced with John Travolta. As guests of President Ronald and First Lady Nancy Reagan, Diana and the *Saturday Night Fever* legend left an indelible memory for each other, and for those who witnessed them.

The dress that drew the most poignant responses was the dark green velvet dinner dress by Victor Edelstein. On close inspection, one can see a child's handprint pressed into the fabric. I couldn't help but think of one of the young princes scampering over to show affection to his beautiful mother. It is both touching and sad to be reminded of what is now no more.

As Diana's life progressed through good times and bad, so did her expertise in fashion. In *Diana: a Tribute to the People's Princess*, author Peter Donnelly wrote, "She provided unending and ample opportunities in the style press; she was our very own Jackie O, our Grace Kelly." In truth, flaunting her beauty and displaying her fashion sense were only two of the many attributes of the complex personality that kept the world fascinated.

Glamour and elegance stimulated an energy that grew and expanded wherever the two princesses went. So vast was their popularity that, as Time magazine reported in 1999, "Like Princess Grace of Monaco, Diana was a celebrity royal." This was due to the complete package each princess possessed, with fashion being a key element.

Again, the different eras of the two princesses has to be taken into consideration. As Judith Quine related to me so well: the fashion of Grace's era was "Before the lionization of fashion, or when fashion became a rock star." Fashion, like so many other capitalistic industries, has skyrocketed, especially in the last twenty years of the twentieth century. This is much like the salaries of movie stars, rock artists and athletes, whose astronomical wealth has handily eclipsed that of previous generations. In the context of their eras, Grace and Diana were superstars of fashion. When "fashion became a rock star," Diana's fashion and style went platinum and won her ever-encompassing adoration. In the generation before, Grace Kelly's fashion and style were equal or above the other renowned women of her era. In the 1950s, when Elvis became the "king of rock and roll," Grace Kelly was the "queen of fashion" even before she was a princess.

The looks and style of the two princesses presented the world with composite attraction and allure. Both men and women admired their physical beauty, and each set a standard for royalty that will never be equaled.

Chapter X - Giving Back: Charities, Causes and Commendations

"Rich the treasure,
Sweet the pleasure,
—Sweet is pleasure after pain."
John Dryden (1631–1700)
Alexander's Feast

Although the population, square mileage, climate and topography of each princess' kingdom were vastly different, the role and duties Grace and Diana played correlated significantly. It is preposterous to compare a small principality like Monaco, whose main industries are gambling, tourism and tax shelters to the British Empire. Yet even though England has long lost its most powerful nation status, it is still one of the centers of attention in Western Europe, and tourism, while not England's main industry, it is still a vital part of their economy. As with Monaco, England's royal family sits at the center of England's tourism industry. Princesses Grace and Diana each became the focal point around which each kingdom's tourist industry revolved.

Politically, the two princesses had no real power or decision-making ability with respect to their nation's policies. Those were left to Rainier and his advisers in Monaco and England's parliament respectively. That didn't dissuade either Grace or Diana from making her mark in the histories of their respective countries, or the world. They took the public relation aspects of their jobs as princesses and catapulted their efforts towards their charity and humanitarian work. This was the most significant accomplishment each of them made during their reigns, and the goodwill they achieved intertwined and fed their ambassadorship. Yet the central point of their work was the help they gave to those who needed it most.

This was a constant that never wavered with either princess. Each of them had a soft and kind heart that beat with devotion and goodness, and they were completely dedicated to their chosen charities and causes. Their involvement also became therapeutic outlets for the heartaches, boredom, and sorrows they suffered. Without these channels, which gave each of them the opportunity to serve others, the mental and emotional consequences would have been even more devastating.

Their spirituality and Christian principles guided Grace and Diana in their service to others. Princess Grace, the devout Catholic, walked as one of Christ's disciples from the time of her childhood training; Princess Diana was the seeker of Christ's love and compassion in her worldwide patronages. Both of them gave back a great deal in return for that which had been bestowed on them throughout their lives. In extraordinary ways, they showed that each person on the planet is worthwhile in the eyes of a princess. No matter what ethnic, economic or social rank from which each individual came, Grace and Diana were always ready to reach out to the unfortunate, proving that in addition to their style, each had immense substance in them as well.

Always the worker, Grace immediately put her efforts into her new career as a princess. Even as a young girl, when she and her siblings sold flowers and gave the meager proceeds to their mother's charity, the sense of helping others was instilled in her. "When she was twelve years of age," biographer Gwen Robyns reported, "Grace was allowed to become a pink girl." So at a young age, she became a wartime hospital volunteer in 1941.

Besides her religion, once again her mother's role-modeling influenced her sense of duty and charity work. Of this aspect, another biographer said, "Grace had a keen sense of duty, inherited from Ma Kelly, who still worked hard for her beloved charity, Women's Medical, in Philadelphia."

Grace, though, went far beyond her mother or other well-to-do women back home. Judith Quine emphasized the importance of Grace's humanitarian and charity work by saying, "It was a well defined priority that was vast, real and devoted." She went on to say that even with all that has been written about Grace Kelly, most people "probably don't know the extent of her work."

In her first year of marriage, while pregnant with Caroline, she threw a Christmas party for the children of Monaco. Howell Conant amplifies others' feelings by reporting that: "Each year, she would organize a party for all the children of the country, and a special party for the orphans." Grace was meticulous to the last detail, overseeing even the choosing of each present, and hundreds of happy faces played and bounced their way through the castle each year, being fed many treats and entertained by magicians and clowns. The first year's party was so successful that it became an annual event.

Princess Grace's discipleship towards orphans didn't end with the Christmas party. Far from it. The orphans of the principality were always a priority for her, and regular visits to the orphanage were always on the princess' schedule. As Conant wrote, "They appreciated her warmth and responded to it." The pain from the loss of their parents brought forth from Grace the tenderness each child was yearning for, and she always gave as much sentiment as she could.

The doctrine of Christ's call to service showed through Grace in many ways. A hospital and daycare center were named after her in 1958. Yet Grace's priority for orphans extended far beyond Monaco. In her estimation, all children were to be nurtured and loved, but especially the poor and unfortunate. "The orphans" were no idle interest to her; the total, unquestioned love her Catholic virtues had taught her was ever-present in her devotion to these children. Visiting the orphanage frequently throughout the year, she would get to know the children individually. To give further help, she established an association called *Mondiale des Amis de L'Ebfance*, AMADE for short. This association helped fight childhood poverty and disease worldwide.

The people of Monaco were her subjects, but this was something she saw as a privilege and honor. Although she was hurt by their slow acceptance of her, the subjects who needed her were always given access. Judith Quine told me that Grace held court every week, open to any citizen "to interact with the people of Monaco." She was grateful to her subjects, and always found time for them. Aside from AMADE, the charity Grace gave her greatest interest to was the Red Cross, which would become one of the Princess of Wales' humanitarian causes also.

However, The Red Cross was Monaco's main charity, and the prince transferred his presidency to Grace after their marriage. As usual, Grace arrived at the first meeting with her game face on—the serious, ready-to-get-down-to-business look, eyeglasses masking her remarkable beauty, showing by her presence that she knew what direction she wanted to take. The women on the committee with her were less formal than she had perceived; a compromise was reached between them, and they set to work.

The work was difficult for Grace, but as usual the Red Cross benefited from her dedication. Anywhere flood, famine, or catastrophe had shown its cruel consequences, money raised by Monaco's Red Cross was there to help. By using her old Hollywood contacts, the annual Red Cross Ball became Monaco's main summer event, and the lucrative fundraiser was able to give relief to many areas in the world. Grace played the major role in the success of every one of these annual events.

Grace was also at the forefront in helping working mothers. Little did she know the role daycare would play in, and become such an intrinsic part of life in her homeland today. This barely recognized standard during her reign would become the rule rather than the exception by the end of the twentieth, and into the twenty-first century.

The elderly were also helped by her kindness. Princess Grace set up a combined residence and visitation service named Cap-Fleuri. Giving advice on decor and equipment made her a strong link in this endeavor. Through this effort, many senior citizens were given comfort and companionship, and the waning days of life for many of Monaco's elderly were preserved with dignity instead of withering away until the end.

In 1964, The Princess Grace Foundation was established. Through her own efforts, she purchased a small boutique in Monaco's village. Here she involved the work of tradesmen, artists and crafters, who were struggling with the sale of their works. After it was up and running, it became quite successful. The proceeds from the shop helped various charities. In 1965, Grace was voted Woman of the Year by the Philadelphia Congress of Jewish War Veterans. This award was given to her in recognition of the devotion and love she had bestowed on children throughout the years. The Princess Grace Foundation is still thriving today, overseen by various family members, and has become one of Princess Grace's main legacies.

Charities for the needy weren't the only area where Grace poured her energy. The theater and the arts still burned an eternal flame inside her. Although her return to the stage and screen was quite limited, she helped many young, aspiring actors and artists in Monaco and France. When legendary African American singer and dancer Josephine Baker moved to France, once again Grace reached out. Ms. Baker had been committed to others her entire life. Her personal charity, the "Rainbow Tribe" of adopted children, had sent her into debt; she was bankrupt. When Princess Grace heard of her dilemma, she quickly came to her aid. Josephine and Grace became close friends and comrades in the plight of homeless children. Josephine, still in her prime until her death in April 1975, gave an astounding performance when the 1974 Red Cross Ball was held at the new Monte Carlo Casino.

Both Grace and Diana cherished their lifelong love of the ballet, and memories of their childhood dancing were always in their thoughts. Hoping to restore the principality's reputation as a center of dance, Princess Grace went to work. Her goal: to revive Sergi Diaghilev's famous *Ballet Russe de Monte Carlo.* To effect this, Grace brought in a respected ballet mistress, Madame Marika Besabrasova, who opened a new school in the old, rundown building. The school was in need of a helping hand and, as usual, Princess Grace offered both of hers. Working together, they were able to revitalize the art form Grace loved so much.

Grace was so dedicated to the rebirth of Monaco's ballet, it was renamed after her, to the *Acade'mie de Danse Classique Princesse Grace.* Students from all over the world came to Monaco to study ballet. Once up and running, Grace immediately enrolled Caroline in the school. Both Caroline and Stephanie studied dance, which became another one of the wonderful art forms their mother bestowed on them.

Princess Grace received two more awards in 1969. In January of that year, the YWCA presented her with its gold medal in celebration of the YWCA's one-hundredth anniversary. Also receiving this award was Mrs. Martin Luther King Jr., who bravely carried on some of her husband's work after his assassination. The second award the princess received in 1969 was from her home city of Philadelphia, given to her for her commitment to the important role of motherhood.

In 1977, Grace used her unique voice to help both Monaco's and other ballet schools by narrating *The Children of Theater Street,* a documentary about Russia's Vaganova Institute. Its director, Robert Dornhelm, had nurtured some of the world's finest dancers. The film became a great success, and Grace's narration won critical acclaim.

Another of Grace's passions was flowers. To get the other women of Monaco and the surrounding area interested in flowers, in 1968 she founded the *Garden Club of Monaco*. At first it was hard to win over the women along the Riviera. However, with some good old-fashioned coaxing and the help her friend, Countess Malvasia, the club was formed. The clubs annual flower show, held each May, became such a huge success that in 1979 a film called *Rearranged* was made. Grace's last film, where she was once again directed by Robert Dornhelm, revolved around the garden club and its annual competitions.

The profits Princess Grace made from her various undertakings were looked down on by upper crust Europeans: according to Judith Quine, "It went against European tradition by turning a profit." It seemed that, in the eyes of European aristocracy, fundraising wasn't a capitalistic endeavor to be run like a business.

Nonetheless, all three of Grace's enterprises—pressed flower collages, art shows and scarves—were successful. This was of vital importance to her for several reasons. For one, there was still American blood flowing through her veins. The lessons of her father and the culture she grew up in were ingrained with the drive for success. Also, the pride and self-esteem she gained reinforced the self-worth Grace was looking for. This was a needed outlet and therapy that showed her that she still had ability. Finally, her Irish American work ethic was the necessary tool that satisfied her purpose. European aristocrats aside, it was a win-win situation for all concerned.

The celebration of America's Bicentennial in 1976 was a very active year for Princess Grace, both duty-wise and professionally. In February of that year, Grace went to Philadelphia to present her Uncle George's collection of literature to the Free Library of Philadelphia. It was a fitting accolade to George Kelly, since the first free library in America was established in Philadelphia by Ben Franklin. There, George Kelly's collection still remains in the archives for all to enjoy.

The year 1976 would usher in another welcome event for Grace— a renaissance from the boredom and longing to perform again. This outlet was poetry reading. From 1976 until her death, she crossed Europe and America performing readings in many famous theatrical facilities.

In 1978, Grace received an honorary degree from Duquesne University, once again for all the work, effort and service over the years to all those whose lives she touched. Princess Grace's final honor came in 1982, when her beloved home city of Philadelphia paid its final tribute, a ceremony held at the Annenberg Institute of Communications as a tribute to Grace's film career. Among the celebrities attending were Bob Hope and Jimmy Stewart.

This honor meant a great deal to Grace, and was also well deserved. From the city's founding by William Penn and the Quakers, Philadelphia has been a cornerstone of liberty and culture in America, where the central theme of freedom beckoned in the city's Independence Hall, and cries for justice were proclaimed from the meetings of abolitionists. Through the years, she had added to the culture of the city she had grown up in, from her acting career to the humanitarian and charity work she accomplished. As Philadelphia said "thank you" to one of its own, her glowing smile showed her joy and appreciation.

Of course, at the time she was so honored, no one knew this would be the last visit from the girl from Germantown. But if she had lived, she would be very proud of the artistic growth and culture of her birth town. On the grid streets, seedy graffiti on sides of buildings has been transformed into beautiful murals handcrafted by many of Philadelphia's artists-in-residence, and various holidays have been filled with performances promoting the history of the City of Brotherly Love.

The transition from star to princess had had its difficulties. It was Grace's choice, though, and her self-discipline and faith carried her through to show an even greater diversity of her talents. The annoyances that caused distress gave her a learning curve of experience that enabled her to show the love and commitment to others that came without question. The honors and rewards she received were fitting, and well deserved. More important, though, was the love she gave willingly from the center of her faith, which was in service to the Son of Man.

♛ ♛

As compelling and dedicated as Princess Grace was to her charities and causes, Princess Diana was even more so. Very few women in history put as much time and effort into charitable causes as did the Princess of Wales. In regard to humanitarian work, Diana's impact eclipsed many political figures, spouses of world leaders, and other royal women. Even First Lady Eleanor Roosevelt, whose efforts and dedication might have equaled Diana's in the twentieth century, could not compete with Diana's stature and popularity. Her name and persona drew money to her causes like casinos to Las Vegas. The funds she raised for her various charities were astounding. Figures ranged from fifty to eighty thousand pounds at a time for each event, and then to millions in her efforts for leprosy, AIDS and the selling of her dresses.

Diana became a workaholic for the charities and causes she was so dedicated to, keeping a full, seemingly inexhaustible schedule. The young woman who in her early twenties had loathed duty and protocol so much now became the hardest worker in the royal family. Having learned that compassion, love, and understanding played a much more important role than intellect, Diana's determination became an unwavering force for those she helped.

This was not, as they say, just for the cameras. Diana did countless work on her own, out of the media's presence. In *Diana: The Secret Years*, Simone Simmons wrote, "Sometimes at night, particularly when she couldn't sleep, Diana would clear out a cupboard and stuff plastic bin liners with clothes she no longer wore. Those nights she would get in her car and drive round London, stopping outside charity shops where she would leave bags in the doorway."

Her dedication to those in need was paramount in every effort she made. About this, Simone said, "Secret nocturnal visits to shelters for the homeless comprised another important aspect of Diana's personal life." Doing this gave her the sense of accomplishment she needed for herself, without the fanfare; her own self-recognition of doing for others was all she needed. Mother Theresa, whom Diana did a great deal of work with, as well many of the other women saints throughout history, surpassed Diana in her years of service and sacrifice; none equaled her dominant supremacy, though. Even so, this didn't make Diana drunk with ego. On the contrary, she used it to her advantage to advance her agenda of care.

During her years as princess before her divorce, Diana became involved with over 150 charities. Some she stayed involved with until her death, while she had to let go of others when her own personal problems became overwhelming.

One of the charities Diana did a great deal of work for in her early reign was Turning Point. This was a charity that helped drug addicts and alcoholics. Diana often held receptions for her various charities at Kensington Palace; Turning Point was among those. Mental facilities like Boardmoor became another one of Diana's causes. This was an institution for the criminally insane. Prime Minister Thatcher was implementing a policy of releasing the mentally ill from institutions. A similar policy was also executed in the United States. These cost-saving measures only increased the number of homeless people wandering each nation's cities, living in the rubble, debris and rubbish of England and America's inner cities. Diana criticized the prime minister's policy, which didn't win her any favor in Parliament.

The Princess attended therapy sessions at Boardmoor, staying off to the side and not getting directly involved with the groups. However, she did counsel some patients about taking charge of themselves and trying to pull their lives together. Even though she had no real training, her own experience and exposure to life's darker side made her able to help those in need.

Time and again Diana went behind the scenes and took risks, visiting patients at various institutions without accompaniment of bodyguards. Upon hearing this, Queen Elizabeth once again summoned her and warned her of the risks involved. In retrospect, the queen was justified. The princess was visiting some problematic and unstable individuals—had any incidents occurred, it certainly would have caused criticism for the royal family as well as danger for Diana. Nonetheless, these were risks she was willing to take, and as the years passed, she became even more bold and daring. Another cause Diana took a direct interest in was that of abused women and children. Visiting shelters for homeless victims of spousal abuse gave this disgrace immediate media attention.

While attention to the problems facing abused, neglected, and impoverished women and children was in its infancy when Princess Grace made her mark, Princess Diana's work came when the final decades of the twentieth century had eroded standards, morals, and ethics to epidemic proportions.

All of Diana's causes were hands-on; getting down in the trenches of each plight was her style. No one could have questioned her character when she became involved with these issues. Even with all her wealth and fame, no amount of money could equal the courage and strong will she displayed. On several occasions and in several articles, Diana told of the therapeutic benefits for her as well. In *Diana: A Tribute to the People's Princess*, she was quoted as saying, "I've had difficulties, as everybody has witnessed over the years, but let's now use the knowledge I've gathered to help other people in distress." No matter what problems her own life held, her reaching out to others in pain was paramount. "She is not just a figure-head president," one biographer wrote. "Her questioning is incisive, and she does seem to have a remarkable grasp of the social services."

When Princess Diana took a stand on an issue, her focus was genuine. If it interested her, she would study and learn more about it. During her visits to the deaf, she studied some of the sign language the staff had given her. She learned it well enough to communicate with patients.

Ironically, the Princess of Wales even counseled couples with marital problems. Relate, whose headquarters are in Rugby, England, is a marriage counseling/social service agency. The director of this organization praised Diana's efforts as perceptive and informative. She never discussed any of her own frustrations, but I'm sure her experiences there gave her insight on how to deal with her own enigmas.

As far as the arts were concerned, the love of dance and ballet burned for the entire lifetimes of the beautiful roses of England and Monaco. Like Grace, Diana also did charitable work in the arts. Though she had done so much in her first few years as princess, 1987 became the year Diana began her ministry to become world-renowned in her efforts towards human suffering. Ballet always held a special place for her from the time she studied it as a girl; that love figured into her charitable efforts.

While all of Diana's charities were worthwhile, six became her focus when she decided to cut back in 1995. Diana had an unending commitment to these six until her death. Those were: The Leprosy Mission, The English National Ballet, National AIDS Trust, Centrepoint, which houses young people at risk, London's Great Ormond Street Hospital for Children, and Royal Marsden NHS Trust at the London Cancer Hospital. The auction of her dresses by Christie's Auction House raised staggering amounts of revenue for these charities.

These charities were all the focal point of the mark she made on the world, an incredible journey aided by the gift Diana knew she was blessed with in reaching out and touching the lives of those who became both her clients and patients. Yet more than just a figurehead, she so many times reached down into the very depths of poverty and despair. In the book *Diana: The Last Year*, it was said that "Diana went, especially in the latter part of her life, where very few people wanted to go."

Diana became a patron for Centrepoint in 1992. Since 1969, when Centrepoint opened in St. Anne's church in London's West End, it became a haven for young people at risk. It is the equivalent of one in New York City, Sister Mary Rose McGready's Covenant House. Both these Christian facilities show the goodness and grace of God's mercy in reaching out to young adults living on inner city streets, where they are vulnerable to hunger, crime, drug abuse, prostitution and the other evils of society that have scourged some of its young. These sanctuaries now give young adults new hope they will be able to break free of poverty and destitution.

Diana's strategy was the same in her efforts for Centrepoint as it was in all her other causes. On one hand, she used the magnetism of her popularity to engage the public at large about this problem; and on the other hand, she worked behind the scenes directly with the homeless youth. In the Centrepoint patron document, 1992-97, it was written, "Diana, Princess of Wales' support of Centrepoint was invaluable and immeasurable."

As with Grace, young children were the most special to Diana. As Fund President of Ormonds Street Hospital, Diana did invaluable work in fundraising, awareness, and personal visitation of sick children. Again, much of her time with the sick children of London went well beyond the time when cameras were clicking or rolling. Diana's ability to nurture children was easy, comforting and carefree. Her natural charismatic demeanor flowed with a gentle love-filled pattern, whether stooping down to touch a child's cheek and softly running her fingers through their hair, or sitting on a sick child's bed while talking, giggling, and exchanging stories. Simone Simmons wrote, "She would stoop to ask the name of every child she met during a formal or informal engagement, and she would remember it." This extra effort bonded each child to the princess, and gave them the thing they yearned for most: attention and caring.

One of the children Diana befriended was a little girl named Danielle Stephenson. From the time they became acquainted, Diana continued her concern and caring for Danielle, who had a heart condition, both when Danielle was in the hospital and at home. Like so many others, Diana would phone Danielle to see how she was doing, and even invited her to Kensington Palace from time to time. These acts of kindness and concern went well beyond someone of Diana's status. The people Diana became involved with, she treated like family. When Danielle had to go back into the hospital on short notice, Diana's concern and help was total devotion. Denise, Danielle's mother, commented, "Then she insisted we bring laundry to her home, rather than taking it back to Southend." That was Princess Diana, the regular person of love and care within the most popular figure of the twentieth century.

AIDS was the first crisis in which Diana became a true pioneer. She was a leader in the struggle to understand and educate society about the disease that became the plague of the final two decades of the twentieth century.

When the full-blown outbreak of AIDS hit the globe in the early 1980's, panic spread like an oil spill from a damaged tanker. America and Western Europe's media exhibited a fright that hadn't been felt since the eradication of other devastating diseases like smallpox and polio. The AIDS epidemic's grasp on society grew into a phobia that quickly led its victims to a quarantined existence. Innocent children infected by HIV were treated as untouchables by paranoid parents who closed the doors of daycare centers, early childhood programs, and even some public schools. This hysteria was reinforced by the trepidation of the death sentence AIDS gave to its victims, a slow "green mile" of pain, weight loss, weakness and death.

In the war against AIDS, she quickly achieved a general's rank. Like other maladies, AIDS hit the world fast and furiously. Its early victims were left in a quandary until medical science was able to determine that the virus was spread through blood contact, and very difficult to transmit. Even when that was clearly confirmed though, the paranoia did not stop. Princess Diana opened her heart and showed tremendous courage and determination, boldly forging a frontier that no one else of her status seemed willing to risk. Due to her efforts, the first ward solely for AIDS victims was opened in England in April 1987. In a pamphlet published by the AIDS Trust, Adler recounted, "I first met Diana, Princess of Wales in March of 1987 when she came to open our AIDS ward at Middlesex Hospital."

When visiting patients, Diana wore no protective clothing. This was during the apex of terror that cloaked every corner of the globe. By showing bravery, Diana became the antidote that calmed the poisoned attitudes of rejection, quieted the strife of prejudice, and replaced it with the awareness of understanding.

Many people criticized Diana and thought her a fool for taking such risks. Naturally, with the stand Diana was taking, Buckingham Palace was inundated with questions about how the queen and the rest of the royal family felt. The queen's advisors felt this was precarious territory that shouldn't be trespassed, and the queen summoned Diana to persuade her to give up this cause. But Diana had done her homework, which proved the victims weren't just promiscuous homosexuals or IV drug users sharing contaminated needles, and she stood firm. Even though she stood alone on this, with pressure coming from all sides (including her husband who, as with most controversial issues, sided with his mother), she never wavered. Finally, the royal family slackened its stance and gave her their approval.

The challenge Diana had met was unquestionably dynamic. Many people didn't understand her taking this stance. Even so, knowing that right was on her side was all she needed. The shy, self-conscious part of her character, which had thwarted many situations and opportunities earlier, was brave, daring, and noble in all efforts she truly believed in. When in 1990 she went to Washington and toured an AIDS ward with then First Lady Barbara Bush, many of the doctors there commented of the genuine concern Diana had, sitting with dying patients, holding their hands and comforting them in their final hours. Even so, she did this purely out of concern for the patients, and not for any personal gain.

The afflicted children, as with any terminal illness, were the hardest to visit. Through the years, Diana became a special friend to a number of them. Many times these grave situations brought tears at the mere thought of innocent children struck down so early. Andrew Morton related once such incident when Diana received a letter from a father whose son was dying from AIDS and who wanted to meet the princess before he died. "After reading his plea," Morton wrote, "Diana personally arranged for his son to attend an AIDS hostel in London run by the Lighthouse Trust which she was scheduled to visit."

Diana's friends thought AIDS was so significant to her because it hit people who had similar interests and careers that Diana loved. Fashion, dance, and the arts in general lost many talented individuals to the disease. In 1991, one of Diana's close friends succumbed to the virus. The death of Adrian Ward-Jackson further reinforced Diana's strides in the fight against AIDS. According to the AIDS Trust pamphlet, "The Princess became Patron of the National AIDS Trust in 1991, and retained us as one of her charities until her death."

Many of her trips during 1991 focused on AIDS awareness. During that year Diana made one of her most informative speeches on all the misconceptions and prejudices against AIDS victims. Her previous loathing for studying subjects that might be considered boring in the first part of her reign now became a passion. To better relay her message, the princess hired film director Sir Richard Attenborough as a speech coach. Her oration improved significantly under his tutelage, and she delivered one of her best speeches on the misconceptions of AIDS and its victims as a consequence. Her travels during 1991 brought the princess to places as distant as Rio de Janeiro and Washington D.C. in her endeavor to combat the modern plague.

Upon her death in 1997, the National AIDS Trust lost its most valuable asset. In tribute to all her efforts and dedication over the years, Professor Michael Adler, chairman of the National AIDS Trust wrote, "The Princess of Wales was the first ambassador for AIDS, showing bravery and complete commitment towards the issue, leaving a legacy which will live forever. We miss her, and thank her."

Even with her involvement in so many charities, Diana still made room for more. In 1989, she began advocating for victims of a disease that has plagued mankind for centuries: leprosy. On a humanitarian trip to Sitanala, Indonesia, Diana visited a leprosy hospital. As always, she touched one of the victims while visiting with him. Photographs of that encounter made the front page of the tabloid the *London Sun.* The headline read: "Don't Do It Di." With that, another round of criticism about the princess putting herself in harm's way began. One letter of thanks, though, set the tone for the strides Diana would make for leprosy.

Doctor Tony Lloyd, executive director of The Leprosy Mission in Peterborough, England, told Diana in his first conversation with her, "That one picture had done more for leprosy in one day than the organization had done in 120 years."

Dr. Lloyd, a Baptist minister whose doctrine in the United Kingdom falls between the Anglican and Catholic Church, asked for the princess' help for a disease that still afflicts victims in both impoverished and modern societies. One of the first things Dr. Lloyd told me in my interview with him was that California still has as many as four thousand cases of leprosy. My own awareness changed instantly on hearing this. Besides awareness, Diana also helped in overcoming the stigma of leprosy, and of course, her involvement dramatically increased the success of the organization's fundraising efforts.

Diana became inspired again, and began a working relationship and friendship with Dr. Lloyd that lasted until her death. Their partnership and the work they did together for leprosy was both a positive benefit for the victims, as well as a spiritual transfiguration for Diana. From April of 1990, when she became a patron of The Leprosy Mission, she traveled with the Baptist minister to various Catholic and Christian missions around the world. This is where she saw firsthand the work and service to Christ so many people throughout the world do in His name, truly amplifying the scripture, "For the Son of Man did not come to be served but to serve and to give his life as a ransom for many."

During her travels with Tony Lloyd, she met and worked with Mother Theresa. The interactions with Mother Theresa reinforced Diana's seeking of Christ's love on her faith journey. Mother Theresa knew the value of each of them when she told Diana, "I can't do what you do and you can't do what I do." Each of their individual strengths moved the world in what God had guided them to do. From then until her death, Diana walked the path for the plight of the outcasts who needed both the power of her influence, and the hands-on kindness of her love.

Besides her visits to India, Diana also made pilgrimages to Katmandu, Nepal and other missions in Africa. In one of his more memorable experiences, Tony Lloyd told me the extent of caring and emotions that overwhelmed the princess at times. On entering a work area for patients in an African mission, she asked the nun giving the tour about a female patient at a sewing machine. As the women toiled and stitched the nun exclaimed, "She came in a leper and went out a Christian seamstress." Diana was so touched and overcome with emotion that she went off by herself to cry.

Diana's genuine qualities of goodness were always evident. "Her mere presence could cheer up the sick without even knowing their language," Dr. Lloyd told me in our interview. "Her goodness at times was even frightening." Her work bonded the components of her personality, and seemed to give pleasure to her being. Diana's love for fun and laughter, along with her charisma, provided joy and energy to all who encountered her. These were perks for all to enjoy as she strove toward her goals, always displaying the characteristics that made her unique. "She was professional to the extreme," Dr. Lloyd said, "and totally dedicated with an intensity which always asked, 'What can I do for you?'"

On several occasions during her work with Lloyd, Christianity was discussed. The reverend saw Diana as a serious seeker of God and Christ, and they talked about prayer a great deal, including the importance it played in each of their lives. Lloyd related that, on two occasions, he personally prayed with her.

Her curiosity about the Gospels came into their discussions also. Her inquisitiveness was apparent when she related that she understood the other thief crucified with Jesus achieving salvation from repenting, "Jesus, remember me when you come into your kingdom."

He replied to him, "Amen, I say to you, today you will be with me in paradise."

But Diana asked Lloyd about the criminal on the cross who didn't believe Jesus was the Son of God: "Are you not the Messiah? Save yourself and us." (Luke 23:39).

Reverend Lloyd was surprised by the question, and wrote her later saying that he couldn't answer her but guessed, "That it was some extraordinary work of the Holy Spirit."

In their next meeting, Reverend Lloyd asked Diana what she thought of his answers. Resting her head on one hand she said, "It will do." Reverend Lloyd then burst out with laughter from the response. This, Reverend Lloyd told me, was Diana's acceptance of his explanation.

Princess Diana's work and patronage for The Leprosy Mission was a two-way street of service to those devastated by this cruel disease. It brought comfort and love from the healing touch of hope Diana was blessed with, as well as the rewards she received in service and the seeking of God's love.

Like all her other causes, the vast void of her death left an enormous challenge to those carrying on her work. The final cause Diana was working on at the time of her death was landmines. Seeing the destruction these had caused in the last twenty years was another of the world's cruelties Diana felt the need to expose. Southeast Asia and the former Yugoslavic Republics had lost thousands of limbs and lives to these cruel weapons. Young men and women, with archaic prostheses, struggled to cope with what their amputations burdened them with. Diana's popularity and determination once again revealed the handicaps of so many people permanently disabled by these bombs.

Once again with respect to landmines, Diana was criticized for her opinion. In his book, Peter Donnelly described one such incident while Diana was on a trip to Angola, saying "Her visit was clouded in controversy when a Conservative minister branded her a loose cannon and others accused her of being uninformed about the landmines issue."

The political controversy didn't sway her, however, for she had learned much about, and become quite capable in the political arena. The reluctant and skittish young woman of the 1980s was now experienced and purposeful. Time had painstakingly transformed a character that was loving and compassionate for each individual victim, as well as tough, assertive and even confrontational to any adversaries. With respect to her untimely death, this was one of the greatest tragedies of all.

In a letter to me, Diana's butler, Paul Burrell, who was her most loyal and faithful employee through the many triumphs she celebrated as well as many of the trials she faced, conveyed to me the total commitment the princess made in her landmine campaign. During his ten years as her faithful servant, he had made numerous trips with her. "The most poignant were the last two to Bosnia and Angola in 1997," he wrote. "The landmine campaign captured the Princess's imagination more than any other, and became her true mission in life."

These visits, only weeks before the fatal crash that ended her life, were the final focus in the unending humanitarian efforts of "The People's Princess."

In her charities and causes, Diana always displayed a humble attitude. Again, this was always to each cause's benefit. The array of flowers and gifts she was given in her sojourns were accepted gratefully with smiles and hugs, but the fanfare she delegated to those she believed deserved it more than her. The media always took care of her recognition at each event, though some reporters criticized her recognition at times. Even so, she never wanted to see the work of those who pledged their lives to the individual organizations shunned. In *Diana: A Tribute*, Julia DeLano wrote, "Being put on a pedestal or hailed as an angel of mercy because of short visits and natural charm in her view devalued the work of those many workers who devoted themselves fulltime to the causes she supported." This recognition was unavoidable, of course, and Diana won many awards. Among these was the Humanitarian of the Year honor given to her by Henry Kissinger in 1995.

All the awards and recognition she received were well deserved, but they were not her focus. The capacity of her name and the mystique of her legend were dominant in the attention brought to each of her causes. Whether standing behind a podium, conversing with potential donors or attending to the needs of those suffering, Diana's power made each issue a main event. But what must be remembered also is the anonymous princess who many nights roamed the streets, back alleys and sat at the bedsides of those who needed the aid she was called to. It all ended too soon, but is being carried on throughout the world in her memory. At her memorial lecture, it was said, "She gave too much, and cared too deeply, for us not to honor her memory with action."

The awareness she drew to the causes she believed in brought each of them to the forefront of priority. Therein lies the key. The intuition of her love and service became a sixth sense, which moved the world in a manner reminiscent of others whose extraordinary attraction magnetized those in their sphere of influence. The results of her acknowledgment directly benefited those in need with the funds necessary to do battle.

Although hard work and effort were an important part of what Diana achieved, it's also amazing how kindness, compassion, and her mere presence attained her goals. Her astounding popularity, together with her efforts to thwart human suffering, knitted a fabric that covered the world with hope, warmth and security. The Princess of Wales, through her own despair and suffering, was able to overcome many obstacles and show the world the love she could give it. With this, along with her beauty, charm, and charisma, she became the most popular woman of the twentieth century, and was able to catapult herself to a status that will live on in history forever.

The two princesses used their names, power, fortune and popularity to leave a permanent impression on those they reached out to. They wore their hearts on their sleeves, engaging a purpose of hope in connection to the dilemmas they served throughout the world. Those worthy portrayals expressed the capabilities each had, and their know-how, concern and endurance.

Although Grace and Diana had different degrees of faith in their Christian beliefs, they always kept God within their grasp. Princess Grace kept Christ in her heart her entire life. As a child of Jesus from Germantown, her awareness of God's presence in her life was established early on. Diana, always the seeker, didn't have the priests, nuns and other Catholic orders to guide her, but did have ministers,

121

teachers and other adults who saw her capacity, and who steered her in the direction of her destiny.

In a discussion of *Two Princesses* with my parish priest, Father Leo Gagnon, I gained even deeper insight into the mysteries of why we are each called to serve in our own various vocations. Father Leo, a kind and gentle man, is by far the most knowledgeable man I've ever known on the history of the Catholic Church, as well as the greatest orator I have ever witnessed. His cerebral knowledge of theology is only surpassed by the love and devotion he shows in his ministry. His hugs during the Rite of Peace transfer Christ's love from this devout Dominican just before the benevolent Eucharist is celebrated, and his hands' tactile blessing softly transfers the Savior's love to the innocent faces of little children brought forward by their parents during Communion. When words of praise and thanks are deserved, Father Leo's vast vocabulary instantly conveys a touching parley.

In my interview seeking his expertise, Father Leo compared the work of Princess Grace and Princess Diana to two other royal women in history, both named Elizabeth. The first was St. Elizabeth of Hungary. Born in 1207, she was married to Ludwig IV at age fourteen. The young couple's marriage, though arranged as was common in those times, was filled with a deep love. During Ludwig's absences, Elizabeth would show great leadership in her duties. Service to the poor during flood and famine were her greatest strength. Ludwig died during the Crusades in 1227, leaving the twenty-year-old Elizabeth grieving and heartbroken.

During the last eight years of her life, the ideals of St. Francis of Assisi, which had been taught to her, became her calling. A devout Franciscan, she tried to live as close to a life of poverty as was possible, giving up her royal life on Good Friday of 1228. She founded a monastery in Eisenach, Hungary and with her inheritance money built a Franciscan hospital in Marburg, Hungry. The last three years of her life were totally devoted to the care of the poor and sick. She was canonized on Pentecost in 1235, and today is one of the most revered saints in Germany.

The other St. Elizabeth was the beautiful queen of Portugal. Born in 1271, her most charismatic quality became her ability to bring serenity and repose to others. Through her prayer, penance, and devotion, the Spanish princess became a peacemaker, and brought harmony to the many feuds in Portugal's royalty family. Also a Franciscan, she attended mass daily until her death in 1336. As in the case of Elizabeth of Hungary, miracles were also proven after her death, and she was canonized in 1625.

The lives of princesses and other royalty in the Middle Ages were vastly different than those in modern times, but the acts of kindness and dedication to the poor, sick, and needy were equally paramount to Princesses Grace and Diana. In the history still to be written, Grace and Diana will take their rightful place in their own service and ministries, as those before and after did. The trails the two princesses walked had different headings, bearings, and topography; however, life led them to follow the same holy principles left by the Messiah in his glory, as well as the Holy Spirit, who ushered the way to their charities and causes. In the end, with God at their sides in service, kindness and love to those who needed them, they reached the same destination. This I relate to in my own faith journey in which I walk as one of Christ's disciples each day.

There is no doubt the two princesses led more comfortable lives from their material wealth than others in service to Christ. Even so, they were among many others who, though wealthy, gave unconditionally of themselves to those in need and received in return the satisfaction no amount of money can buy. They followed the example of Jesus at the Last Supper and washed the feet of so many in need of their service. Even their penetrating blue eyes, which had the capacity to freeze those admiring their beauty into an almost-hypnotic state, transferred their love to those they helped. No matter what their own plights were, love was always the beginning and the end in all they accomplished.

Chapter XI - Friends and Companions

Like everyone does, Grace Kelly and Diana Spencer had their good times and bad. While they experienced triumphs from the talent, fortunes, and hard work they were blessed with, they also endured trials all the riches in the world couldn't abate. They enjoyed awards, praise, and admiration everywhere they ventured, along with periods of deep suffering and melancholy. Fortunately for them, they had many resources along with strong wills that helped them to pull themselves back up. Among these resources were their friends, who supported and kept them on the path they were destined to lead, and who were witnesses to many of the triumphs each princess achieved. Some were from their childhoods; some were social acquaintances they met in their journey through life; others were loyal colleagues in their employment or those with whom they worked.

Like everyone, Grace and Diana's cycle of friendship was an ongoing entity. The abundant harvest they both enjoyed was a direct result of the commitment they gave to each who was fortunate enough to have them as a friend. They were both "people persons." Even though the mobs that couldn't get enough of them were a constant annoyance, the people truly close to them gave laughs, cheers, and tears to their lives.

In spite of their remarkable similarities otherwise, this is where each princess contrasted somewhat. With Grace, the friendships she made lasted until her death. Even though the ocean between them did see a fading of some of her close friendships in America, including those of some of her bridesmaids, she still kept in contact with most of her old friends from her first life. Her life as a princess brought many new friends who shared many precious moments with her, and she cherished all of her friendships.

With Diana, the circumstances were different. Mistrust, misunderstandings and paranoia on her part left gaping holes in some of the friendships that at one time were as close as a family bond. There were vastly complicated reasons for this, especially in the final years of her life. For one, her immeasurable popularity became too much of a temptation for some of those close to her when the almighty dollar was within their grasp. To Diana, the breaking of this first commandment was unforgivable, which is why when her sudden death came, it left some of her relationships without closure.

Like all of us, the two women enjoyed the pleasure and peace friendship brings, including tight commitments where love, support and understanding grow like sunflowers in July. Of course, like the sunflower, which withers and dies with the shortening days of autumn, so do some friendships. As time and seasons pass, though, new friendships germinated for both princesses. The one constant, like so many things that paralleled in their lives, was their devotion and loyalty to the individuals who counted on them. Zealous, steadfast assurance, loyalty, and trust never wavered for those they had faith in, even though some, especially with respect to Diana, became a disappointment.

Grace Kelly left an entire world behind her when she agreed to become Princess of Monaco. She reflected upon this a great deal in her private moments; staring out at the ocean from the deck of the *Constitution*, she knew her new world and new life would bring many adjustments.

Her feelings came to fruition soon after her ascension to her new life. From the beginning of her reign until the end, many lifelong friends as well as new ones shared her life. Loyalty was a creed for Grace set firmly in her Catholic roots. The teachings of Christ intrinsically emulated the goodness Grace found in so many individuals, synchronized in the Beatitudes she followed in her relationships with those who became companions.

Through the years, Grace was able to see many of the old friends on her trips back to the States. In particular, she was able to keep in touch with her bridesmaids who had traveled across the ocean to help her begin her new life. For the most part, though, she was away from the family and friends of her first life. Naturally, she needed to find others to fill the void. With all her public and social events, committees, and charity work, many opportunities for friendship presented themselves to her. Of all the people she came in contact with in her new world, three became significant.

125

The first of these was Milica Banek, the widow of a Yugoslavian shipping magnate. So wealthy was her husband that, during his life, the economy of Yugoslavia was directly related to his business. Grand parties were a regular occurrence at her estate, and she became a real social butterfly after her husband's death. Banek was nearly seventy years old when Grace met her, but the age difference presented no problems. Their friendship was a boon to Grace in a more practical way, too: European through and through, Banek helped Grace a great deal in her adjustments to being a European wife.

The second woman was another Eastern European. Ania Chervachidze was an exiled Russian princess, one of the fortunate royals who had escaped the purge of the Bolsheviks. A very sweet but sophisticated woman, Chervachidze had lived life among the riches of Russia's Czars until the Great War brought so many monarchies to an end. Her home sat above the Monte Carlo Beach Club. From there, Grace and many other guests enjoyed lunch and dinner parties.

The third friend was someone she brought from the States, and someone she could count on the most. Her name was Phyllis Blum, a very outgoing and gregarious person who grew close to Grace quickly. Blum had helped Grace disassemble her New York apartment and pack for her new life. Considering Grace's packrat nature, this was quite a task. Grace knew she would need a personal secretary in Monaco, and Phyllis fit the bill perfectly. Phyllis spoke French fluently, which was critical to someone who became Grace's right hand. Also, she was American, which gave Grace that "someone from home" she could relate to among all the Europeans. The two of them teamed up in many a success during Grace's reign. In fact, a great deal of Grace's success with the Red Cross was a direct result of Phyllis's help.

Each princess had English nannies who were extremely competent. While Diana had her problems with Barbara Barnes, Grace and the children's nanny, Maureen King, became good friends. They were very compatible in their philosophies, and together did a fine job in the children's early development.

During the summer, Grace saw many of her Hollywood friends who had come to the Riviera on vacation. Many of them supported her Red Cross work by attending the ball each August. These included Frank Sinatra, David Niven, Elizabeth Taylor, and many others. This good mix of pleasant visits and helping others kept all these famous people friends for life.

Other friends from Grace's first life remained close, and visited or had Grace as a guest often. Among these was sportswear designer Vera Maxwell. Maxwell became a friend during Grace's rise to stardom. In 1955, Vera and Grace received the Neiman Marcus Fashion Award, and an immediate connection was made between the two women when they stayed together in Dallas to receive the awards. Grace, already well read and a student of literature, made an immediate connection with Maxwell there, since they shared a love and passion for Shakespeare.

Maxwell was immediately taken with all the positive qualities Grace possessed. "I remember at the time thinking what a remarkable young woman," she was quoted as saying. "Not because she was a supreme actress but just because she was a marvelous person." A lifelong friendship ensued from that time. On some of her trips back to the States, Grace would stay with her. Maxwell's private apartment gave Her Serene Highness privacy from the public and paparazzi.

Yet of all of Grace's friends, whether from her life before or after she became a princess, Judith Balaban Quine was her closest and dearest. In the many passages of this book dealing with my interview with her, as well as the quotes from *The Bridesmaids,* I can hear Judith's cultured voice in each reference sharing all the moments of love, respect and affection this resident of Beverly Hills had for her *best* friend.

Over the years, she and "Judybird," as Grace affectionately called her, shared an remarkably close bond, and they considered each other family as the decades rolled by and their children grew up. Even though an ocean separated them, Grace and Judy still managed many letters, phone calls, and visits. Hurt so much by the loss of Grace, Judy composed many letters to Grace in *The Bridesmaids* as therapy from the heart, but also to stay in touch with the spirit of the friend who was taken away from her.

Of her six bridesmaids, Grace's marriage was the only one that survived. In one way or another, all six intimate friends' marriages dissolved. Yet their friendships endured.

Over the years Grace saw Rita Gam many times in New York or other places where their paths would cross. Gam's career went on, and she had many successful achievements in show business.

Of all her bridesmaids, Carolyn Reybold had suffered the most. After a divorce, the loss of one of her daughters in an automobile accident, and bankruptcy, she became homeless. According to Judith, "Someone had recently confirmed to both of us that Carolyn Reybold had been living for a time in a women's shelter." This revelation carries some irony; before her death Grace visited her in shelters on her travels to New York, proving that no matter how far down a friend would go, Grace was always there for them.

Another author who became a close friend of Grace toward the latter part of her life was Gwen Robyns. The English author covered every square mile of Philadelphia and Hollywood to learn all there was to know about Grace, spending endless hours talking and interviewing family and friends of the Princess of Monaco. The thorough investigation uncovered many of the details and relationships of Grace's past, so much so that Grace asked to meet with her to ask her to tone the manuscript down. Grace knew the publicity from the book would be embarrassing for her and her family. Robyns agreed to Grace's wishes. Grace never forgot this, and became indebted to Robyns in her remaining years. They even collaborated on a book together, *My Book of Poetry and Flowers*, in which Grace shared her love for flowers and poetry with Robyns' assistance. Grace and Gwen Robyns remained in close contact with each other until Grace's untimely death. Their friendship formed a solid intimacy of commitment and trust.

Perhaps appropriately, the most defining article I found about Princess Grace's friendship and commitment to others was a passage in Gwen Robyns' *Princess Grace*: "There are lesser known friends, too, who have experienced the depths of her friendship. Lady Doverdale passed away. But she did not die alone. Princess Grace sat with her for almost two days."

Love displayed like that comes from within those hearts whose devotion cannot be measured, only admired.

Both Grace Kelly the actress and Princess Grace were one in the assurance she pledged to those who were her friends. Once her gregarious nature made a connection with someone and a friendship developed, an earnest giving of herself was always first and foremost. Any of those who were among her closest friends were truly blessed by receiving her friendship. Like the waters that sustain each life, Grace always poured homage from a pitcher that never ran dry.

The Princess of Wales likewise made many new friends during her reign. She had an advantage over Princess Grace in that old friends were easier to stay connected to, since she didn't have to relocate thousands of miles across the ocean to ascend to her new life. Even though she was confined much of the time to that new life, Diana made time now and then to see her old flatmates. Catching up with Annie Bolton, Virginia Pitman, and especially Carolyn Bartholomew was an early outlet for Diana's new containment. Of the three, Carolyn spent the most time and stayed the closest to Diana over the years. Their friendship remained so close that Diana chose Carolyn to be Prince Harry's godmother.

Having friends from her first life close enough to at least phone and visit with once in a while was more important for Diana than it had been for Grace, especially during their early years as princesses. Although Grace had many lonely moments and adjustments in her new life, these had been even darker days for Diana. There were endless problems filled with despair, disease, and depression, times when she had to reach up just to touch bottom. With no one to relate to, including her husband, Diana withdrew and felt sorry for herself. When she and Charles had one tiff after another, she had no one she could really count on or to tell her story to. Her friends were there to listen, but that wasn't enough.

Her family took the edge off somewhat. Diana always had a close relationship with her sister, Jane Fellows. The wife of the queen's private secretary cared, listened, and helped Diana as much as she could. It still wasn't enough, though. She needed a confidant she could relate to as a young woman—a peer who would befriend her and show her the fun and interesting side of her world. Suddenly, like a messiah, one appeared. Her name was Sarah Ferguson.

Related to Diana distantly, Sarah was the daughter of Charles' polo manager, Major Ronald Ferguson. Fergie, as she is known by most, had been around the royal family most of her life. With polo being one of Charles's favorite pastimes, he was often in the Major's tutelage. Sarah was raised by her father for the most part. Her parents had separated when she was thirteen. Like Diana, it was her father who did most of the parenting after Sarah's parents divorced.

Early in her relationship with Prince Charles, Diana was formally introduced to Sarah at one of Prince Charles's polo matches in the summer of 1980. The introduction became an instant friendship for Diana and Sarah. A bond formed quickly and welded tightly—so much so that the relationship between Diana and Sarah became as intimate as that of any of Diana's sisters or other friends.

With similarities that molded an enduring coalition, the mutual spark between Diana and Sarah quickly grew into a bonfire. For more than a decade, the two commoners who became part of the royal family formed a partnership that brought excitement, intrigue, sorrow and support of each other. In *Duchess: An Intimate Portrait*, Andrew Morton wrote, "Sarah was a Best Friend who played a vital role with keeping Diana in touch with ordinary life at a time when her new responsibilities and position threatened to engulf and overwhelm her." As if preordained, their feminine souls guided and attended to one another's wants and needs, a welcome codependency that would help them endure the rigors each would experience as their individual romantic relationships withered.

Diana and Sarah's friendship couldn't have been formed at a more crucial time. Had Sarah Ferguson not been there for Diana, Diana might have gone down for the third time any number of times. Within a year after they became friends, Diana was already beginning to feel the misery of her marriage. Sarah had also been raked over the coals in her romances. During the critical first months and years for Diana, when bulimia, depression, and loneliness had a strangling grip on her, Sarah gave her a good deal of the lifesaving support she so desperately needed. Of that, Andrew Morton wrote: "Throughout her difficult and often lonely adult life, Diana has had no more stalwart friend and advisor than Sarah."

Diana played a matchmaking role in making Sarah Ferguson the Duchess of York. "The Princess of Wales is an incorrigible matchmaker," Andrew Morton wrote, "who delights in waving her magic wand over friends and watching the resulting chemistry."

Diana knew Sarah had endured a lot of heartache in her relationship with Paddy McNally. Like so many other women who get involved with older men who have money, Sarah put much more into her relationship with McNally then she received. Diana, who knew all the circumstances, set to her task. Prince Andrew and Diana were always very close, going back to the days before she began her romance with Charles. The two even shared a brief infatuation before Charles came into the picture. With Diana's coaxing, the romance between Prince Andrew and Sarah blossomed until they became man and wife on July 27, 1986. Princess Diana's potion worked.

In the spring of that same year, with Sarah now engaged to Prince Andrew, Diana poured her heart out to Sarah, relating all her unhappiness and misery. This occurred at a dinner party attended by Sarah, Andrew and a psychic named Penny Thornton. After Diana's confession, Sarah advised her to seek Thornton's help. Not knowing which end was up at this point, Diana accepted immediately. Diana contacted Thornton without a moment's hesitation and was instantly in her care.

In their first meeting, Diana held nothing back. Thornton's astrological advice was that Diana and Charles were incompatible. While I personally think any first-year psychology student could have come to that conclusion, Thornton was no phony or quack. In essence, she steered Diana in the direction she needed to go—to relax and not take everything in the world she'd married into so seriously, and to take stock of herself and begin to use her captivating qualities to help others. This is when Diana's real transformation began. The Diana the world couldn't get enough of began with this renaissance, and began to bring forth the potential that had been waiting to blossom.

The closeness and friendship Diana achieved with Sarah was a welcome release from the drudgery her life had become. Their relationship helped Diana grow, and also cope with all she'd been through. It didn't end the war, but helped form a truce, ceasefire, and outlet for the dilemmas that never seemed to go away.

When Sarah Ferguson became the Duchess of York, it was a remedy that became instant relief for the Princess of Wales. Fergie was a bold and outgoing individual; she had guts and spunk, as well as natural athletic ability. Riding and skiing were two areas she excelled in; in her youth, her father's influence nurtured her tomboy traits.

Fergie's strong personality and experience had another side too. Although she was a commoner, she knew the royal family inside and out. She had witnessed all the etiquette and protocol for years, and it neither intimidated nor daunted her. She was her own person—a person who wasn't going to change her style because of what she considered an artificial, archaic code of behavior. This played perfectly in helping Diana make her transformation.

In her relationship with Diana, Fergie was the dominant partner. Her more prevalent nature was the lead Diana needed to follow. Older palace aides noticed the bonding of the two young women, and didn't approve. They saw Fergie as a bad influence on the Princess of Wales. There was no stopping it, though. Sarah's influence began to extricate all the marvelous traits Diana had kept locked up inside her. Suddenly, the dreaded social events Diana felt so uncomfortable at became fun. Her spirits climbed steadily and her attitude changed positively. Their duet performance was just to the two friends' satisfaction.

The changes in Diana were noticeable to all in her sphere of influence. Becoming her own person gave her new assurance in her relationship with the queen and her royal advisors. No longer was she going to quietly obey, or be frustrated by orders and decorum. Her opinion would now be heard. Life was not dangling out of reach anymore, but suddenly within her grasp. By merely extending her arms, she clamped her hands around and seized it.

In the beginning of their marriage, both Sarah and Andrew were good friends with Diana. The trio shared many moments, especially social, and whenever Charles was away, Diana would chum with the two newlyweds. In Diana's transformation, the shoe slowly but surely went on the other foot in her relationship with Charles. Now it was the Prince of Wales who wished his wife was home evenings. It was too late for that, though. Diana's new vitality was on cruise control, and the road ahead led to adventure.

Diana's friendship with Fergie added a new cast of characters that formed a gang for the women to be out and about with in the world. In their presence, Diana was able to carouse, laugh, and joke, and the two women reverted back to almost-teenage conduct on some of their escapades. They even pulled off a number of pranks in their newfound excursions.

Some of their behaviors were definitely irresponsible and immature. Fergie and one of the other women dressed up as police officers and crashed Andrew's bachelor party at the Club Annabel. Diana wasn't in uniform, but went along to participate. As it turned out, Andrew's group wasn't there, and the snooty club members didn't take kindly to the antics. The prank also made the papers, which didn't go over very well at Buckingham Palace.

On various ski trips, Diana and Fergie would disguise themselves and go out and about into the nightlife; as the years passed and Diana's popularity grew, disguising herself would become an even more necessary strategy to hide from all those trying to smother her. These antics did involve the consumption of alcoholic beverages to loosen up their inhibitions; however, nothing bad ever happened in any of these capers. In essence, they were a good escape for Diana from the stuck-up, frumpy world she loathed so much.

The newfound independence Diana found with Fergie opened even more holes in the already weakened dike of her marriage. The prince didn't think by any stretch of the imagination that the future Queen of England should be engaged in pillow or snowball fights. Queen Elizabeth and the rest of the palace staff were quick to generate a negative opinion also.

Again, there was fault on both sides. Diana was bored and had little to no romance and passion in her marriage. These factors quickly led her down the dreaded path of depression. Had Charles participated in some of the activities the princess enjoyed, dancing or socializing with her generation, things would have been better. Then his young wife might not have rebelled so much. This was all well beyond the Prince of Wales however, as his heart was always elsewhere romantically, along with his willingness to compromise.

Diana wasn't innocent either. She was definitely rubbing her new life in Charles's face. But lashing out at him only made their situation worse, further eroding the already damaged downward slope of their marriage. These were choices the two made which would eventually end a marriage that once looked so promising.

As Diana tried to divert some of her problems through her newfound pleasures, Sarah Ferguson's problems were beginning.

Sarah was popular in her own right, and received some of the overflow of Diana's popularity as well. This made her prey for the press also, which eventually got her in more hot water than anyone in the royal family. By the time it all played out for the Duchess of York, her world would completely fall to pieces.

Mixed into the total mess would be the affairs of both Sarah and Major Ferguson, Sarah's father, who would become the focal point of a scandal that would eventually lead to his dismissal. Ferguson suffered from an affliction of many men, both famous and ordinary: women. His indiscretions finally caught up with him. Unfortunately, he didn't have the title a John Kennedy or Bill Clinton had, which would lead to his ultimate downfall. The tabloid newsmagazine *People* ran a story about the major and his exploits at a brothel called the Wigmore Club In the book, *Diana: A Princess and Her Troubled Marriage*, it was said, "The article, which was to ruin Ronald Ferguson's life and cast him into royal limbo."

Yet no attention would have been paid to these occurrences if Sarah hadn't been a member of the royal family. Sarah didn't have the lens power of Diana, but was still under the public, press, and tabloid microscope. This period was the beginning of the ammunition, which Sarah herself provided much of, that turned into an arsenal the entire press ran with. A pulverizing barrage continued bombing until there was total destruction in Sarah's world.

This was hard on both Diana and Charles. Diana and Major Ferguson never had a good relationship. As biographer Nicolas Davies stated, "Despite Diana's affection and friendship with Fergie, she disliked Major Ferguson intensely, finding him seedy." Her close relationship with Sarah, though, added further anxiety to the situation. For once Diana was on the royal family's side on an issue. Charles, once again, was in a no-win situation. Torn between loyalty and duty, he knew that eventually duty would win out. For a while, Charles tried to see if the Major's scandal would die and go away, while Major Ferguson thought that his close relationship with Charles would protect his position. It did for a while.

Diana took a very hard line with her views. At the awards ceremony at a polo match, Diana turned her back on the major as he approached her, never speaking to him again. This caused increased friction between the Prince and Princess of Wales. Arguments between Charles and Diana occurred about what should be done. As Nicholas Davies wrote, the dialogue of their disagreements went, "How can you do nothing when he acts in such an insulting way towards the royal family?"

The major's position couldn't camouflage him in the end, though, and there was still pressure being applied from all sides. Since he held no royal title, lay members outside the royal family were able to solve the problem discretely. Finally in 1988, the Guard Polo Club committee voted not to renew his contract, and the damage control done by staff and lay people quieted any disparagement nicely. Charles and the royal family were once again off the hook by way of their power combined with the loyalty of those who served them. This was another of the many lessons Diana and Sarah learned in their tenure.

Unfortunately, the "Major Ferguson scandal" was only the beginning of the dilemmas and predicaments for the Duchess of York. Through the next four years, Sarah and Andrew's marriage would deteriorate even more than Charles and Diana's. Prince Andrew had some flaws: he was neglectful and naïve, and it seemed he was married more to the Royal Navy than he was to his family. For months at a time he would leave Sarah with the children while he was out to sea, and Sarah wasn't cut out to be a navy wife.

Like Diana, friendship helped replace the absence of romance and passion somewhat. However, loneliness paid frequent visits to Sarah during all of Andrew's absences. When a spouse isn't happy, her eyes and desires are bound to wander. For Fergie, a man named Steve Wyatt filled the void.

Mr. Wyatt, a young gentleman from Texas, was good-looking, rich and interesting. The Duchess met him in November of 1989 while on an official visit in Houston, Texas. To say Sarah was infatuated with him is an understatement. As the relationship evolved, the two were spending more and more time together. Andrew was cavalier and almost oblivious to the entire situation, giving proof to the old saying that some people can't see the rug being pulled out from under them until they hit the floor.

Andrew thought his wife's friendship was all very innocent…until he discovered some pictures of them on vacation in 1992, showing Wyatt and the Duchess in some extremely compromising positions.

Then, the blinders came off. The pictures were devastating to him. In disbelief and completely traumatized by the discovery, he immediately distanced himself from Sarah, which put the final nail in the coffin of their marriage. In some ways, Sarah Ferguson was given the same treatment her father had been given when he was removed.

As with Diana and Charles, Queen Elizabeth had many talks with Sarah and Andrew, urging them to make their marriage work out. Sarah even met with the queen herself in February 1992, and explained her plight. However, later that year, Sarah and Andrew separated. This was a major blow to the queen. She saw the marital problems of her two sons as a threat to the royal family itself, and the role-modeling and examples her two sons were exhibiting to the British Empire were in exact contrast to what she had expected.

By now all the problems of the royal family were flashed daily in print and on television. Even across the Atlantic, North America was getting its daily reports. The queen felt she should have insisted that her sons abide by the old traditions and not marry commoners. This twenty-twenty hindsight had some validity; however, this was the modern world. Most of the monarchies of Europe went to their death in World War I. Arranged marriages between royals seemed archaic as the twenty-first century approached.

As it turned out, Sarah wasn't the only feather in Major Ferguson's cap, or Mr. Wyatt's, both had had a relationship with a woman named Lesley Player: in Mr. Wyatt's case, during the same time as Sarah. In the end, it just caused more grief for all concerned, and Sarah continued feeling that the royal family and staff had never really supported her.

Once again, one of the halves of the wedding of the century was caught between a rock and a hard place—only this time it was Diana's turn. In this case, Diana was alone on the other battle line in supporting Sarah. Almost Diana's entire family was against Sarah, including her brother-in-law Robert Fellows. Both he and Charles Anson, the queen's press secretary, put on a denouncing smear campaign about the duchess, going so far that Queen Elizabeth had to step in and make Anson retract his words.

Sarah became very depressed and, as Sarah had done for her years earlier, Diana tried to do all she could for her friend. This was a daunting task, since Sarah realized that the separation from Andrew would cause her total banishment from the royal family—the same fate Mrs. Wallis Warfield Simpson had suffered when Edward VIII abdicated the throne in 1936. As Diana would later also feel, the constant pressure and invasion had done a real number on Fergie.

There was even more scandal to surface for Fergie. Foolishly, the Duchess had allowed her psychic, Madame Vasso, to tape their meetings. *Maclean's* magazine told that, "For six years, she prodded the Duchess to talk about her extramarital lovers and gripe about her in-laws, enduring a barrage of whining about the royal life." When the opportunity arose and the temptation of money was offered, Madame Vasso's greed was immediate. Voicemail conversations were sold over phone lines telling of all Sarah's affairs and feelings of jealousy towards Diana. Totally foiled, Sarah's royal world was terminated.

Sadly, her friendship with Diana would terminate also. At times, Diana and Sarah did act immaturely. They each made mistakes and paid dearly for them. Even so, when all the sinners involved in each of their problems and marital collapses began throwing stones, the damage was irreparable, and the friendship that was wound so tightly in love, support and trust became unraveled by mistakes, misunderstanding and stubbornness.

Diana had many other friends from the time of her marriage, through her divorce, and until her death. All were important in the love and support they gave to Diana in dealing with her immense problems. This group of people became the supporting cast for the leading lady whose splendor was unmatched. But even on the sloop that sailed so majestically through pristine seas, the friends who kept Diana's keel from capsizing knew her solitude and isolation. Her life was filled with moments of adoration and praise from the world at large; other moments were filled with the hurt engulfing a soul that searched so often for elusive serenity. Each one of these friends received warmth, appreciation, and love from the princess, who never forgot any kindness done on her behalf.

Angela Serota met Princess Diana in April of 1991. This was when AIDS was Diana's primary humanitarian work. As Adrian Ward Jackson's life slowly deteriorated from AIDS, Serota kept

Diana informed of all that was happening to him. Together, Angela and Diana kept as many vigils as possible for their dying friend. When the end was near, Angela and Diana said the Lord's Prayer together as a blessing for their dying friend. Until Diana's fateful end, she and Serota remained close friends.

Mara Berni was another of what might be called friend-therapists for Diana. Berni, along with her husband, owned the San Lorenzo Restaurant in the Knightsbridge section of London. Berni quickly became friends with Diana from the understanding and care she felt for Diana's problems. She truly knew the confinement, pressure, and difficulties Diana was burdened with. As their friendship progressed, Diana became a regular customer at San Lorenzo, welcoming Berni's advice for the multitude of things always troubling her.

Lucia Flecha deLima, the wife of the Brazilian ambassador, had been a friend of Diana for some time. She was older than Diana; her friendship was like the one Princess Grace shared with Vera Maxwell. DeLima's greatest act of friendship towards Diana was at one of Diana's lowest points—the first Christmas after Diana's and Charles's separation in 1993, when Diana had agreed to leave William and Harry after church and have them go with their father to the queen's Norfolk retreat. Loneliness entered again without knocking, only this time it had left the most popular woman in the world alone on Christmas Day.

DeLima's husband had been transferred to Washington in November, which had been another painful separation for Diana, so Diana flew to Washington the day after Christmas to spend a week with the couple. Diana stayed through New Years with her friend, even though she still felt blanketed with grief. By her own admission, "I cried all the way out and all the way back, I felt so sorry for myself."

DeLima and Diana remained close until Diana's death. In fact deLima was one of the last people to speak with Diana on the day of the accident. Like all the others who loved Diana, Lucia deLima lost one of the dearest people in her life.

The closest friend Diana had just before her death was Rosa Monckton. A devout Catholic, Monckton talked with Diana a great deal about spirituality, her friendship and patronage with Mother Theresa, and how Diana, a seeker of Christ, kept a statue of the Savior and a set of rosary beads on her desk which had been given to her by Mother Theresa and Pope John Paul.

One of the prime trials Diana helped Monckton with was when Monckton miscarried her child at six months; as always, Diana was there in her friend's struggle and grief. So close were these two that Monckton accompanied Diana on one of her last vacations before her death, a cruise to the Greek Islands in the summer of 1997: the same summer when Diana and Dodi Al-Fayed's romance began.

Diana had complete faith and trust in Monckton, and shared her feelings regularly. According to Donald Spoto, the author of *Diana: The Last Year,* the time of these two women's friendship was precious to both of them: "No one was as loyal to Diana as Rosa Monckton, and none was more aware of her thoughts and feelings." After Diana's divorce, Monckton saw the positive transformation in Diana, and how her charity work became her main lifeline. When Diana was killed, Rosa Monckton's broken heart fell in line with so many others.

Diana's fashion, humanitarian and charity work bridged many new friendships. Various friends from these endeavors teamed up professionally and personally to elevate her with their own blend of accomplishment and love. Liz Tilberis, Catherine Walker, Sam McKnight and others helped give Diana her stunning looks as well as their fraternity. Tony Lloyd, Nancy Lynn, Victor Adebowale, Derek Bodell, Michael Adler and countless others were fortunate and blessed by Diana's companionship and camaraderie in service to those in need.

Of all the Princess of Wales' staff, one stands out in loyalty and dedication above the rest. This was her butler, Paul Burrell. Much like Princess Grace's relationship with Phyllis Blum, Paul Burrell was an intricate part of Diana's life, both personal and professional, and served as the lifeline for Diana in all her wants and needs, both socially and politically. He enhanced Diana's ability to entertain guests to a level coinciding with other extraordinary women in history. Paul Burrell's expertise and dedication amplified her magnitude to the stature of twentieth century women such as Princess Grace, Queen Elizabeth, Margaret Thatcher, Jackie Kennedy, Nancy Reagan, Barbara Bush, and Hillary Clinton. Mr. Burrell's assistance helped to loft Diana on her own pedestal above any first lady, monarch, or head of state.

The chemistry between the princess and her butler was a unique blend of hands-on cooperation. Mr. Burrell's insight into the princess's personality relaxed Diana when guests arrived. One-on-one lunches with the likes of Oprah Winfrey, Barbara Walters or any of the princess' friends were the atmosphere Diana felt most comfortable in, where she and her guests enjoyed private, discreet moments away from all the perverse mayhem of the world outside. In the environment that Burrell so skillfully created, she was able to be at ease and project her keen sense of style and humor.

When Diana did host a formal dinner party, Paul Burrell was at her service as well. Tables were set with precious china and stemware; cloth and linen blended perfectly with polished silver, candles, and flowers. Eye-pleasing decor completed the distinct arrangement of soft light and pleasant conversation for all to enjoy. With most of the gatherings for her charities, Diana's perfectionist nature did frazzle her nerves at times. On occasions when their rare disagreements occurred, Diana always apologized to Paul. Burrell's loyalty and devotion was with Diana to the end. Even after her tragic death, he immediately flew to Paris to stand guard, and remained with Diana until Charles, accompanied by Diana's sisters, arrived to bring her home.

The tireless and caring eighteen years of service Paul Burrell gave to Diana and the royal family was homage above and beyond the call of duty. In his letter to me, Burrell's last line conveyed how much Princess Diana meant to him on both a personal and professional level: "I am proud and always humbled to know that 'my boss' described me as 'her rock.' They were her words, not the media's, from some reporter writing a story, she said it and that is why they mean so much to me."

Princess Grace and Princess Diana turned the world on in many ways. With beauty, charm and compassion, they dazzled. The various gifts they bestowed on each person their lives touched can only be calculated in love and memories. They had many true friends, because they knew how to be true friends. As Walter Winchell said, "A real friend walks in when the rest of the world walks out." The two princesses "walked in" countless times when those whose lives they touched needed them most. Their gregarious natures were one of their strongest characteristics, not just to their adoring fans, but also to the family and friends fortunate enough to share their lives with them.

The support each princess gave her friends was as strong as a cathedral's foundation. Not that they were perfect or without flaws: Like everyone else, their egos and self-doubts gnawed and perforated their characters at times. This was more so in Diana's case, but true to some degree for both women. The triumphs and trials they endured, however, gave them the strength to do the work God intended for them with the help of friends and companions.

As far as friends are concerned, I've always liked the "bus" analogy, and believe it relates to all people, no matter who they are. We all drive our own bus. During our lives, people get on and off at various points. Some get on and off like commuters, while others stay on for some time and then disembark. All our passengers, though, have some unique way of touching our lives. The sad part is that some are thrown off for one reason or another. The ones still on at the end of the line are the ones who will miss us and keep us in their memories and hearts.

The lives of the two princesses, as well as those of any who follow the path our Creator lays out for us, are nurtured by the love, support and assistance of others. Whether as part of our chosen profession or vocation or our leisure-time activities or hobbies, the help and sharing of others brings meaning and purpose to our existence. Grace and Diana were among the luckiest people in the world, for the love they gave the world not only transformed the lives of those they helped, but was also given back to them as well.

Chapter XII – Smothered

Of all the people who have made history throughout the centuries, Princess Diana received more press and media coverage than anyone, both before and after her death. Someone else may someday come along to exceed her popularity, though I don't think it will happen in my lifetime. Diana's popularity grew as rapidly as the age of technology that tried to capture her every moment. Although not garnering the same record-setting exposure of Diana, Grace Kelly was also near the top in the coverage she received during her life.

At times, Grace and Diana gave ammunition to the media's ongoing assault. However, most of the invasions they had to put up with were due to the media's pursuit of the almighty dollar. Each princess became the bounty, or prize, for the media's relentless chase. In this, each princess' magnetism became a drawback that restricted any private or normal life they may have wished for.

In this fast-moving age, the rich and famous have become commodities for various money hungry members of society. These include both the individual-picture and writing stalkers, as well as the companies or corporations some of them work for. Once a person's notoriety can achieve monetary rewards for any member of the media, the feeding frenzy begins, and their exploits cross any lines, boundaries, or laws to satisfy their economic goals.

This is a jaded part of the puzzle each person of fame is too often subjected to. Like a chronic condition, each acclaimed individual must learn to live with and tolerate all the negatives that go along with the endless pursuit. Only when their era has passed, and their glory has fled, can a true peaceful existence be found. Unfortunately, for Grace Kelly and Diana Spencer, that time was never realized.

Grace Kelly's problems with the media followed her from the time she first became a star until her tragic death. Yet there were some idle periods along the way. For the most part, though, the frenzy was overwhelming, at times hurtful, and fairly constant.

The future princess of Monaco did supply the media and press with material to carry out their missions at times. From 1954 to 1956, the beautiful young actress' inappropriate affairs created copy for the early gossip columnists. Fortunately for her, the media hadn't yet become the predators that hunted each individual of fame so relentlessly by the end of the millennium, when the combination of technology and capitalism drove the greed of the media to gain profit from revealing the personal and private lives of each princess.

After *Rear Window*'s release, Grace Kelly's career was on cruise control. She was featured on the cover of *Life Magazine* in 1954, and this began a growing need by the media and press for her attention. Grace had "been around" the media "block" a few times already, and handled all her seekers well at first. Those interviewing her when she first became a star found her cool, reserved and a bit distant. One biographer wrote: "It was Grace who had the correct and intriguing mixture of fire and ice."

In truth, the mature young women wanted her demeanor portrayed that way, so when any personal questions were asked that she didn't care to answer, she could simply change the subject. From early on, Grace Kelly set up a defense perimeter that tried to keep out things she didn't want to reveal to the public. It worked for a while; however, like all those of her stature, the tactics of those vying for a story broke through the perimeter and uncovered embarrassing situations.

Grace took a different direction from her counterparts in making herself accessible. Most up-and-coming stars were much more accommodating to the microphones, lights and cameras. The All-American Girl, as she was portrayed so often, was very independent. Having made a clean break from her family financially, she wasn't about to run at every beck and call of the media. This attitude made it difficult for both the media and the public relations personnel of her studio. At times, when she was overworked from such a hectic schedule, she could show a formidable temper.

By 1954, Grace Kelly was the number-one female box office attraction in the industry, and some of her leading men became some of her biggest fans and supporters. William Holden commented that her beauty was only one of the outstanding qualities that set her apart from others, saying, "I've never known a young actress with so much know-how."

Kevin Noa

Like so many others that made their mark throughout history, Grace was in the right place at the right time. Always polished and knowing how to carry herself, she became a symbol and role model for women worldwide. Her romantic behavior during her acting career was a great risk, however, and could have caused irreparable damage. In that respect, she was very lucky.

The media of the 1950s wasn't nearly as bold and brash as they are today. Nonetheless, they still had their ways and methods of working their trade. As Grace entered her period of superstardom, she found out how fragile one's image was. The wall she built between her and the media was frustrating for those who interviewed her, according to one writer, like "Chipping away at granite with a penknife." Eventually some broke through though, and so began the hurt, aggravation and humiliation she would encounter through the years.

Some of the relationships she had during her movie career, especially the ones with married men, would have filled the headlines of tabloids of Diana's era or today. Fortunately for her, the appetite for such journalism wasn't as great as it is today. As another writer put it about those times, "There was a shame attached to the repeating of gossip." But by no means did she get off scot-free.

Of all the research I've done, albeit with some conflicting, the one thing each author who ever wrote about Grace Kelly had the same philosophy of was her taste in men. She was attracted to men much older than her who had power, position, and sophistication. All these central themes lead back to her struggle growing up with the distant relationship she had with her father. Yet the age difference wasn't as problematic as the fact that almost all of the men Grace had torrid relationships with as a blossoming star were either divorced or still married. This wasn't a girl-next-door image, especially for a Roman Catholic in the 1950s. Had it not been for her family and friends pulling in her reins several times, her pure image could have suffered irreversible damage.

Although various spins were put on Grace Kelly's social life, the press and media still won many days. Her affair with Ray Milland came extremely close to putting a permanent tarnish on her image. "She had come within an ace of wrecking her reputation," as one account described that situation. Her family did some damage control

144

to keep the relationship under wraps. A leak did spring, however, from one of the tabloids of Grace's era called *Confidential*. In its articles, the tabloid reported that Grace had ruined Milland's marriage.

Some friends of Ray Milland's wife took extreme exception to the infidelity he shared with Grace, as did Milland's wife, Mal. "Out!" Mal Milland was quoted as saying, "I have all her letters, and I can sue you both." Again, Grace's friends and public relations people were able to keep the story low-key.

Not all the butting-into her personal life by Graces' parents was destructive, after all, and sometimes Jack and Margaret Kelly's henpecking did keep the beautiful young actress from real disaster. In the Milland episode, bowing to her parent's wishes was a wise decision.

Grace's very next adventure, also one that put her into hot water, was her romance with William Holden. Again, *Confidential* landed a major scoop in the form of two Hollywood stars engaged in adultery, because William Holden was also married. The magazine boldly reported: "Bill Holden's highly recognizable white Cadillac Eldorado convertible had been seen several times outside the apartment."

Although Holden had been a playboy for years, as usual most of the blame fell on the woman. Fortunately, after the romance was exposed, again Grace was fortunate in that *Confidential* cut her some slack. Yet the story that ran did strongly imply that Grace walked a fine line in her romances: "As long as the men were not officially married, she did." Even though she never had a truly scathing article written about her, statements like this still left questions in the minds of the public.

Even the 2001 miniseries about Judy Garland's life made a remark about Grace's sexuality when Grace won the Academy Award over Judy Garland in 1954. Her sexuality, however, wasn't even close to some of the labels cast on her. Oleg Cassini plainly spoke that "Grace would only sleep with a man if she truly believed it would end in marriage." She truly loved these men, which caused a great deal of suffering and heartache for her. This was the big-time, though, and the "reputation Russian roulette" she toyed with came frighteningly close to firing a bullet from its chamber.

145

In the summer of 1955, Grace rekindled her romance with Jean Pierre Aumont. The report by the press on this situation wasn't damaging, but more of an aggravating invasion. *Time* magazine ran a picture of the pair dancing at the Cannes Film Festival. Various paparazzi had their shutters clicking, too, and a picture of them enjoying an intimate lunch was captured. Rumors once again spread about an engagement. This upset Grace, but this was actually only a faint shadow of what lay over the horizon for her once she met her prince.

Grace did a marvelous job of keeping her engagement to Rainier a secret until the right moment. But when the simultaneous news was announced in America and Europe, all hell broke loose. Although still very young, Grace was a seasoned veteran by now in the ways of the media and press, and she knew what was coming. Rainier was not, though, and got a blitzkrieg indoctrination on Henry Avenue. Their engagement interview was crowded, aggressive and persistent. This was Rainier's initiation into the world of fame, which was going to follow him for the remainder of Grace's life and beyond. They both prevailed though, and between the rumors and headlines, the endurance and stamina of the future couple were remarkable.

Ma Kelly also got into the act. When Grace went back to Hollywood to do her final film, *High Society*, her mother gave a series of interviews to a reporter from William Randolph Hearst's *King Syndicate*. Without even telling Grace about the interviews, Ma Kelly gave her version of Grace's life, including her accounts of Grace's fragile childhood. Also included were her teen years, during which Mrs. Kelly claimed Grace had received marriage proposals as early as fifteen. The most damaging words she revealed, though, were Grace's romances from the past seven years until she met Rainier.

All these biographical details were spread throughout newspapers in the United States and Europe. In the book *Princess Grace*, author Sara Bradford writes about the published interviews, "Day after day for ten days in mid-January saw the private life she had striven so hard to keep private."

This was not a freebie by any means; Mrs. Kelly was paid well for these interviews, and gave the proceeds to her charities. But by going behind Grace's back as she did, Mrs. Kelly dashed any hope Grace might have had of keeping her personal life private. Yet again, Grace had to work and live in an atmosphere of guilt and anxiety, and the first few weeks of the filming of *High Society* kept her looking over her shoulder.

Prince Rainier didn't stay for the entire filming of *High Society*, and when he took his leave to return to Monaco and prepare for the wedding, he tried to escape unnoticed. The press caught up with him when he changed planes in New York and, as usual, a barrage of questions was thrown at him. This was only a small annoyance compared to what lay ahead for Rainier when he returned home.

Along with all the fanfare and discord Grace and her guests had to endure as the *Constitution* embarked, there was the scheduling of various appointments to keep the journalists onboard the ship satisfied, or at least under control. This caused a few hectic moments on the voyage, but for the most part it was pleasant.

Once everyone arrived in Monaco, the entire ordeal became at best controlled chaos, and at times total bedlam. Over 1500 journalists invaded the two and one-half square mile principality, each of them with one common goal: a story at any cost. The dream Grace Kelly had for a solemn, spiritual and moving experience looked more like a P. T. Barnum enterprise. "By the time we pulled up in front of the Hotel de Paris," Judith Quine recalled in her book *The Bridesmaids*, "more than eleven hundred journalists had arrived in Monaco, nearly twice the number that had covered the earlier Geneva Peace Conference."

The thirty-one countries represented by the press just added to the stress level. By the time of the actual ceremony, Grace had lost ten pounds since her departure in New York. Dark circles appeared under the stunning eyes and perfectly textured skin, evidence that lack of sleep and constant engagements had left the bride weary. Having had her moments of friction with gossip columnists, she spoke only to Dorothy Kilgallen before the wedding.

The groom wasn't faring any better. There were paparazzi everywhere. It was so bad that the palace staff clashed with them a few times. As the wedding day drew near, Rainier grew so frustrated he banned all press from the garden party after the civil ceremony. It was only at Jack Kelly's insistence that Rainier changed his mind. When Rainier finally agreed to daily press conferences, things calmed down a bit.

There was no way, though, that a daily question-fest would satisfy the by-then 1500 journalists; so as usual, those that couldn't get a story made one up. Some reporters criticized Monaco in general, saying it was rundown and in need of renovations. They were even some remarks made about the castle itself needing a facelift, which admittedly it did. The spectacle-ridden spot the small principality turned into was at times a complete frenzy. Even the residents of Monaco got in on the act of scalping tickets and selling expensive souvenirs. Then as now, the capitalistic aspect of human nature always comes to pass.

All in all, the wedding wasn't an enjoyable time for either bride or groom. As the years went by, Grace and Rainier, each with bad memories of it, didn't bring it up in conversation very much, as though it was something they more often than not tried to forget.

The next time the media swarmed upon Monaco like a colony of bees was Grace's first pregnancy. Every opportunity the press was offered would send a multitude of cameras and questions directly at Grace and Rainier. Rainier's decision to have the princess give birth in the castle was a good strategy. It denied the press another photo opportunity, and kept the last moments of labor easier for the first-time mother.

Becoming royalty never calmed any of the attention Grace had during her Hollywood days. She thought that things might settle down once her marriage had been established. This was never to be, though. Grace was even more popular and sought-after as Princess Grace than she had been as a Grace Kelly, movie star. Wherever Grace went, either by herself or with her husband, legions of media were always present. There were times they couldn't even go outside while traveling. With their secret service accompanying them, they were rarely alone.

Rainier never reached a comfort-level with the media. Most of their trips were filled with fond memories, but sometimes the adoration just got out of hand. As much as Rainier dreaded visits to America because of the crowds, some European trips were even worse. On their 1957 trip to Italy, the police had to literally surround them from the advancing paparazzi. In 1961, Grace and Rainier made a tour of Ireland so Grace could retrace her ancestry. On arrival, the Emerald Isles gave them such a welcome that over one hundred people in the crowd were injured. According to one report, "In Dublin itself the crowds were unbelievable." Grace and Rainier's Rolls Royce was actually stopped and rocked by the crowds.

In spite of, or perhaps because of Grace's popularity, the Prince of Monaco had married one of the most famous women in the world, and this attracted attention like squirrels to acorns. Grace became the best public relations boon Monaco ever had. This was as true for heads-of-state visits as with public events. When Rainier had a critical meeting about Monaco's future with Charles DeGaulle, Grace warmed the atmosphere and charmed the general immediately.

The strife and turmoil that became one of the darkest hours of American history became double jeopardy for Grace during her reign. On the fateful day in Dallas when an assassin fired bullets from the Texas Book Depository, the world was shaken like an earthquake. Grace took John Kennedy's death very hard; the Irish Catholic U.S. President and the Irish Catholic Princess of Monaco were good friends. But the sting of John Kennedy's death was only the forbearer of one of the cruelest moments Princess Grace suffered at the hands of the press.

November 22, 1963 was a national holiday in Monaco. Grace and her children were at the carnival before John Kennedy, eight time zones away, was even awake that morning. While at the carnival, Grace took a couple of shots at a target-shooting booth. A photographer snapped a picture. What happened next, which Judith Quine described in her book *The Bridesmaids*, was devious and low:

> "Without ever bothering to mention the time difference and the fact that the Kennedy motorcade was hours from starting when the photo was taken, newspapers carried the picture of Grace with a rifle pointed towards an automated gallery of ducks and pinwheels (the target off camera, of course)."

This photograph mushroomed into various vindictive stories of Grace being callous, and a gun lover. This was a deep, uncalled-for blow that Grace never got over.

When the news reached Monaco, a week of mourning was declared. Because of all the confusion and upheaval, Grace didn't attend John Kennedy's funeral, which only circulated more rumors and lies. But in the face of such scurrilous behavior on the part of the press, in early December of 1963, while America was still reeling from the tragedy, Princess Grace traveled from Monaco to place a wreath on the grave of the fallen president.

Some of the worst episodes were yet to come for Grace in her dealings with the media when it came to her children. In *Grace*, Robert Lacey wrote "Grace and Rainier had thought long and hard about the problems of bringing up their children in the spotlight." Yet times were much more arduous with Grace's children than Diana's in dealing with the media. There are several reasons for this. Grace lived longer than Diana and experienced the rebellious teenage years most children go through while growing up. Also, the playground atmosphere of Monaco as compared to the more stoic traditions of England made a difference. In many respects, the carefree, liberal French Riviera is by no means a place for instilling values and morals in children. As Judith Quine told me, it is "...nothing to see eighty year old women playing cards topless at the Monaco Yacht Club." This is the atmosphere, though, that the impressionable children of Princess Grace grew up in.

Environment aside, the number-one reason the Prince and Princess of Monaco had so many mortifying episodes was the fact that they had two girls...two beautiful young girls who loved the party- and night-life all rich and famous children seem to adore. This goes well beyond any aspects of lifestyle, though. Human nature, without any question, is always going to tip the scales to the side of the female of our species. Nature and God's lure from the beautiful mother and daughters created a second generation of endless bondage for those vying for the shot or story that would sell for big money.

History repeated itself for Grace with her own two daughters. Just as Grace's concerned parents had intruded into her personal life, Caroline's various deeds during her rebellious period gave fits to both her mother and father. To make each and every situation worse, the press covered all these various events like a blanket, reporting such things as this: "Tall and graceful, Princess Caroline's Mediterranean looks, with her dark blue deep-set eyes, owed more to the Grimaldis than to the light skinned fair-haired Philadelphia Kellys'."

There was little control of the media outside of Monaco, so when Caroline moved to Paris, she played right into the press' hands. Being captured smoking, drinking, and sunbathing nude sent shockwaves all through Western Europe and America. Tabloids by now were coming into their own, and Caroline Grimaldi gave them plenty to write about, and of course exaggerate. All Grace could do was suffer the embarrassment and try to spin whatever damage control she was able to come up with.

When Grace and Stephanie went to Paris to live with Caroline, the coverage grew even worse. There the paparazzi were so oppressive that Stephanie had to hide in the trunk of the car just to go to dance lessons.

Although Caroline hated the invasion into the fun-filled life she wanted to lead, she had to accept that she'd been born into a world that watched her every move. Yet the first daughter of the world-famous movie star-turned-princess did little to change her habits, even when Grace moved to Paris to keep an eye on her. The Paris nightlife still saw the intriguing young woman at various nightclubs wearing various arousing fashions. Grace, Rainier and Caroline had many go-rounds about her behavior, with little noticeable effect.

In my interview with Judith Quine, she told me one of the most hurtful incidents was when Caroline's dress slipped at a Paris nightclub, exposing her breast just as one of the ever-present cameras clicked. "With anyone else," Judith told me, "it would have been no big deal."

This wasn't anyone else, though. In a flash the picture was traveling, printed in various tabloids of Europe.

Put mildly, the young princess was by no means as timid as her mother had been at her age. There was little adherence to any advice given to her. More often than not, her argumentative nature would hold steadfast in the face of any attempt by her mother to reach a compromise. With all the seething publicity pouring down on her family, Grace admitted to the press what a difficult time she was having with Caroline. She confessed how some of the differences in their personalities clashed. However, Grace also acknowledged how she saw a great deal of herself in Caroline at this age.

Things became even worse when Caroline met Philippe Junot . For the press, that relationship brought once-in-a-lifetime photographs of Caroline and Philippe sunbathing nude. According to one source, "These explicit photographs showed a naked Caroline reclining on deck with Junot kissing her bare breasts." I don't even think Bill Clinton on his best day could have wiggled out of that one.

Predictably, this pushed both Grace and Rainier right over the edge. Yet as hard as Grace and Rainier tried to cool the romance between Caroline and Junot, it was no use. They finally bowed to their daughter's wishes and reluctantly gave them their blessing for marriage.

With their unquestionable love for their firstborn, Rainier and Grace gave Caroline a lovely wedding and for once kept the media under control. Rainier did a good job keeping his first daughter's wedding from turning into a fiasco. Both Rainier and Grace abhorred the thought of a repeat of what had taken place twenty-one years earlier, and banned all helicopters and souvenir sales from the ceremony.

It's too bad the marriage ended the way Grace predicted it would. Once again, when the marital difficulties of Caroline and Philippe became known, the press did its best to bias and slant every aspect of their troubles.

The years toward the end of her life were the hardest and unhappiest for Grace. She had a whirlwind of problems, both personal and family, and the press kept up its tenacious behavior all the way through to the end. The "anything for a story" attitude was always present with the world-renowned star and Serene Highness, who had to deal with the constantly embarrassing and humiliating invasions into her private life.

Diana's indoctrination into the media's obsession came in one tidal wave. In her case, the coverage reached a peak immediately and never let up. As months and years passed, the swells became bigger and bigger until Diana was picked up and swallowed in the undertow. The relentless sea of press, television reporters, and photographers went to any extremes to achieve the goal of capturing any facet of the young lady, who would become the most popular woman ever.

Once the media got wind of her and Charles being an item in September 1980, the barrage of coverage never stopped. The most menial day-to-day tasks of going to the store or a friend's house became endless intrusions into the life of "The People's Princess." With each move Diana made outside the few places she could feel secure, dollar signs motivated all those rolling tapes or clicking shutters.

After the press' discovery of their romance, Diana was met each and every day by some form of the media. Just trying to leave her flat and enter her economy car became a daily chore. In *Diana In Private*, Lady Colin Campbell describes the pressure Diana withstood by saying, "Every day an army of pressmen and photographers were camped outside Coleherne Court."

The onslaught was relentless. In the beginning, Diana had a fairly good relationship with most of the reporters. It was aggressive from the start, though, and as the relationship of Diana and Charles progressed, so did the reporting.

The first controversial story came on November 5 1980—two months after Diana and Charles became an item. This is when The *Sunday Mirror's* front-page story reported that Diana had driven from London for a romantic meeting with Charles aboard the royal train. When the story broke with allegations against Diana's morals, she was devastated. But, as reported by Nicolas Davies in his book about her marriage, "The story was false; the incident simply never happened." Diana thoroughly refuted the story, saying she'd been in her flat the entire night after attending Princess Margaret's fiftieth birthday party.

In these early days of what was to become her royal life, she had some needed support. As the story unfolded, Queen Elizabeth immediately authorized her press agent to demand a retraction from the paper. Also, Diana's mother, Francis Shand-Kydd, wrote a stern letter to the *Mirror's* editor. In it she complained about the harassment and deceit her daughter had to deal with. She went on to complain about the constant invasion Diana had to live with from dawn to dusk each day. Sixty members of Parliament drafted a motion criticizing the deplorable treatment the future princess was receiving. It did little good, though, in changing any of the media's reporting policies.

In addition to being an additional attraction for the shutter-hounds, Diana's young body and long legs were allies to her during this period. Several times she used her wit and athletic talent to avoid the endless onslaught. Andrew Morton wrote, "While once she and Carolyn abandoned her car and jumped on a red double-decker bus to evade photographers."

At times these escapades were fun for the future bride and oftentimes her accomplices. Another time, when she wanted to return to Sandringham after visiting her flatmates during Christmas 1980, she borrowed her grandmother's car to avoid the prowling poppers. Diana, accompanied by whoever was willing to help her at that moment, made a game out of outwitting the various media. Sometimes Carolyn would leave in Diana's car to throw the reporters off her trail.

As time went on though, this necessary subterfuge became one sweet pain in the behind. Diana's first real public media nightmare occurred in March of 1981. Coincidentally, this is when she and Charles attended Princess Grace's poetry reading at Goldsmiths' Hall in London. Diana wore a strapless, backless, black gown that would have turned any man's head. Charles' opinion of the gown caused the first real quarrel for the engaged couple, and his criticism of her color choice made the already nervous Diana a wreck. She was totally inexperienced in answering media questions and had to fight through all her anxieties. This, of course, was the time she confided in Princess Grace how she hated the stalking of the media.

The days leading up to and the wedding itself, from an organizational and media aspect, went much better for Diana and Charles than they had for Grace and Rainier. London had the capacity to manage many more people than Monaco, which helped a great deal. Also, there were many more staff and lay people in Great Britain to facilitate a successful celebration. Not to say Diana wasn't a bundle of nerves; but as far as the media was concerned, they didn't add any further burdens that day.

The apex, which Grace Kelly had already reached, was even greater in the case of Diana as far as popularity after her and Charles' honeymoon. The ordinary manner with which she bonded with people made even the most simple citizen or subject feel worthy. Her focus, always based on the appeal and affinity she shared with each person she touched physically, emotionally, and spiritually, caused her popularity to climb logarithmically to a degree that could have only been measured on a Richter scale. Magazine covers were inundated with the new cover girl the world had crowned "most popular."

The fission with which the Princess of Wales' popularity grew was unstoppable. Nothing could halt the chain reaction of energy released from the frenzy. Like an atomic bomb, the mushroom cloud could only expand upward once the atoms began splitting. The toll this took on Diana, however, made her implode to a point that cost her dearly.

On her first official state visit as Princess of Wales in October 1981, Diana suffered a major anxiety attack from the swarms of people and personal problems that had come with her new life. Bulimia had now taken its firm hold of her; she was dreadfully thin and weak from what was to rule her life for so many years. Not knowing how she was going to take another step or force another smile, she tortured through the various ceremonies, pleading in vain for help. The crowds, apprehension, and Charles' unabated sense of duty only made the misery even worse. The dues she paid early on were far beyond anything she was prepared for.

As time grew near to Diana's first Christmas as princess, the media's dogged pursuit became unbearable. Rumors of her unhappiness began to surface. With the press sensing controversy, they attacked. According to Nicolas Davies, "Editors ordered all royal photographers and reporters to keep a close eye on the Princess of Wales and to photograph her every move."

Charles became concerned about the effect this was having on Diana. He sought help from his mother, who had a talk with the press corps about toning down their unceasing coverage of her daughter-in-law. The press did adhere to the queen's wishes for a while; but Diana's growing popularity—and the money to be made from it—was too tempting. Davies reported, "But she had become such a hot property magazine editors at the time reported that a cover of Diana in color boosted sales by a remarkable ten percent."

There was no stopping it; Diana became the most sought-after person the world had ever known.

Diana's first pregnancy became another media circus. Every day, newspapers and television searched for the latest doings of the expectant mother. After William's birth, rumors of Diana's health problems began to travel. With her emaciated look, various stories surfaced about her having anorexia. While this story was uncharacteristically close to the truth, the various other fact-laced fictions only added to all the other problems and trials the new mother was going through. There were no bubbles or encasements Diana could use as an escape mechanism to hide away as she tried to extinguish her pain.

In February 1982, she and Charles flew to the Bahamas for a holiday to relax and unwind. Naturally, the paparazzi were closely trailing their every move. Two tabloids got a glimpse of the five-months-pregnant Diana bounding through the surf. Needless to say, the photographs weren't flattering, and the outrage felt by the future king and queen ended any thoughts of an amiable relationship with the press.

The press criticized Diana's shopaholic habits, as well as her outbursts of temper in dealing with staff. She was marked the villain when Charles had to curtail some of his friendships. According to Andrew Morton, "Gossip columnist Nigel Dempster described her as 'a fiend and a monster.'" Reports of her various outbursts brought headlines of "Malice in the Palace." It is no wonder she had suicidal thoughts, and her suicide attempts are at least partially understandable. Had any of these tries at the ultimate escape been successful, some of the blood spilled would certainly have been on the media's hands earlier than August 31, 1997.

In the epicenter of her melancholy, Diana's loyal nature never left her. No matter how nasty the storm became, she always showed appreciation for those who helped her. When Princess Grace was tragically killed in 1982, Diana insisted on attending the funeral. Some of the royal staff didn't think it was a good idea. This was during the time when Diana was easily intimidated by the royals, so while it took tremendous courage on her part, somehow she gathered the valor to tell any and all against her wishes that she was going. The paths of the two princesses had only crossed a couple of times, but Diana felt a bond of friendship and devotion for the help Grace had been to her when she needed it.

As it turned out, the press rewarded her bold decision. Their positive reaction gave Diana a needed boost in the middle of all her turmoil.

Trips to Australia, New Zealand and Canada became the next swarm of people and media to test the frazzled nerves of the young princess. The oppressive heat, combined with the crowds of over a million people vying for a glimpse of the world's renowned maiden, again vexed her entire existence.

The most valuable pictures of Diana were the ones caught in private moments. These yielded the most money for those paparazzi sly, clever, bold and obnoxious enough to acquire them. Even simple get-togethers with old friends always had the enemy lurking about. Sometimes photographers were caught and their films confiscated. Most times, though, the deeds were captured and consequences of what was printed had to be dealt with after the fact.

Through the late 1980s, the antics of Diana and Sarah Ferguson kept the cameras clicking and the reporters writing. The fooling-around the two women engaged in at times produced the needed pictures and text each reporter could twist and spin to their hearts' desire. Andrew Morton related once such incident, saying, "Photographers captured the moment when Diana and Sarah poked their friend Lulu Blacker in the backside with their rolled umbrellas."

For average people, these are antiquated occurrences, but with the Princess of Wales they were front-page news. Should she have been more careful? Absolutely! But she was human; and with that vulnerability was bound to come mistakes we all make. Only with Diana, for every mistake she paid an elevated price. Even before her affair with James Hewitt, reports of her being too friendly and cozy with friends out in public or at social engagements would start the rumors and print. It never stopped.

The controversy, discord, disputes and fracases over the years were a mere warm-up for the final two-year war that took place in 1991 and 1992. When the real breakdown in Charles and Diana's marriage came crashing down like delicate china falling off a wall, headlines abounded as quickly as presses could print them. When the final moments came, and Charles and Diana went at each other like two gladiators of ancient Rome, all gaskets blew and all warheads exploded around the Prince and Princess of Wales as well as the entire royal family.

Hitting the tabloids at full stride, reports of Diana refusing Charles' wish to give her a thirtieth birthday party got the ink flowing quickly. The release of Andrew Morton's book, *Diana, Her True Story*, only added rocket fuel to the inferno. Charles' loyal spin-doctors fought back with their own accusations about Diana, and a series of articles in *Today* portrayed Diana as neurotic and hysterical. It also accused her of much the fault in the marriage's breakdown.

Charles' public relations people fought back hard and fast trying to elevate the prince's image. Charles had an army of media and political advisors trying to win favor for him. It was of no use, though. After all, he didn't have the one thing Diana always had locked up: the people.

The mature Diana proved to be as shrewd and cunning a foe as any politician or diplomat in history. Her mere presence was no match for anything Charles' cronies had up their sleeves. A poll in the *Daily Express* put the blame for the breakup of their marriage squarely on Charles. Diana was number one with the people, and there was no changing that. Even when the rumors and stories about her relationship with James Hewitt appeared, the public didn't waver. Of course, Charles had his own blockbuster to deal with when he foolishly made romantic calls to Camilla Parker-Bowles on his cell phone. What would become known as the "Camillagate Tapes" were revealed by the *Daily Mirror* on Charles' forty-fourth birthday. The taping of the lust between Charles and Camilla was like stealing candy from a baby, and the modern age of technology once again showed Charles that the days of keeping one's infidelities under wraps were gone. Once the tapes were revealed, separation of the prince and princess was inevitable.

Thrown in with all these situations were Andrew's and Sarah's doom and the queen's wanting the public to pay for the fire that engulfed Windsor Castle, for which the queen paid a price of rejection by many of her subjects who were out of work during the recession of that time. All this staged more episodes for the royal soap opera, with the media having endless information with which to write their scripts.

With all the mistakes and controversies Charles, the queen, and Sarah had made during 1991 and 1992, there was no way they were going to gain an upper hand on Diana. The difference was that the public perceived Diana as genuine. She had proved this many times by her words and deeds. Over and over again, her work with the downtrodden and her dedication to her sons reinforced the image that she was no phony. Traveling with regular people and friends gave her a persona with qualities resembling some of the philosophies of Christ, Gandhi and Martin Luther King. King The motherly qualities she exhibited to her admirers were examples for women to imitate and respect. No matter what bait was thrown at her by the press or the royals' instigators, the public wasn't biting. The stuffed shirt, pompous attitude of the royal family was no match for average people who had toiled and sweated for what they earned in life.

The end of Charles and Diana's marriage brought the worst of times for the princess in her dealings with the paparazzi. Without the police protection she had while part of the royal family, the media became even more savage than ever. Some of the tactics and plottings pulled by various reporters and paparazzi were the work of the worst forms of life on this planet, instigating lowlifes whose cameras, pencils or monitors were tools to gain monetary satisfaction at any physical or emotional price. Of this situation, Lady Colin Campbell relates, "We editors listened at the stories of how street gangs of paparazzi worked. How they pushed and jostled her...if she stepped on to the streets."

The techniques used by these scum should have landed them in prison for long sentences. At times, cars carrying these parasites would pull beside Diana's car and yell vile words and phrases at her. According to Diana, "They scream obscenities at me hoping I'll lose my temper and give them a sensational photograph." It is truly a disgrace that a person of Diana's stature had to endure the intimidation and outright sexual harassment conveyed on her by these scoundrels.

During my interview with Tony Lloyd, he related to me some of Diana's anxieties and frustrations with the media, "How Diana felt the media committed face-rape against her." He went on to comment that, as he left Kensington Palace after some of his visits with her, he felt, "It was sad that the most popular women in the world was alone and by herself much of the time." But there was no other choice; she had to endure the isolation because of the constant surveillance of the media.

Dr. Lloyd also told me of one experience in which Diana became very anxious and distraught at an impending intrusion by the media. On a humanitarian trip to Hong Kong, a slew of reporters were waiting as their plane landed and approached the gate. At that point, he said, "She became very frightened of the reporters and cameras." The tension eased as they disembarked, though the unexpected stress Diana lived with each time she ventured into the outside world could appear in any given situation.

After the final episodes of her marriage played themselves out in brash fashion, Diana didn't quietly slip into obscurity. Although someone with less-dazzling qualities might have faded out of the limelight and into a more tranquil existence, Diana's spotlight grew with even greater candlepower. She was no longer a royal by then, and had lost her title of Serene Highness, yet as far as the people of the world were concerned, this was only the end of a chapter, and they were eager to turn the page.

Diana's unending and cumbersome dealings with the media compelled her to create her own form of ambiguity, in the form of disguise, for Diana had found love again. This time, it was heart surgeon Hasnat Khan who captured her romantic affections. She had met him while visiting the husband of her acupuncturist, who was recovering from heart surgery.

During their relationship, they liked to dine and listen to the jazz the doctor enjoyed. Even though these various pubs were darkened establishments and nighttime retreats, she still couldn't enter without her facade. Yet according to Simone Simmonds, this was effective enough: "In one of her wigs and suitable make-up she was quite unrecognizable."

Diana was both clever and sly, and became quite adept at cloaking herself. With her bravado, she was able to relent in the relaxing and fun atmosphere each night and enjoy these times with her newfound love.

Diana wasn't ready for the quiet, private life Jackie Kennedy was able to achieve after years in the spotlight. She tried to cut down somewhat on her humanitarian work, but knew she couldn't fade into the background either. As much tension, hurt, and chaos the media had brought to her over the years, she knew her calling to those she helped, and had to keep her popularity at the level it was in order to achieve the fundraising her prominence endowed. Yet notoriety was simple for her to maintain; her sons, her work and her mere presence kept the ball right on rolling. If she dreamed of someday having an ordinary life, the dream was smashed in a tunnel by those who pursued her.

👑 👑

> "One writes of scars healed, a loose parallel to the pathology of the skin, but there is no such thing in the life of an individual. There are open wounds, shrunk sometimes to the size of a pinprick - but wounds still. The marks of suffering are more comparable to the loss of a finger, or the sight of an eye."
>
> *Tender Is The Night*, F. Scott Fitzgerald

I don't think any woman in the past century—with the exception of Jackie Kennedy or Queen Elizabeth—could parallel Grace Kelly or Diana Spencer in dominating every engagement she attended. At the height of each one's popularity, I believe it is safe to say that her husband couldn't have had a better partner on his arm in regards to diplomacy.

Nonetheless, fame, glory and splendor have no gray areas, only black and white. Grace Kelly and Diana Spencer, like all their counterparts, were codependent on the very thing that gave them the most trouble. Without the promotion, publicity, and campaigns various forms of the media and press touted for each, they surely wouldn't have achieved the prominence that enveloped them. This frustration was true for them, and all those who suffer the clutches of fame.

Yet in their cases, it went way beyond an annoyance. The turmoil each of them had to put up with in their dealings with the media traumatized any peaceful existence they longed for. The endless stalking choked their freedom to a point that made them captives of their popularity. Their independence was constricted by the truths that

161

ordinary people never saw printed about them, and the untruths that abounded in each fabrication. Unfortunately, compromise wasn't feasible in the cutthroat world each princess reigned in. The nature of the beast compelled those covering each icon's actions to forge an overzealous path whenever a situation arose.

So stifling was the emotional pain Princess Grace tolerated at the hands of the media that she fantasized and envied the impoverished she reached out to help in her causes. In Judith Quine's book, she wrote, "Grace told me only recently," I mentioned, "that she was grateful for what she had but that sometimes-when she saw bag ladies on the streets-she envied their anonymity and their freedom."

With Diana, the loss of freedom was even worse. She was inhibited from exploring independent post-divorce life without hiding from the world. Finding her way through her final years had to be done in the dark hours of late night, when many vying for monetary trophies were asleep, or masquerading herself externally to cover who she was from the rogues of constriction. As Simone Simmons said so well, "It's hard for the rest of us to imagine how desperately Diana missed the simple freedoms which most of us take for granted."

Those liberties would never be realized for either woman. The two princesses paid a price for fame with emotional wounds: bone-deep punctures leaving scars that never healed. For Grace Kelly and Diana Spencer, the media left marks of emotional pain that reached the depths of all five senses, inflaming the peace each hoped for, and smothering any repose they surely deserved.

Chapter XIII - Nothing Lasts Forever

Romances and marital relationships spawn one of the greatest problems facing society today. The catastrophic number of divorces is a direct link to the immorality and values that have been lost. Drugs, teen pregnancy, crime, and violence all can be traced back to the declining family unit. These societal factors were prevalent in each princess's reign. For Princess Grace, the trend began in the tumultuous 1960s, when she expressed her shock and horror at the changing values of her birth country, and kept right on going through Princess Diana's reign, her own divorce, her death, and into the new millennium.

The breakup of families is like a dead tree whose branches snap off one by one in a heavy wind, finally toppling to the ground when the final decay reaches the inner core. Very few sprout new life from the roots and stumps that remain. The majority atrophy further, until their final decomposition returns to the grounds from which they sprouted.

The tree of Grace's marriage was still alive at the time of her death, though, it had withered somewhat over the years. Grace had left her life as a movie star to be challenged by a new foreign land and life. For over two-and-a-half decades she pursued, endured, and achieved an array of successes and turmoils both public and personal. She never wavered in her values, faith and dedication to her children, or in dealing with her family problems. Grace faced and met these challenges until fate's cruel hand opened the door of tragedy.

Diana Spencer's tree began to die immediately after her marriage. Though much of it was not her fault, she wasn't totally blameless. By 1984, shortly after Harry was born, the branches had all withered and the trunk's demise was inevitable. Even so, it would take ten more years before complete weakening would topple her tree and send it crashing to the ground.

The two women, who dazzled the world with weddings that had shown so much potential, had many of the same problems that plague any couple. Whether exchanging vows in city hall during lunch hour, or staging an extravaganza witnessed by millions of people around the world, the institution that gathers two to be as one separates and ends far too many times.

♛ ♛

Grace Kelly did not take growing older gracefully. With the onset of menopause—the "angry jaws" as she referred to the change of life—she underwent some difficult times. Also, over the years the relationship and marriage between Grace and Rainier had definitely changed. Part of the closeness and intimacy they once had reversed its current; they had drifted apart. Even so, her family unit, which meant more to her then anything else, remained intact. The romantic part of their marriage, though, lacked the fire and passion Grace had adored so much during her young adulthood.

The last six years of her life were filled with peaks and valleys, positive and negative events and circumstances which both elated— and burdened—one of the twentieth century's greatest icons.

With the approach of her fortieth birthday, Grace felt that she hadn't done enough creatively since becoming a princess. This was to change, though. It wasn't easy as she struggled and worked at an evolving renaissance. While creative fulfillment had ebbed and flowed over the years of her reign, she never quit, and her faith, talent, and fortitude opened new windows to the doors that had shut. As Judith Quine related in her book, "Grace had begun to loosen up her life to make more time for other things—for new attitudes."

Rainier had buried himself in the business dealings of Monaco. With the slow waning of the relationship between them, Grace needed an escape, a way to channel her energies away from all her problems. Her solutions came from several directions. The world she had left behind as a mature but still young woman now became her therapy and strength, and the talent she had locked away was reopened to become the focal point of her purpose.

The three principal endeavors the Princess of Monaco engaged in during her final years were her flowers, films, and poetry. All three had a double benefit, as they were also a big part of Grace's service and fundraising work. She loved all three, and her passions became her ambitions and gave a distinct vantage-point for the years she had left, a relief from the paradoxes she faced which interconnected all the other positive values she held so dear.

From childhood, when she would clip unsuspecting neighbors' flowers and sell them to help her mother's charity, Grace always had a love for flowers. Her Germantown upbringing supported and encouraged her in this; from my visit there, I was assured there are many beautiful gardens in the picturesque neighborhood every summer. I'm sure that Grace, as a child, had a variety to choose from.

From the time she became princess through the establishment of The Garden Club of Monaco and until her death, Grace grew, nurtured, and visited some of the most beautiful gardens on earth. She labored with the joy of bringing life to the gardens of the palace and Roc Agel, as any proud homeowner who runs their fingers through the soil and makes the landscape flourish. "Hobby" is too simple a word for Grace's passion; it was an intricate part of her being which became another of the many branches of talented gifts she was blessed with. Grace's flower fetish blended with her beliefs, language skills, intelligence, and creativity.

Grace's passion extended to floral preservation. Mrs. Henry King of Philadelphia is the woman who got her interested in pressed flowers. Under that tutelage, her garden room at Roc Agel became a sanctuary for the peace and delight she enjoyed through the making of each collage. It is said that a person has found a positive passion when they rise before the sun to do it. Many days found the princess up at four or five in the morning working at this avocation.

Through her friendship with Gwen Robyns, Princess Grace collaborated on a book called *My Book of Flowers*. Published in 1980, it revealed the experience and knowledge Princess Grace had gained over the years as well as exemplifying the love she had for flowers, poetry, and herbs. The book, through its description, showed the expanse of culture she had nurtured during her reign.

One of the wedding gifts my wife and I received in 1983 brought me into contact with Adele Richards, one of the women Grace exchanged ideas with on her flower collages. Adele had done a flower collage of our wedding invitation, which was given to my wife and me by my mother's best friend.

While living in Utica, New York, Adele lost her home in a fire. When she moved into an apartment and began missing her former garden, she began to walk the country roads of upstate New York and gather flowers to press. She became so enthralled with pressed flowers that it became more than a business; she began teaching it as well. One of her students suggested she write to Princess Grace, and she did. Grace responded immediately and invited her to visit on her trip to Europe in the summer of 1979.

When they met, Adele brought Grace a variety of flowers native to New York. Grace was both thrilled and appreciative. She also brought a bar of soap with pressed flowers that she showed the princess how to make. Grace made the pressed flowers soap, then immediately showed it to all the members of her garden club, where it became one of their fundraising products for the revival of Monaco's ballet.

Like everyone else, Adele found Princess Grace warm and friendly. Speaking of their meeting, she said, "She made my husband and myself feel welcome and at ease." The motherly side of Grace entered their conversation as Grace told of her excitement in expectation of Stephanie coming home from camp. Although a European princess, Adele felt that "the Princess still had a real American side to her. She was very gracious and thoughtful. She made my husband and I feel so welcomed, that upon leaving my husband simply said, 'See you Grace.'"

Over the last couple of years of her life, Grace and Adele corresponded often. A newspaper article about their friendship was titled *The Princess and the Pen Pal.* Adele received several personal gifts from Princess Grace before her death. Among them are one of her famous scarves and a signed copy of *My Book of Flowers.* Like everyone else, Adele was shocked by Grace's tragic death.

In her final years, Grace came out of retirement to rekindle some of her first career. This established a rejuvenation of her performances. Although it was on a different level than before, these experiences gave Grace a clarity and new resolve for the accomplishments that awaited her.

Grace traveled a great deal during this period. She also spent a great deal of time at the family's apartment in Paris, which was both an escape from Monaco and a way to keep an eye on Caroline. This was during Caroline's youthful "party time" phase.

Grace wanted Caroline's higher education to be at an American Ivy League school. Instead, Caroline wanted to study and live in Paris. This was the beginning of so many stressful decisions about her two girls that Grace would have to deal with. Grace and Rainier would experience episode after episode of upheaval with the two young beautiful princesses from the time Caroline graduated from St. Mary's, until Grace's death.

After the French paparazzi laid siege to the royal family of Monaco's apartment in Paris, Grace immediately moved there with Stephanie as she had originally planned. John Glatt referred to this when he said, "She [Grace] had grown bored with Monaco and was looking forward to the freedom that Paris would give her." So 26 Place de l' Avenue Foch became the headquarters and rejuvenation-point of her creative talents.

Perhaps nowhere else in the world could have re-ignited her smoldering creative spark. Just a short walk from the Arc de Triomphe, the Paris apartment of Monaco's royal family leads to one of the most beautiful spans of the urban city's glory, des Champs-Elysees, where the wide avenue's shops, restaurants, and cafes draw endless crowds of citizens and tourists. A cultural haven matched by very few world cities, as the sun sets each night, the "City of Lights" explodes in grandeur and history.

Here Grace felt refreshed by the memories of her first life, reminding her of the young movie star relaxing in one of the quaint cafes she was filmed at so many years before. This, a second chance to work, relax, and live the life she had loved in her youth, it wouldn't totally mirror what was before; instead, it would exhibit the qualities that were far from over.

In 1977, Grace's narration of the documentary *The Children of Theater Street* put her back on the road professionally—not the superhighway she'd known in the mid-fifties, but more like a picturesque country route she could travel at her leisure.

Four years later, *Rearranged* became the last film of her extraordinary career. In the film, Grace played herself opposite Edward Meeks. Meek's wife, the romance novelist Jacqueline Monsigny, wrote the script. The film was a humorous, almost-ludicrous story about an absentminded professor who mistakenly ends up at Grace's annual flower-arranging show instead of a scientific conference. The 1981 film was never released to the public.

These two films were by no means the Hollywood productions of her earlier years. However, they gave Grace satisfaction as something to hold on to as the clock ticked.

Another rebirth that magnified the performing spirit within Grace was poetry reading. Here again, the unique quality of her voice, combined with the acting skills she perfected so long before, transposed the star of stage and screen to a new role. The unique combination of talented artist and noble representative became so successful for Grace that she toured Europe and the United States each year until her death. She was welcomed and adored wherever she went. Being back on the road really lifted her spirits; she was able to shop, dine, and spend time with old friends. Seeing and visiting with the people she loved helped her recapture some of the magic of her youth.

As the American Bicentennial approached in 1976, a man named John Carroll was looking for someone to read poetry at the festival in Edinburgh, Scotland. Gwen Robyns, an old friend of his, put the bug in Carroll's ear to give Grace a try. Both Carroll and Grace showed an immediate interest. Carroll wanted Grace to read for him, so they met for lunch. He asked her to read a poem for him called "Nod." Grace, at first rusty, needed some coaching, but only a few constructive suggestions and a bit of practice brought back the legendary voice.

Grace and the other actors performed to rave reviews and sellouts. With each performance the Academy Award-winning actress became more adept at another art form, and her newfound occupation led her, for the next six years, on tours from Western Europe to the United States.

In March of 1981, Princess Grace gave her most famous reading. The guests of honor for this performance were Prince Charles and the young woman he was betrothed to, Lady Diana Spencer. By fate, this performance began the short but critical introduction of the two princesses. Held at London's Goldsmith Hall, the facility was filled with an excited crowd that night—Charles and Diana had just announced their engagement. In a dazzling display of irony, Diana privately confessed to Grace her unhappiness with the sudden influx of media attention she was receiving. Grace's intuition noticed her plight immediately, and as Grace had done so many times through the years, she led Diana to the ladies' room. There, Diana opened up and poured out her heart to Grace. The older woman's reaction was chronicled in this passage from *The Royal House of Monaco*: "When she was finished blurting it all out and was in tears, Grace put her arms around Diana, held her and patted her on the shoulder like a mother comforting a child." Grace humorously but nonetheless straightforwardly gave her the bottom line: "Don't worry, dear. It'll get worse."

How right she was.

From that moment on, the special bond between the two was welded like reinforced steel. Diana never forgot the kind and loving manner with which Grace helped her, and the two of them became compatriots in the unique lives that were so similar. Several years later, Diana told biographer Andrew Morton: "I remember meeting Princess Grace and how wonderful and serene she was. But there was troubled water under her, I saw that." Little did Diana know that the troubled water under Grace would soon flow swiftly under her as well.

The time Grace and Rainier spent away from each other towards the end of Grace's life hurt both of them. Rainier never understood Grace the artist, or her love for the arts. It was somewhat disappointing to Grace in that Rainier only came to one of her poetry readings. This was when she did a recital in London with the queen mother as the guest of honor. During the performance Rainier feel asleep, which he often did when he was bored.

This had to have hurt Grace, who had so beautifully and eloquently won the adoring praise of so many audiences. Nevertheless, she still had the gift of making entrances that sent gasps through an audience, as well as other projects which also helped fill the void of the devout Catholic princess. These included becoming the first woman to sit on the board of directors at Twentieth Century Fox.

In 1982, Philadelphia paid tribute to one of its most prized possessions when "the girl from Henry Avenue" was given a tribute to her film career. This was another heart-warming event, and Grace was both humbled and touched in accepting this precious honor from the citizens of her hometown.

Even with all that Grace had given back in return for the riches and rewards the world had bestowed on her, a final gift she treasured and adored was a gift she gave to herself—the creation of her own theater. The former convention hall in Monaco was renovated to revive the theater Grace had such an affinity for. In that small playhouse, she worked to recreate the mood of her summer-stock days. Under her leadership, the small playhouse quickly gained notoriety. Grace even had visions of acting herself once all the kinks had been worked out. Sadly, though, the tragic accident that took her life occurred before she could ever see herself on that stage.

As much as Grace and Rainier tried to keep the weekends to themselves and the children, conflicts would arise. When this happened, Grace felt trapped by a world that was keeping her away from the once-precious normal life both she and Rainier had wanted for the family.

Judith Quine had a different opinion on this. She surmised that Grace wanted to escape from Monaco and Rainier's mood swings. While meeting Grace for lunch one day, Judy commented, "We smiled for a moment at the irony of Grace's life, the unreal fantasy of it that warmed the dreams of women all over the world and the reality of limitations her position placed upon her."

Much of the world changed drastically in the sixties, and the change carried even further into the seventies. These changes were not a welcome period for Grace. As she grew older, many of her views and ideologies stayed far to the right. The conservative philosophies she believed in became a sounding board at many social events. Not that she stood up on a podium or soapbox; however, when discussions turned to politics she was quick to respond.

Many of society's changes astonished Grace, as they did almost any mature adult of this period. Dressing down, long hair on men, drugs, sexual freedom, and both parents working made Grace witness the values she had grown up with disappear. She made her feelings known to old Hollywood friends about her disenchantment with the films being produced during that time. Gone were the romantic love stories and mysteries she had played in, replaced with films containing foul language, sex and violence that devalued the film industry as it had devalued so many other institutions. Anything that was contrary to tradition or Catholic doctrine made her skin crawl; however, she was in the good company of other decent people worldwide.

I got a kick out of a passage in *The Bridesmaids* in which Judith told of a conversation that got heated at a California dinner party. It seems Judith and her husband Don owned the rights to one of the many films made over the years depicting Christ in a different light. This one portrayed him coming back in modern society. He had various roles, which included a home and family. Grace wasn't pleased at all, and said, "Why would you make a picture like that today?" Any devout Catholic only sees Christ the way He is represented in scripture and doctrine. I am not passing any blame here, only the defense mechanisms the Catholic Church and its parishioners always seem to take the fall for whenever those of different faiths or Hollywood itself questions our divinity.

Grace also criticized working mothers, even though she was one herself. The picture she painted, though, was of women throwing their children into daycare and then neglecting them. Even with all the duties and obligations that had befallen her through the years, she was a model mother who gave her maternal all to her children.

There were a few younger men who Grace kept company with during the final years of her life. Some who knew Grace referred to them as her "Boy Toys." There's no doubt she was seen in public with different younger men from time to time. Some authors, books, and even some friends said these were more than friendships, but there was never any definitive proof on the part of the rumors or the princess herself. What is known, however, is that the romance that had been such an intricate part of Grace since she first went to New York as a young aspiring actress was still alive. However, to what extent she broke her marriage sacrament is unknown. Prayer, confession, penance, and reconciliation were disciplines she relied on during her entire life. What she told her priest during reconciliation was between them and God.

Menopause was especially hard on Grace. As middle age wore on, the once beautifully contoured frame now showed weight gain. Mood swings also caused burdensome episodes. She tried hormone therapy and everything else that was available at the time. Mother Nature won these battles, though. When she was reunited with Don Richardson, the first real love of her life, he commented, "but there was something very tragic about her," and added that Grace was very unhappy near the end of her life.

As much as she tried to fill all the voids and personal problems with meaningful work, the problems still had to be dealt with. Even so, the trials she had been put through only increased in volume during her final years. One of the big disappointments for Grace was Caroline not looking to her mother when all of her own problems occurred. After Caroline's first term at *Ecole Libre des Sciences Politiques* in Paris, she decided to quit. Because she neglected her studies, her grades were poor. After voicing their disappointment, Grace and Rainier decided to do what they had planned in the first place: Caroline would enroll in Princeton, and the Kellys would keep an eye on her.

Just before Caroline was to leave for the States though, she fell head over heels in love with Philippe Junot. That brought an abrupt halt to any peaceful solution, and from that moment forward things only became more chaotic.

From the beginning of Caroline's romance with Junot, Grace knew it was doomed. Like all young women in love, there was no use trying to reason with Caroline. She manipulated her parents in different ways and ended up marrying Junot. But the marriage was a disaster that ended in divorce. There was fault on both sides between Caroline and Junot. Neither was ready for a real committed marriage. Realizing this, Grace broke with her traditional Catholic values and gave her approval for the divorce.

Another dirt-covered mound of trouble was Grace's family dilemmas back in the States. The plights of some of her own family members could have been used as scripts for an Emmy Award-winning soap opera. Her brother Kel's life began taking a nosedive in 1968, and kept on descending. Leaving a wife and six children, Kel deserted his family and began living his life as a playboy. His excuse? That his father had always pushed him in directions he never wanted to go. This was a typical copout used by many other irresponsible midlife-crisis men. Revenge for his sins, however, was going to be assigned by someone he least expected—his mother.

Kel's occupation was running the Kelly family's brickwork business. He also was a Philadelphia city councilman. In 1975, he decided to run for mayor. Grace came to Philadelphia and campaigned for him, but the anger his mother had for the hurt he had caused prompted her to play her trump card. Ma Kelly's practical and stern personality didn't mince any words with Kel's political backers when, in no uncertain terms, she told them they shouldn't endorse her son. If they refused to heed her words, she was ready to go public to tell why she felt that way. She also pledged to back his opponent if they dare try to continue their support.

This effectively ended any hopes of John B. Kelly Jr. ever becoming mayor. Ma Kelly's rationale was that all the antics Kel had pulled in recent years would come out during the campaign, and she didn't want the family's reputation dragged through more mud. Obviously, Ma Kelly was no Rose Kennedy. When his mother did this to him, Kel was devastated, and never recovered from his mother's betrayal. As time went on, Kel plummeted even further until, while out jogging in March of 1985, he suffered a fatal heart attack.

The whole ordeal was very stressful and nerve-wracking for Grace. Being put in the middle of the entire situation only added more baggage to her other problems. The once-strong Kelly family was falling apart.

As usual though, Grace didn't quit. Grace counseled one of her nieces, Kel's daughter Lizzie, who had become a victim of the Kelly family turmoil by developing anorexia. With her own world turning upside down, Grace brought Lizzie to Monaco to advise her and help heal some of her wounds.

To add to her burdens were the problems of Grace's oldest sister, Peggy. Peggy had had a drinking problem for years, which had cost her two marriages. Naturally, it had also affected her children. Like many other children of alcoholics, one of Peggy's daughters eloped as a teen to escape from her mother's drinking problems.

The stoic Henry Avenue family had seen its day. Like so many other notables throughout history, the promising life of the pretty little girl with white gloves was in disarray; the Kelly family's problems sent Grace into some of her depressions. Of this forlorn circumstance, Robert Lacey wrote: "That she was having to put on a good face on many unhappy things."

Sadly, like other famous people before and after her, Grace faced many of these problems alone. Hollywood Boulevard is filled with the broken hearts, psychological disorders, and catastrophes that became the fate of so many. From Elvis Presley to Marilyn Monroe, the suffering of the rich and famous has no boundaries.

For Grace, though, the professional always surfaced. Like so many with her type of character, there are no options of giving up. No matter what life might throw at you, you catch it, put in your bag of troubles and deal with it. This true piece of the Cross is part of every true Catholic. Is it foolish? Is it too much? Many would shout a resounding yes. But Christ's mysteries are far deeper than that. It is the strength of His love that replenishes and guides you in your prayer and faith.

Grace Kelly held those beliefs. Some days the "weight of the wood" is unbearable, while other days you walk with God in happiness and harmony. If there is an Eleventh Commandment for Catholics, it is this: Thou shall help and serve, no matter what. That service which I know Grace had is at times exhausting and burdensome: but most times, both during and on completion of each mission, the joy and love is well worth the effort taken in example from the one who washed His disciple's feet.

During the last few months of her life, the Prince and Princess of Monaco found peace with each other. Although the fairytale dreams had long come to an end, each of them seemed to have compromised and adjusted to the strengths and weaknesses each possessed, and a love based on companionship now satisfied their needs. Like her parents before her, the little girl from St. Bridget's well knew the meaning of "Till death do us part." There was still love and respect between the pair, but the raging, romantic fire Grace had cherished in her youth now burned with less intensity. Rainier was to find out that the beautiful American actress he'd fallen in love with meant more to him than he knew. These feelings would come to the forefront when his princess was killed.

For the Princess of Wales, disillusionment was one of the kinder nouns that described her marital problems. Genocide might be a more appropriate term. It is amazing that Diana endured all she did during her years as royalty and survived. It was also a miracle that the marriage of the Prince and Princess of Wales lasted as long as it did.

The anguish she encountered is almost unbelievable, yet part of the responsibility for this rested on her own shoulders. At times she could dish out her own misery on others. Still, the kaleidoscope of problems, obstacles, and dilemmas she overcame were truly gargantuan. The naive young woman still showed fortitude in overcoming the physical and mental oppressions set before her, making her a true survivor.

From the time Charles and Diana's courtship began in 1980, until their irreconcilable problems put the final nail in their coffin, Diana had done more than a lifetime of suffering. The bulimia, which began before her wedding, was to be a constant intrusion into the princess's life for years to come. Between their official engagement in February and the wedding in July, Diana's waist went from twenty-nine inches to twenty-five and one-half. This was only the beginning of what this disease would do to Diana both physically and mentally.

Another major problem that would haunt the shy young bride-to-be was her future husband's deception. In public, Charles professed his love for Diana, but Charles' heart was really pledged to Camilla Parker-Bowles. Diana got her first real evidence of this two weeks before her wedding, when she found out about the bracelet Charles had made for Camilla. When Diana confronted him about it, quite an argument took place between the two. These encounters would occur more often and escalate as time went on.

The hot-and-cold attitude the prince took toward Diana never allowed her to stand level ground. Yet even though Diana felt in her heart she was making a mistake, she knew it was too late to turn back. With her nerves wound up like a too-tight guitar string, the days before the wedding became increasingly difficult. On the early morning of her wedding day, Diana felt surprisingly calm. However, she couldn't get the thought out of her head that she was a sacrificial lamb. "So walking down the aisle," she told one magazine writer, "I spotted Camilla." It is truly sad to think that even as she walked up the isle, instead of thinking happy thoughts, she was panning the crowd for someone she already knew as a rival—a rival that was going to encroach on her personal relationship and intimacy with Charles all through her marriage.

Even sadder is the fact that Diana was truly in love with Charles, and believed that when they were married he would pay more attention to her. This was not to be; even on their honeymoon, the competition for Charles's love was apparent. Before entertaining Egypt's President Sadat, Diana discovered Charles had a set of cufflinks and pictures, gifts from Camilla. This caused another rift between the two.

With all the entertaining, the newlyweds had limited private time. By now Diana's bulimia was compelling her to purge four times a day, which made her moods go up and down like a yo-yo. After the cruise, Diana and Charles returned to Balmoral. The cycle of bulimia was turning faster and faster. With the deprivation of nutrition she became thinner and thinner. By now the thoughts of Camilla were even invading the princess's dreams. Lacking the means to deal with her problems, Diana became more and more miserable. She was given little or no support from Charles or anyone else in dealing with her problems.

Charles, like other members of the royal family and staff, thought Diana would make the transition to their way of life easier. In particular, Charles was totally devoted and steadfast to his mother, making Diana always feel she was third in line in her husband's loyalty to his parents. In truth, the princess took a backseat in Charles' relationship with both his parents and Camilla.

By October 1982, Diana was in such trouble that she went back to London to seek help. There, she was analyzed by several psychiatrists. The doctors wanted to give her medication, but she refused. Instead she felt time would ease her burdens. This may have been her greatest mistake, since mental disorders like bulimia and clinical depression cannot be simply willed away. Although mental illness is so frustrating because it isn't an exact science, the trial and error experiments each person suffering from this too-often debilitating condition must endure are terrible. However, it is a necessary process each person afflicted with the demons must go through.

The period of time between William and Harry's birth were some of Diana's darkest days—so dark that she eventually forgot all the details of them. During various interviews with author Andrew Morton, it was difficult for her to remember any details.

Diana felt Harry was a true blessing, since the six weeks prior to Harry's birth were the closest she and Charles ever were. However, as soon as the second prince was born, the marriage again took a turn for the worse and steadily went downhill. Diana knew her second child was to be a boy from scans the doctor did. She kept it to herself, though, and didn't tell Charles. For good reason apparently: Charles, who had wanted a girl, showed his disappointment immediately. This was it for Diana, who said of that dark time, "Something inside me closed off." She knew Charles had been seeing Camilla, and this latest criticism became the beginning of the end for them.

Harry himself was a complete joy for Diana and Charles. Diana even remarked that she thought Harry was closer to Charles than William. Any joy between the prince and princess, however, was over.

Diana's problems were still playing havoc with her life. Various people knew from her behavior that she needed help. In fact, anyone connected with Charles and Diana would have had to be deaf, dumb, and blind not to know their marriage was in deep trouble.

Even though her sister, Jane Fellowes, and Sarah Ferguson were there for her, she still experienced terrible misery. Jane Fellowes found out about Diana's second attempt at suicide by seeing one of her wounds. The princess had a v-neck top on, which revealed an incision Diane had inflicted on herself with a penknife. She had also made another incision down her thigh. There was a great deal of blood from the wounds, she confessed to Jane. Naturally, this astonished her sister. Once again, the despondent princess was making a desperate cry for help.

Behind the front of happiness lay feelings of guilt and worthlessness, made worse by Charles' lack of compassion. At the 1986 Exposition in Canada, Diana, still in the clutches of bulimia, collapsed from exhaustion and a lack of food. Charles gave her no sympathy, "He said I could have passed out quietly," she said of the incident.

In the late 1980s, Charles and Diana toured Spain and Portugal. In retrospect, Diana felt this was the last time she felt any closeness or chemistry with Charles. By now her popularity was gaining new heights, and with each appearance, people simply adored her more.

Inside Windsor Castle, it was a completely different story. Much of the time she was treated like an outcast and an oddball. With all the publicity and warmth she received, she still felt deep inside that she would never be queen. But by now Diana had broken out of the shell of the timid and troubled young women. She still had a great many problems, but was ready and able to stand up for herself now.

Charles and Diana were invited to Camilla's sister's fortieth birthday party. There, with all the courage she could muster, Diana confronted Camilla with the feelings and torment that had built up inside her for years. Her decision made, she found Camilla downstairs, deep in conversation with Charles. "They tried to stop me from going downstairs," she said of her friends' warning. But upon finding them together, she knew it was time to act. She entered the room and said, "Camilla, I'd love to have a word with you if possible." In a panic, Charles and the other men retreated upstairs. When the room was cleared, Diana told Camilla that she was well aware of what had been going on for years. In a sarcastic manner, she told Charles's mistress that she was sorry she was in the way. After the confrontation, they went back upstairs, and the party dispersed shortly thereafter.

Charles was fuming on the ride home. Diana stood her ground, though. The effort cost her dearly; she hardly slept, and cried most of the night. During their argument she told Charles that she had told Camilla that she loved her husband. It was a great relief to her to finally vent the feeling she had bottled up inside her for the last seven years. Of both difficult conversations, she said, "I'd done something, said what I felt." However therapeutic, what Diana had done came far too late. By now, Charles and Diana's marriage was dead in the water, and it was only a matter of time before it would officially end.

Charles' opinion was that their marriage was so troubled because Diana was always sick. Diana did have many problems in the physical, mental, and emotional triangle. I'm sure this wasn't easy for him. However, had they had a loving relationship—if Diana had been shown the love she deserved—the outcome could have been quite different.

This, too, wasn't to be. The two of them were never on the same page when dealing with each other: sometimes not even the same book. Without sharing, and compassion for each other's needs, they simply were never able to resolve or compromise any of their difficulties. In the end, Diana was only able to respond in kind.

With Diana's heart so wounded by the endless problems in her marriage, and with long-held romantic desires gone unfulfilled, her eyes began to rove. For several reasons, Charles would never meet the passion she had longed and dreamed of. Finally, an opportunity presented itself, and the temptation was too great to resist. Starving for intimacy, she latched on to the intrigue and promise of passion that lay before her: His name was James Hewitt.

Captain James Hewitt came from a military background. His father was a Royal Marine who by nature believed in a disciplined environment throughout all aspects of life. The captain's mother was loving, warm, and affectionate. James had two sisters, one being his twin. After training in various military schools, James Hewitt joined the Life Guards of Buckingham Palace in 1978. From there, due in part to his splendid horsemanship, his career advanced.

Hewitt's somewhat sheltered upbringing and strict background didn't leave much time for socialization; he didn't have a girlfriend till age nineteen. Princess Diana was to become the first real love of his life.

The first time Diana and Hewitt's paths crossed was at a polo match between Charles's team and the team Hewitt was on. Diana was very upset and anxious that day, and Hewitt noticed the princess's despair. He wanted to help, but was too busy with the game. Diana's beauty and vulnerability, however, remained stored in his psyche.

After this first encounter, they didn't come in contact with each other until 1986, when they were reintroduced during an event at the Mayfair Drawing Room. This meeting lit the candle that would burn for a long time. Captain Hewitt's enchantment with Diana began to churn into emotion at Sarah's and Andrew's wedding. The sight of Diana, looking stunning as usual, caused his yearning for her to grow stronger. Fate would gently push along the inevitable.

By 1986, Hewitt was put in charge of security at Buckingham Palace. One day he spotted Diana sitting barefoot on the stairs, and "She took his breath away." Their conversation turned flirtatious, fueling the passion each of them was now feeling, their small talk and body language showing a longing that, for each of them, became unrelenting.

Being who each of them were, their intelligence had to take priority over their emotions. They needed a route to begin their romance, and that was provided by riding lessons. Diana called James a short time after their talk on their stairs and made an appointment for her first lesson. Coyly making sure everything remained aboveboard, the princess brought Hazel West, her lady-in-waiting and also a proficient horsewoman, along with her. The captain was eager to welcome them. Leaving from Windsor Castle's Combermere Barracks each morning, the three would ride on the trails of Hyde Park, trotting and cantering among the beautiful flowerbeds and trees set in the busy streets of London. The landscape transposed its energy to the two attracted riders.

As the lessons progressed, the bond between the princess and captain grew stronger. In *Princess In Love*, Anna Pasternak wrote, "These meetings, she was soon to tell him, were becoming an integral and much-needed release from the tensions that characterized her daily life." The natural progression of their relationship now more personal, Diana curiously asked James if he had a girlfriend. Once it became clear that he didn't, the foregone conclusion began.

This is where Diana's path began to mirror her mother's. Not feeling any love for or from her spouse, her young heart longed for romance. As the conversations between Diana and James became more personal, Diana began to open up and tell him some of her pent-up feelings. The trust and safety she felt in confiding to Hewitt became a needed release, and she related the sadness of her childhood, especially her parents' divorce, and how she had to protect her younger brother who was even more hurt by the family's destruction. At first James didn't completely understand her hurt. But he continued listening and, as time went on, it became clearer.

One day, while Diana was melancholy, James asked her what was the matter. While he listened intently, Anna Pasternak wrote that Diana told him, "All she could see was the tunnel of misery stretching ahead of her," meaning that she felt extremely guilty realizing that William and Harry might have to go through the same things Diana had. While Diana poured her heart out about her loveless and trouble-filled marriage, James held her hand and completely focused on each phrase. Every move still had to be made cautiously, but there was no denying it—they were falling in love.

180

As the trust and bond blossomed, James also confided in Diana. Hewitt was very close to his mother, and like most women, including Grace and Diana, her children came before anything else. There was turmoil also in the captain's family, which eventually led to his own parents' divorce. This had also caused James to withdraw from the hurt he felt. The common bond of family problems made their cohesion even stronger.

Diana told James how she hated the phony displays of public affection Charles showed her at times. To her, these must have been much like Bill and Hillary Clinton's handholding act while toting a Bible into church each Sunday. For years, Diana had shown a jealous nature for Charles' friends, who seemed to be able to make him happy when she couldn't. But now that once-insurmountable problem seemed less important. Now, Diana had found someone whom she could please, someone who made her forget about her troubles.

The momentum built steadily between Diana and James, but the pinnacle began when Diana invited James to dinner at Kensington Palace. According to one account, James was "delighted by the invitation." Understandably so. The habitat each had fantasized had become reality: an intimate, romantic cuisine, with candles and flowers creating a climate of passion. The princess was so moved to ecstasy by their lovemaking, tears of joy and a release of so much lonely tension flowed like a swift river. The pledge of love that had brought them together became a sanctuary for the love, romance, and sentiment locked away in their hearts. Although the key was sinful, its turning opened a door Diana had never experienced. They were the first real shared loves of each other's lives.

Diana and James's affair steadily developed. They talked with one another twice a day. The praise and recognition Diana yearned for by someone she loved romantically finally became a reality. The captain bolstered her self-esteem and helped the stage fright Diana always experienced. As their secret relationship blossomed and became more confident, the princess became more assertive, and she began to stand up to the royal family. Charles' gallivanting and the stuffy standing orders of the queen would now be met with hard questions.

In 1987, Captain James Hewitt was promoted to major. Naturally, Diana was proud and thrilled for him. Their involvement grew, so much so that Diana, James, William, and Harry became their own family unit. Weekends at Highgrove became a frequent occurrence. At the time, Barbara Barnes was still the boys' nanny, and knew what was going on. In this regard, however, she was loyal to Diana's secret love, and kept it to herself. The once-lonely weekends when Diana and Charles were apart became purposeful now for the princess. The fulfillment, comfort, and safety Diana felt yearned for each week's end.

As the relationship progressed, Diana's intimate feelings for the major reached a crescendo. At one point, she confided in the major her innermost secret—the disease that had plagued her for so long. To him she confessed all the turmoil and suffering her bulimia had caused her. James was shocked, but with the love he felt for her, he vowed to help her. Finally she felt "...the relief at last that someone was supporting her." The psychological battering that had attacked her for so long was soothed by James' compassion. For the first time in years, she was able to keep food down. At least for a period of time, she was able to negotiate a psychological peace with herself.

The relationship was by no means a utopia, though. Carrying on an adulterous affair with the most popular woman in the world had several downsides. First and foremost of these were the necessary secrecy, and the anxiety it produced. Both of them knew well the consequences awaiting them if they were exposed. Diana's situation piled an enormous amount of responsibility on the major, and his guilt-induced pressure began to build, so much so that James needed an outlet for his frustrations. Relief came in the form of his father. The major's confession to him came six months into the affair. Yet this turned out to be a positive aspect in their relationship. Diana understood perfectly and was glad, and James was able to calm some of his concerns.

James's mother also became a confidant to their liaison. One weekend, Diana and he met at his mother's home. The princess wanted very much to make a good impression on her. Diana was put at ease quickly by Mrs. Hewitt, quelling Diana's feelings of apprehension.

While together in the throngs of love, Diana and James became a team, a partnership working mutually in support of each other. That reassurance gave Diana the strength to begin to sort out her other troubles. With her unlimited financial sources, she tried quite a few of the alternative therapies that became so popular as the century closed; to cope with her problems she tried massage, acupuncture, and aromatherapy. While not cure-alls by any means, all these newfound assets became very helpful to her. This success also made her realize that all these, coupled with self-reliance, would further erode the stockpiles of anxieties she still dealt with each day.

The love and relationship the couple experienced couldn't continue an endless, blissful path. Like all affairs, there was a great deal of baggage that had full suitcases added to it as time went on. Even though Diana had pledged her heart to James, the seething rage she felt for Camilla still plagued her. Also, James felt out of place and tormented when he had to witness Diana and Charles together. Being the other man is no different than being the other woman. For a time these apprehensions were kept under control. As time passed, though, these problems began to take their toll.

The affair between Diana and Major Hewitt was still in full swing in 1988 when an avalanche involving Charles' skiing party met with some tragic results. When word of the incident first reached all concerned, details weren't clear on whom was injured or killed. Finally the tragic news came that Hugh Lindsay, one of Charles' close friends, had been killed.

This was a reality check for Diana and James. What if Charles had been the one killed? They both knew that a permanent scourge would have been put upon both of them if Charles had died and their affair was revealed.

Even with all the joy Diana's relationship with James Hewitt brought, she still agonized a great deal over the slow but steady death of her marriage. The pressure of the goings-on around them lead to inevitable friction between them. Their first real quarrel was over Diana's incredible sexual appetite. This tiff became a sharp turning point in their relationship. As related in *Princess In Love*, "As he heard the mistrust in her voice and saw her fury, for the first time in their relationship he felt angry and let down."

During the argument, Diana became so upset that she ran off to be by herself. Allan Peters, her bodyguard, scolded her when she was found. Jeopardizing her own safety had put Mr. Peters in a very precarious position. Again, Diana's temper had gotten the better of her. Humiliated by the entire ordeal, she had Peters transferred.

Eventually, when things calmed down, Diana apologized to Peters for both her behavior and her knee-jerk reaction.

Like Princess Diana's marriage, her relationship with Major James Hewitt began a progressive deterioration. But there were still some good moments left. One event they were able to enjoy was Raine Spencer's sixtieth birthday party. Held at Althorp, the five-hundred-guest event allowed time for Diana and James to be with each other, and she was able to break away from her usual mob and show him the home she grew up in.

Even so, the web of deception and secrecy progressed, the ever-mounting circumstances like a wind from an approaching storm becoming more and more forceful. Charles' fortieth birthday party was another awkward event for both Diana and James. Held in November of 1988, the formal affair included some of England's entertainment giants. Elton John and Phil Collins headlined the party, along with political and royal guests.

The final gust that toppled them began with the transfer of Major Hewitt to Germany. The long distance between them, an intermission before the final act still to be played, caused Diana to begin to distance herself from James.

In fact, the major's eighteen months in Germany gave both of them time to reflect on what had been. During the separation, the major began to date another woman, Sophie Von Reden. Diana's world, as usual, was filled with her work and problems. Like all deep-rooted loves, however, theirs wasn't leaving without a fight. During each day of the eighteen-month separation, they each crossed the other's minds several times a day.

Although the affair between Princess Diana and Major Hewitt was doomed from the beginning, the love between them was real, a deeply bonded commitment that couldn't be turned off and on like a faucet. On Hewitt's return, after not seeing each other for eighteen months, the enraptured feelings and passions sprang back to life. Their love still had a few final scenes to play.

The major was so mixed up emotionally that when the Gulf War broke out, he fantasized about being killed in battle. He perceived this as a way to die tragically, but still be able to go to his grave with his heart pledged to Diana. Once more, Diana showed her loyalty to the man she truly loved: during the Gulf War, she wrote him daily. This tender ritual became another romantic chapter for each—the stoic warrior in a faraway land being thought of and agonized over by his sweetheart back home.

As she had done so often in her life, Diana turned to Christ while the Gulf War was fought. The structure and love of the Catholic Church drew Diana, and according to Anna Pasternak, "Diana would creep into churches and light candles for James." It was an insightful and esoteric period for both of them. More fittingly, it became their final chapter.

The once-strong rope that could handle the weight of circumstances in their relationship was now weakened to its last strand. The inevitable discovery of their relationship by too many people finally broke it. A former girlfriend of the major's, Emma Stewardson, told the media of her love affair with James, as well as his relationship with Diana. As Anna Pasternak related, "For now that their secret was out there would be no peace." It was as if this final tidal wave of unwelcome publicity was staged for their foregone ending.

When the Gulf War ended, Diana cried with relief. Upon his return, James went to Highgrove to be with her. Each knew the sad reality of this meeting. Their relationship had to end; James had lost his promotion because of all the negative publicity. So after five years, their relationship ended in 1991.

There were to be no bittersweet secret memories of their relationship, at least for James at first. Driven by greed, he would become one of the princess's biggest traitors by selling his story and love letters to both authors and tabloids. Even after Diana's death, he published his own version of his relationship with Princess Diana. The book didn't do well, though, after his reputation had been tarnished by his avarice. Like most intimate liaisons of deceit, Diana and James's finished with the profound wreckage of hurt, and like all emotional disasters, there was nothing left to salvage.

Even the queen could see the handwriting on the wall. Although she had tried many things to keep Diana and Charles together, she now knew it was hopeless. Queen Elizabeth knew of all of Diana's problems, included the bulimia. When she had to relate to others why the marriage had broken up, bulimia became her main reason, perhaps because it was easier for her to use than other reasons. She surmised that Charles just couldn't deal with the list of problems the Diana put on Charles' shoulders, especially the bulimia.

Diana's bulimia *was* a major problem in the marriage; however, it was well under control by the time Charles and Diana decided to separate. 1988 was the turning point for the young woman who had to bear so much weight in becoming a member of the royal family. Yet instead of fighting everything and everyone, Diana began to adapt. Former flatmate Carolyn Bartholomew had a heart-to-heart talk with her, telling her how dangerous the bulimia was to both her mental and physical health. Carolyn finally convinced Diana that she needed professional help. Diana knew she was right, and finally got the help she needed.

Diana began treatment with a psychiatrist named Maurice Lipsedge. Their sessions immediately focused on Diana's suicidal thoughts and attempts. When Dr. Lipsedge asked, "How many times have you tried to do yourself in?" Diana admitted that she had tried to take her life four or five times.

Dr. Lipsedge did a marvelous job with the princess. In their weekly sessions, the isolated, lonely feelings that the depression brought were dealt with, and after six months she was much better. Through this methodical process, she made steady progress and was able to regain her self-esteem. With her outlook on everything much improved, the disease that had consumed so much of her life for much of a decade was under control, and her purging went from four times a day to once every three weeks. This gave her a new outlook, and strength to confront the problems and difficulties she had to deal with.

The progress Diana made in her therapy was a needed pillar to help support her under the weight of the future. Problems that had once so overwhelmed her could now be dealt with. This was by no means a magic wand. There were still several painful hurdles to jump. Yet those six months gave her the strength to prevail for what was to come.

The deathblow to Diana and Charles' marriage was struck when Andrew Morton's tell-all biography of the princess was released in 1991. Aided by the extraordinary research he had accumulated, Morton revealed to the world all the hurt and deceit that had plagued Diana. Charles also had a coming-out. In taped telephone conversations, Charles admitted his longtime infidelity with Camilla

Parker-Bowles. With taped telephone conversations and secret interviews with the princess, enough dirt to have filled a silo came pouring out.

By now, Charles and Diana had grown ice-cold towards one another. The walls they had built around one another were plainly apparent to anyone by now, especially the media. On a visit to South Korea in 1992, reporters called them "The Glums." One month later, the separation became official.

In an interview in 1994, Charles admitted his infidelity and said he had never loved Diana. Further, he revealed that the only reason he married her was because of the pressure his father put on him. Like so many separations, once fingers are pointed and accusations are made, the gloves come off, and anger and hostility become the smorgasbord of revenge. Charles and Diana's banquet table was filled with a variety of charges. Diana fired back after Charles spilled his guts and said that William should be the next king. By now, the queen had heard quite enough. To avoid further humiliation and exposure, the queen insisted they divorce.

This marked an end to the most flamboyant marriage in history. The failure of her marriage was extremely painful for Diana, and she would grieve almost until her death. A couple that had redefined envy had now given way to the mortal emotions that pander to no one. Diana wasn't just fighting Charles at the end of her marriage, but the entire bureaucracy of the royals.

Tony Lloyd compared her courage to that of Sir Thomas Moore who had stood up to King Henry VIII during the king's purges. Not that Diana was going to be carried off to the Tower of London; however, even outnumbered in everything she had to deal with, she still showed how resourceful she could be. Her popularity, along with the backing of the public, saved her reputation and earned her a fair settlement in the divorce.

In spite of her other successes, Diana endured tremendous emotional pain. Tony Lloyd, who worked with her, revealed to me one of the struggles she went through during the time of her divorce by saying, "She became very silent at lunch once when her divorce was imminent."

Naturally, as in all divorces, there were innocent victims who had to endure heartache also. With William and Harry, it was no different.

William, being the older, had to bear more of the brunt. In his mother's sorrow, William had tried to ease her pain. At times, when Diana would go into the bathroom to cry, William would pass tissues under the door.

For the most part, the boys shunned stating a preference or special allegiance for one parent over the other. In *The Day Diana Died*, Christopher Andersen wrote, "William and Harry had both resolutely refused to take sides in the divorce." But seeing his mother in such pain, William did once ask his father, "Why do you make Mummy cry all the time?"

Like all children of divorce, both young princes searched for outlets—particularly adults they could feel secure with and talk to. This need wasn't fulfilled for either of them by relatives. Queen Elizabeth and Prince Philip had neither the personality nor compassion for the situation. Instead, the boys turned to adults they had become close to at school, and also their nanny. In William's case it was Andrew and Shauna Gailey, his housemasters at Eaton. For Harry it was Gerald and Janet Barber at Ludgrove. These couples, along with Tiggy Legge-Bourke, provided the necessary love, therapy, and comfort the boys needed.

Even to those such as myself who are experienced in working with children who have gone through this modern epidemic, it is surprising at times how well some children adjust to divorce. Usually these are children with strong personalities, proper upbringings, and most of all the support of both their parents and other extended adults. This was the case for William and Harry: even though their parents' divorce did have its rough moments, overall they came through it fairly well.

In February of 1996, Charles and Diana met in St. James Palace to negotiate their divorce proceedings. Diana, who had come far from the naïve young woman she once had been, was shrewd, cunning, and resourceful. She lost some things, but retained others. The divorce meant separation from all ties with the royal family. Diana would never be queen. She did retain her title as Princess of Wales, but wouldn't be referred as Her Royal Highness anymore. In the financial settlement, she made out very well. Her take was 26.5 million, which kept her quite comfortable during her last eighteen months. Of all else, she had her freedom—and at last, a chance to pursue happiness.

The two princesses had now come full circle. Their spherical patterns traced similar arcs at times, while other times each one's circumstance would stray toward its own radius. Yet for the most part, the accomplishments and setbacks they experienced traveled a corresponding spectrum.

Grace and Diana both accomplished a great deal in the many endeavors they were involved in. Each showed an extraordinary amount of strength, fortitude, and persistence to meet their challenges. Though unique and extraordinary in many ways, they still were vulnerable to the problems and predicaments that everyone meets on their journey through life.

The unhappy times of each of their marriages pushed them towards the outlets they both pursued, perhaps proving that women are far more loyal than men romantically. Even though some men stray no matter what, when a woman's needs are met romantically, it leaves them satisfied and secure. Each princess had different degrees of frustration in their relationships with their husbands. Their loyalty, though, would have stayed steadfast had the satisfaction and security they craved been met.

Through their years of royalty, each knew the dreams and hopes that shone in some ways and faded in others. What had once showed such promise was now a distracted institution for one, and a conclusion for the other. Even though the worlds in which they lived looked as inviting as anyone can imagine, the results of each prove that life makes no one any promises—that each fate and destiny are determined by a set of circumstances we can only expect and make adjustments to when the dreams fail to meet expectation. When changes invariably hit us right between the eyes, we must grieve, make our peace with God, and go on. Nothing lasts forever, as Grace Kelly and Diana Spencer both found out.

Chapter XIV – Accidents

Of all the similarities integrated into the lives of Grace Kelly and Diana Spencer, the way they died was more coincidental and ironic than any of their other comparisons. The set of circumstances that led to each of their tragic deaths showed a frightening awareness of the cruelties and occurrences that we have no control over. The dice rolled for each one of us every day brings changes and revelations that only destiny or providence has the power to control. Like theirs, our lives are but a present existence that can at a moments' notice be altered or ended by the fate that hangs over each head. Whether each person believes what happened to them was done by spiritual intervention or random acts makes no difference—the end result is that one never knows what is around every corner or bend.

With various defense mechanisms, we try to bring peace to the unknown events that can lead to our demise. In the case of Grace and Diana, fate ended each of their lives in a tragedy recognized by the far too many who had to pick up the shattered remains of life and love taken away before its time.

Like each person who dies accidentally, Grace and Diana each had a bizarre set of circumstances that fit together like the pieces of a jigsaw puzzle. One "what-if" either way might have spared them. However, what-if's are mysteries that are only discovered after it's too late. When the last pieces of their puzzles were pressed into place, disaster was the outcome.

Some comparisons are obvious. The two princesses were both killed in automobile accidents. Both accidents were within two calendar weeks of each other, towards the end of summer, and each accident happened within French borders. This is just the beginning, though, of the explicit similarities that ended their lives.

The lone survivor of each tragedy has helped very little in confirming the true circumstances that led to the tragedies—one because of the severe injuries he sustained in the tunnel of death, the other because she has kept it to herself the past twenty years.

To add to the many "what-if" scenarios for both, speed played a role in each victim's tragic ending. Neither Grace nor Diana was wearing a seatbelt, which tilted the odds even further toward the fate they were dealt. Had they been wearing seatbelts, it has been theorized that they might have survived. Also, neither accident scene had guardrails where the airborne vehicle of Princess Grace left the road, or where Princess Diana's fatal impact occurred. That, too, would have given them much better odds.

Critical mistakes were made in regard to the first medical treatment each princess received, which will be detailed below. Both princesses were brought to Catholic hospitals. Each received their final blessings at the time of their deaths from Catholic priests. Princess Grace, being Catholic, received the sacrament of the Anointing of the Sick, which used to be called the Last Rites. Princess Diana, being a member of the Church of England was administered the nondenominational Extreme Unction ritual.

Rumors, innuendoes, and controversies surrounded each accident as planned sabotages. In Princess Grace's accident, the rumors of foul play were ruled out fairly quickly and were accepted. The rumors of Diana's accident come back full-force each year on the anniversary of her death, due to Mohamed Al-Fayed's claim that sabotage was behind the death of Diana and his son.

In both cases, the public was kept in the dark a great deal. The first reports that surfaced from each tragedy were that neither princess was hurt very badly, which caused confusion on all continents. In the end though, the result was loss of life, and the world mourned deeply from each loss.

In Princess Grace's accident, the set of circumstances leading up to it seemed fairly innocent. Stephanie, at seventeen, was in full rebellion at the time her mother's tragedy was about to occur. As with her sister Caroline before, her young, arrogant independent attitude led her to have many a go-round with her mother. Stephanie, with second-guessed permission from Grace and Rainier, was allowed to vacation with her boyfriend Paul Belmondo in Antigua. Grace and Rainier didn't want a similar disaster to what had occurred between Caroline and Philippe Junot. By giving Stephanie permission, Grace and Rainier felt they would avoid the blackmail-marriage routine Caroline had given them.

The plan quickly backfired. On returning from her holiday Stephanie—who was already enrolled in the Institute of Fashion Design in Paris—announced that she now wanted to attend racing car school with the nineteen-year-old Paul. Grace's reaction was expected and according to biographer Robert Lacey, "…her mother, for once, had had enough." In short, Grace put her foot down and forbade this from happening.

This refusal set off a series of torrid battles between mother and daughter that still weren't resolved by the time Stephanie was to leave for Paris. In addition, Grace had been experiencing a great many headaches that were going to play a key role in her calamity.

On the day the accident occurred, September 13, 1982, Grace was taking Stephanie from Roc Agel down to Monaco to get her off to school. This was likely a welcome opportunity for Grace; many things between them were still unresolved, and Grace wanted to bring some kind of peace and closure to their differences.

Grace had some dresses that needed alterations, which she spread out in the backseat of the vehicle, a Rover. This left room for only two: one passenger and the driver, so Grace told her chauffeur Christian Sylvestri, "It's just easier if I drive." Grace hardly ever drove anymore, but the ride down to Monaco would give mother and daughter time to talk and try to settle and calm the friction. Implementing this strategy would give her privacy for what Stephanie and she were going to discuss. Sylvestri reluctantly agreed.

The drive downhill to Monaco from Roc Agel is precarious, with steep drops and sharp turns. It winds through hills and valleys lined with knolls, rock formations, and various picturesque dwellings leading down to the sea. The road's turns and curves test the ability of both driver and vehicle.

While negotiating the steep angles and sharp turns, a truck began to follow the Rover. When the truck began to follow Grace's car, the driver noted that it made the first turn without any apparent difficulty.

After that, however, things became more and more reckless. The Rover was now all over the road, weaving back and forth, crossing the centerline, and even clipping the rocks on the opposite side of the road.

Yves Phily, the truck driver, sounded his horn to get some kind of response from the erratically behaving vehicle. Grace's car did straighten itself out momentarily. When it was time to brake for the next turn, though, the car accelerated instead, and disaster was its only course.

With the Rover going much too fast (seventy to eighty kilometers per hour was the estimate), it left the road and became airborne. The car had such momentum from its speed that it sheared of the top of some trees before bouncing and somersaulting off several rocks and other foliage. When it finally came to rest, it was on its roof, and tilted toward the front of the car.

Stephanie, hurt but still conscious, was able to crawl out of the rubble and make her way to a nearby farmhouse. Near hysterics, Stephanie begged the occupants to call her father, which was done immediately after she told them who she was.

Even though they were still within France, it was Monaco's emergency personnel who were first to arrive at the scene; the report had been picked up by the radio frequency from the French Police. Rainier arrived about thirty minutes after the accident. By now, Monaco's fire department had gotten Grace out and was getting her into an ambulance. They quickly rushed Grace and Stephanie back to the hospital in Monaco named after Princess Grace.

Without the safety of a seatbelt, Grace had massive trauma. She had suffered fractures in her thigh, knee, and arm, and also head injuries. It was the head injuries, however, that concerned the medical personnel the most.

The preliminary examiner at the emergency room diagnosed a brain injury. A brain surgeon named Dr. Jean Duplay was immediately summoned from Nice. When he arrived, two problems confronted him immediately. The Monaco doctors had already made a major mistake—they had administered a narcotic drug called Gamma O.H. for pain. By doing this, they had sent Grace into an even deeper coma. Also, Dr. Duplay discovered that Grace's hospital didn't have a CAT-scan machine. Grace had to be transported to the other side of Monaco to a clinic that had the machine. This necessary move only lost more valuable time.

The CAT scan showed two key findings. The first was damage to Grace's frontal lobe that had occurred from the impact of the accident. However, the second, even more troubling, showed that, deep within Grace's brain, she had suffered a slight stroke. This critical evidence—along with Grace's family history of cardiovascular disease, a high cholesterol diet, her recent, frequent headaches, and the stress she endured toward the end of her life—confirmed the most probable theory that she had suffered a slight stroke as she tried to negotiate the treacherous road.

Once Grace was brought into Monaco to be treated, Rainier worked to keep everyone in the dark as to what occurred. Captain Roger Bencze, the chief detective doing the investigation outside Monaco, had his hands tied in many respects. Without a clear report, rumors flew wildly in the newspapers and tabloids of what happened. Stephanie was at the center of many of them. Some of the media printed and reported that Stephanie had been driving. These assumptions couldn't be denied, because Rainier never allowed Stephanie to be interviewed. To this day, the one critical witness who could confirm or deny all theories has not spoken.

The reports on Grace were so played-down that initially her close friends thought she had merely broken a leg. Judith Quine heard the news as she was on her way to the Indianapolis Airport to fly home to New York. The young man driving her and her husband Don to the airport commented, "I'd heard she been in some kind of accident." To quell their instantaneous alarm, the driver assured them immediately that the news reports said she only suffered minor injuries. A relieved Don told Judith to make the time to visit Grace during her recovery.

The shocking truth would come some hours later.

With the dismal facts shown by the CAT scan, the doctors told Rainier that, even if Grace were to survive, paralysis and other mental and cognitive functions would significantly impair her. Slowly but surely, throughout the night of September 13th and into the following morning, Grace's condition deteriorated. Grace's fate had played its last hand and lost, and the inevitable became reality. As was stated in *The Royal House of Monaco*, "Grace was clinically dead—she was only being kept alive by machines."

Caroline had flown back from England. Along with her brother, Albert, and their father, they kept vigil at Grace's bed throughout the night. Stephanie was in another hospital room with the injuries she had sustained. She would make a full recovery, but was incapacitated from the accident on that night.

With their last hopes dashed, the two children kissed their mother good-bye and left her alone with their father. At noon, Rainier told the doctors to remove Grace from life support. Grace Kelly, Princess Grace, Her Serene Highness of Monaco, world-famous actress, wife, and mother, died at 10:35 PM on September 14, 1982.

All the rumors and theories about Grace's death turned out to be false. No wrongdoing was found. Officers Roger Bencze and Noel Anton, who were top-of-the-line traffic accident investigators, went over the scene and the Rover with a fine-toothed comb. With respect to all mechanical features, one account stated, "It was also clear that the prince's garage had serviced and maintained the car in very good condition." So the rumors and hearsay of sabotage or foul play were ruled out quickly.

The circumstances and events that led up to Grace Kelly's fate were comparable to the many occurrences that happen when a medical emergency befalls someone operating a motor vehicle. Thankfully, Grace was the only victim to lose her life in this catastrophe. Stephanie made a full recovery, and no other cars had been involved. Yet in the final analysis, by the providence she was called home to, the world lost one of its most renowned figures.

Of all the tragedies of the twentieth century, of which there have been so many, the only one that equals Princess Diana's was the day in Dallas when Camelot was extinguished by shots fired from the Texas Book Depository.

Diana Spencer's death was a true catastrophe in every sense and aspect. Though no longer Princess of Wales, she still commanded enormous power by her mere popularity and presence, and the world remained at her beck and call. She was still climbing to new heights at the point her life ended, which made her tragedy all the more shattering.

If her story were fiction, the events and circumstances that led to her death would read as well as any best-selling novel. It had all the elements necessary: love, danger, mystery, intrigue, and tragedy. If Mary Higgins Clark, Danielle Steele, and the spirit of Alfred Hitchcock had collaborated as a team, I don't think they could have imagined or written a better plot. Unfortunately, it was real, and left real pain for all those who loved her.

Diana was still active in all of her six main causes when she reached her fateful end, including a new focus—the landmines that had killed and maimed so many in Southeast Asia and the former Yugoslav republics. With this and all the other causes she poured her considerable energy into, Diana still could raise awareness and money with only the sound of her voice.

Like Grace, Diana also had an uncanny set of circumstances fall into place at the wrong time that led to her tragic end. Things were rolling along much better for her; the seemingly insurmountable problems that had plagued her for so long were all either gone or well under control. She was spending carefree days with her two boys, and having glorious times basking in the summer sun. Most important though, romance had entered the scene. In the years of feeling trapped and stifled by her position and the royal family, Diana had dreamed of escape, an escape to a new life and land where she could be appreciated and valued for her work without the constant surveillance she always dreaded. Finally, the stunning and beautiful world figure had met a man that complemented the mature, confident idol the world admired. His name was Emad Dodi Al Fayed.

Dodi Al Fayed was worldly, experienced, and confident. The son of Mohamed Al Fayed, one of the world's richest men, Dodi had known the good life from birth. Dodi and the princess had first met ten years earlier at Smith's Lawn, where Dodi's polo team was playing against Charles'. The spark between them was ignited when Dodi's father invited Diana and William to the family's summer villa in St. Tropez. After that mid-July weekend in 1997, the romance was on.

Of average stature and build, Dodi's dark, short curly hair gave easy view of the middle-eastern complexion below: olive skin, dark from the sun and sea that were second nature to him, deep eyes trimmed with thick brows set equally on each side of a sizable nose, and a firm, strong chin showing a pleasure in and fervor for life.

Dodi had tried his hand in a few enterprises. He'd lived and worked in Hollywood for a while, and had a brief career in the film industry as a producer. Some of his films included *Chariots of Fire* and *Hook*. For the most part, though, his main hobbies were living the life of the young, rich playboy he was.

Like so many things that were left without closure when Diana was killed, the exact extent of her relationship with Dodi Al-Fayed died, along with other mysteries from other notable tragic deaths. The media in general, as well as all the various authors who have written about Diana since her death, have given different theories on where Diana and Dodi stood with each other at the time of their deaths. It has been proven that Dodi was about to ask Diana to marry him, had the ride back to his apartment not ended their lives. In divergence with that information, Simone Simmons wrote that Diana was on the rebound from Hasnat Khan, and was using the relationship with Dodi to make the doctor jealous. There is evidence for both theories; however, the exact nature of Diana's feelings will remain an enigma. The car crash left an unfinished end to their story whose tragic end will be discussed, speculated, and debated, but never truly revealed. Suffice it to say that, at the time of their deaths, Diana and Dodi were romantically involved.

Being who Diana was, as soon as news of the world's most popular figure in a new relationship reached the media, any and every tool of the press descended upon them. This onslaught was to play the pivotal component in the drama leading to the catastrophe.

For much of the month of August 1997, Diana and Dodi had been enjoying themselves on the Mediterranean, living the life Princess Grace and many of the rich and famous dabbled in each summer, and enjoying the various beaches, boats, and water activities that were so much a part of their lives.

On Saturday morning August 30, 1997, Diana and Dodi flew from Sardinia to Paris. They were to spend the remainder of Saturday there until Sunday morning, when Diana was to return to England to see her boys.

From the moment their plane touched down in Paris and they left for their first stop, the paparazzi were in hot pursuit. "Step on it!" Dodi angrily ordered Dourneau, the driver, at one point. "Lose them."

Dodi wanted this night to be special, and had lost his patience with the paparazzi. During the next several hours, his frustration would grow until his plan of action would spell disaster.

The first stop for Diana and Dodi was the Villa Windsor. The former home of King Edward VIII had just recently been purchased by Dodi's father. The Villa Windsor is where Edward VIII had lived in Paris after he shocked the world in 1936 by abdicating the throne because he'd fallen in love with a rich American aristocrat named Wallis Warfield Simpson. With marriage to Mrs. Simpson out of the question, Great Britain had made the king choose between love and country. He chose love.

Since they were planning to use the magnificent home in the future, Diana and Dodi were overseeing the villa's redecorating. After checking appliances and measuring for curtains, they left for the Ritz. They each made what was to be their last phone calls to friends and relatives from one of the grand suites of the stunning hotel.

During one of Diana's phone conversations, with friend Annabel Goldsmith, she revealed that although she was happy in her relationship with Dodi, marriage wasn't in her plans. "I'm having a wonderful time," she said, "but the last thing I need is a new marriage." She also admitted in her last phone conversation with Richard Kay that she was going to withdraw from public life. Meanwhile, Dodi was preparing his plan to ask Diana to marry him.

The Trot Von Dom Square, where the Ritz is located, became the base of operations for all events leading up to the accident. The beautiful, majestic architecture there pays tribute to two of Frances greatest heroes; portraying the high pedestal statue of Napoleon, along with the various Sun King medallions on each lamppost of Louis the XIV. It is a breathtaking sight both day and night. While researching this book, I carefully gazed at its splendor each time I was in it during my trip to Paris, and was captivated by its grandeur and architecture. It is another piece of Paris that regales the traits of the upper class.

Located in the square is a high-class jewelry store named Repossi. In the early evening, while Diana was having her hair done, Dodi visited Repossi to acquire the $200,000 diamond ring with which he was going to ask her to marry him later that night. "When Dodi came out," Christopher Anderson wrote in his account of Diana's last day, "he obviously had something with him and he was happy."

At 7 PM, Diana and Dodi left for his apartment near the Arc de Triumph. Henri Paul, Dodi's bodyguard, watched them leave, thinking his work for the day was through. The second piece of the puzzle of death was now about to be put into place.

When the couple arrived at Dodi's apartment, the paparazzi were already there, cameras ready. Trevor Rees-Jones and three other security men were forced to push a path open so Diana and Dodi could get in. Dodi's plan, which he revealed to his butler, was to leave the ring in his bedroom and pop the question to Diana when they returned from dinner. In his book about Diana's last day, Anderson wrote, "The ring was on the nightstand in his bedroom, and Dodi had checked to make sure they had several bottles of Dom Perignon on ice to toast the big moment."

At 9:30, Diana and Dodi left his apartment to have dinner. But the paparazzi had found out where they originally planned to dine, and Dodi's anger grew again as they approached the Chez Benoit restaurant. "Furious that his perfect romantic evening was being irrevocably spoiled," the author wrote, "Dodi ordered Dourneau to turn around and head back to the Ritz."

After fighting their way through the crowd in front of the Ritz, they finally got inside, where they could get some privacy. By now paranoid that there could be paparazzi in the hotel's dining room, Diana and Dodi went up to one of the imperial suites and had their meal sent there. Everything might still have been fine had Dodi not let his ego and temper get the better of him.

After they were done eating, two more decisions were made that began hammering the final nail in Diana, Dodi, and driver Henri Paul's coffins. The first was totally Henri Paul's fault. Mr. Paul had consumed a variation of alcoholic drinks and prescription drugs when he thought he was done for the night. Because of his inebriation, he had no business agreeing to drive Dodi and Diana back to Dodi's apartment. With all accounts, accusations, innuendoes, and fabrications since the accident, one thing is undeniable: Henri Paul was intoxicated before getting behind the wheel. As was reported in *Time* magazine, "A second analysis of his blood had confirmed the original test taken on August 31. Paul had between 1.75 and 1.87 grams of alcohol per liter of blood, nearly four times the legal blood alcohol limit of 0.5."

A second inalienable fact was Dodi's impatience. Dodi called his father just before leaving the Ritz. His father suggested with all the problems they had had that night, they should just lay low and stay at the Ritz. Dodi explained that was not possible—their luggage was back at his apartment, and they had an early flight in the morning. More crucial than that, though, the ring was at the apartment. Finally, Mohamed Al-Fayed agreed but told his son, "Now look, don't try any tricks when you leave the hotel." Dodi had already made up his mind, though, and that, combined with the impaired Henri Paul, the disaster was launched.

At midnight, they were ready to depart and return to Dodi's apartment. Then, the deadly sequence began. Not following his father's advice, Dodi wanted to avoid the cameras. The decision was made that one Mercedes Benz would leave the front of the Ritz with Dourneau and a man named Wingfield. Dodi and Diana would leave by a back entrance with driver Henri Paul and bodyguard Trevor Reece-Jones in another Mercedes. The ruse was intended to make the paparazzi believe that the first car was carrying the couple the mass of photographers and reporters was yearning for. Some of the stalkers took the bait, but not all.

Henri Paul's drunken state only inflamed the crowd further. As Anderson relates, "Paul, who made no attempt to conceal his glee at the impending game of cat-and-mouse," went so far as to tease the photographers outside.

Along with Henri Paul and Trevor Reece-Jones, Diana and Dodi passed through the revolving door at the back of the hotel and into another Mercedes. It was now 12:20 AM. Diana and Dodi were in the backseat, with their escorts taking the front. Not one of them began the ride with their seatbelt fastened.

So began the ride that would end Diana's life, just as it had ended Grace's life fifteen years earlier.

The Mercedes traveled down the Rue Camlon and turned right on 321 the Rue de Rivoli. Now on the main Paris thoroughfares, the paparazzi that hadn't been taken in by the diversion began pursuit. At least one motorcycle was hot on their tail. Making a right turn onto the Cours la Reine, the vehicles were now running parallel to the Sene River and picking up frightening speed. The first motorcycle was now joined by another, and one car. Through a first tunnel and back again to street level, the acceleration continued.

As the car sped towards the Place de l'Alma death tunnel, their speed reached dangerous levels. The paparazzi were close behind. One motorcycle was especially close. As Anderson relates in his book *The Day Diana Died*, "[Reports] put the motorcycle at thirty to forty meters behind the Mercedes."

Just outside the tunnel there is a dip in the road, which would effectively end any control Paul might have had left of the car. With its speed being estimated at perhaps 110 miles per hour, the Mercedes clipped the phantom white Fiat which has never been found. It was theorized that the impact of the Mercedes slamming back down on the roadway after the dip might have deployed the airbags. But whatever happened at this point, thus began the series of chain reactions that would end the lives of three people.

Now inside the tunnel and traveling at breakneck speed and with possibly impaired vision, Paul swerved left and clipped the white Fiat. The momentum caused the Mercedes to glance off the third pillar inside the tunnel. Paul slammed on the breaks and yanked the wheel in a last ditch effort to regain control.

It was too late, though. Within seconds the Mercedes smashed head-on into the thirteenth pillar, then spun around and rear-ended the opposite wall, where it came to rest.

On my personal observation, both traveling through and looking from one of the tunnel's on-ramps, it is clear the pillars are perfectly square. Their shape only added to the inevitable. With the pillars being square, the car's front-end hit at full impact, with the vehicle crashing head-on into the thirteenth pillar at eighty-five miles per hour. "The entire trip," Anderson wrote, "from the back of the Ritz to the moment of impact—had taken less than three minutes. It was 12:23."

Late-night strollers along the river heard the force of the crash loud and clear, and they all said the noise was terrifying. With such force, the impact crushed the front of the Mercedes like an accordion. Driver Henri Paul and Dodi Al-Fayed were killed instantly. Diana and Trevor Reece Jones were alive, but seriously injured.

Some of those walking along the river rushed to the tunnel's opening after hearing the dreaded sounds. An emergency physician named Dr. Frederic Mailliez was returning from a party. When he saw the commotion he pulled over. The experienced doctor quickly surmised that Dodi and Henri Paul were dead. But just before the crash, Trevor Reece-Jones had fastened his seatbelt. That decision saved his life, making him the lone survivor.

Quickly, Dr. Mailliez returned to his vehicle and called for help, then returned to the wreck with an oxygen mask he had in his trunk. So focused on his work, he didn't realize he was giving first aid and comfort to Diana Spencer, the former Princess of Wales. He wouldn't find out until the next morning whom he'd rendered aid to. Later he reported that she was semiconscious before the first ambulance arrived, which took about six minutes. As police sealed off the area, seven paparazzi were taken into custody as part of their suspected preliminary involvement in the accident.

It took almost an hour to extract Diana from the twisted metal and glass. When they finally got her out, they followed a different set of procedures than we have in the United States. Valuable time had already been lost extricating Diana from the vehicle, but instead of rushing her to the hospital as quickly as possible, they tried to stabilize her at the scene. Just like Grace in 1982, this would be the critical mistake the first medical team would make on Diana, which would forfeit any chance for her survival. The medical team worked on her for over an hour before taking her to the hospital; with the internal chest injuries and bleeding there would be no hope.

Finally, she was taken to *Pitie Salpetriere* Catholic Hospital. The ride was agonizingly slow, though. In the book *Death of a Princess*, the reason was explained in this way: "On doctors' instructions, however, the ambulance proceeded slowly in order to avoid bumps and accelerations that they feared might harm the patient in such a fragile state."

Diana and the medical team finally arrived at the hospital one hour and forty minutes after the accident, at 2:02 AM.

Without having worn her seatbelt, Diana had suffered major trauma to her torso. The force of the crash had damaged her pulmonary vein. Internal bleeding and lost time made her blood pressure almost nonexistent as her heart finally stopped beating. The medical staff, which included Doctors Bruno Riou, Jean-Pierre Benazet, Pierre Coriat, and cardiovascular surgeon Alain Pavie, tried valiantly for two hours to bring the heart that had given so much love to so many back to life. When conventional methods didn't work, the surgeons opened her chest and tried to massage it manually. All attempts, though, proved futile.

At 3 AM, Father Yves Clochard Boussuet, the resident priest at the hospital, was awakened and told that Diana needed the Last Rites. With Diana not being Catholic, Father Yves administered the nondenominational Extreme Unction ritual instead.

Finally, at 4 AM on Sunday August 31, 1997, Diana Spencer was declared dead. At 4:20, the British ambassador approached Father Yves, who told the ambassador that Diana had died, and to pray for her soul. The announcement of her death was released to the media at 6 AM Paris time.

After she was pronounced dead, arrangements that would focus the attention of the world for the next week were begun immediately.

Even though lives are lost by accident every day, it is still shocking when the curtain closes forever on those taken before their time. In the realm of life, different philosophies prevail when the ultimate end concludes. Some would say it was their time to go, while others will ask why. Whatever each perspective accepts, ultimately our mortality is measured in a way only the mysteries of God or providence control. Like most tragedies, the fate of the two princesses was not deserved, either by them or those that loved them.

Of the numerous circumstances that surrounded each accident, the one thing I personally believe is that is what they were: accidents. The rumors, allegations, and accusations that have been spun since their deaths don't have enough credible evidence to carry any real weight. The conspiracy theories—especially in Diana's case—are thin, considering the little circumstantial evidence available. In retrospect, the two women, revered and renowned the world over, proved through their own mortality that no matter what status or hierarchy one achieves, all of us are susceptible to the dangers that can snuff out life in one quick, shattering moment.

In the case of Grace Kelly and Diana Spencer, the what-if's were communicated to all because of who they were. In both accidents, had guardrails extended at the sharp corner of the steep road, or in the tunnel, the outcome could have been completely different. If seatbelts had been worn, they might have survived. This is neither here nor there, though; what happened, happened. None of us are getting out of here alive. This is something mankind will never abolish, no matter how advanced the human race becomes. In the cases of Grace Kelly and Diana Spencer, two lives that moved the world in so many ways, fate's power brought their worlds to an abrupt end.

Chapter XV- Grief, Sorrow and Comfort

The end of the lives of Grace Kelly and Diana Spencer signaled the finish of two figures who captured the very essence of renown. I truly believe that the appeal and enchantment they displayed won't be duplicated in quite the same way ever again. Some greater accomplishments, by both men and women, have been made in history. In the case of the two princesses, though, the spot-lit focus each of them received was in direct relation to the beauty, charm, class, compassion, and personality that surged from them: a concentric flow that surrounded everyone everywhere they appeared.

The sorrow and grief expressed by those who loved and admired them were fanfares of display that showed the popularity of these two women's processions-in-tribute that displayed what each of them meant to all the lives they touched.

The new millennium will bring its own heroes and icons. Time will steadily march on like an eternal Roman legion. Technology, modern science, and medicine will continue to advance. Through all these interactions, accomplishments, discoveries, and revelations, new individuals will rise and claim their place in the sun. For the two princesses, whose rays enveloped each hemisphere, the light and warmth will always remain, a shining beam that illuminated each and bonded their lives with so many similarities it marvels both comprehension and recognition.

Grace's death was the beginning of a dramatic change in the Grimaldis' lives that carries until the present day. After the machines were turned off and Her Serene Highness, The Princess of Monaco, took the last breaths of life, the dreadful tasks began. The first of these was Rainier having to break the news to Stephanie. From *The Royal House of Monaco* comes perhaps the most accurate account of her reaction: "On hearing the news the young Princess let out a terrible scream," John Glatt wrote. "She started crying uncontrollably and as her father held her hand tightly, he too broke down in tears."

When word finally reached the world's media, shock and grief was sounded on each continent. As a result of the rumors that had cascaded across the seas and oceans, confusion and bewilderment took hold of those close to Grace. Her close friends had no idea how seriously injured she was: they had thought the injuries were no more than a broken bone here or there. When they finally learned the reality, they were astonished and bewildered.

Judy Quine and Grace's other close friends in the States were heartbroken when they heard the harsh, accurate, final report. Especially Judith. Thinking Grace had only broken her leg, Judith had sent a jovial telegram, which read, "Up, Up, Up. Dance, Dance, Dance."

At 5:30 the day after Judith and her husband returned to New York, her daughter called Judith at work with the dreadful news. "'Mom', my Amy said, her voice cracking with tears she could not contain, 'Grace is dead.'" Judith, hysterical, ran down the hall, trying to get hold of a radio. Consoled by her husband, she said, "It's not fair. She didn't get to be a grandmother."

Like Grace's friend Judith, when word first reached the Kelly family at their summer home in Ocean City, New Jersey, they were led to believe Grace was going to be fine. When Grace's family returned to Henry Avenue, their shock was immense…and their anger. Grace's remaining family couldn't believe that Rainier had all life-support turned off without their consultation. They would learn later that Rainier had made the only sensible choice.

Very little could have consoled Grace's friends. Huddled together in grief at Judith's daughter's apartment along with Rita Gam and others, they got in touch with Grace's family in Philadelphia. Then Judith remembered the telegram she'd sent. The guilt she felt was actually the first therapy for all of them as Rita Gam began to giggle, explaining how Grace's good-natured sense of humor would have had her spirit in stitches looking down upon them. It was a small but soothing moment for what was to be a long period of mourning.

Ironically, before leaving for Monaco to join some of the other bridesmaids who'd made the journey to see their friend become a princess, Judith had an appointment at the Plaza Hotel and returned to the very spot where she had first met Grace. As she relates the experience, "She was over there," I whispered, pointing to the exact place where Jay had introduced us in the receiving line." On the journey to Monaco and the proceeding days, Judith Quine, Rita Gam,

Jay Canter, and the other friends from America who loved her so much kept repeating a phrase, "It doesn't seem real."

"A-teams" of morticians and make-up artists did their best to restore Grace's damaged exterior for viewing. Try as they might, they weren't able to cover the massive damage all areas of her head had sustained. Her hair, which had been shaved to try to save her life, was replaced by a wig that didn't nearly do her justice.

The wake was held in a small chapel inside the palace. An honor guard stood valiantly as the procession of mourners filed past the open casket: the normal practice for a Catholic death. Monaco had become completely silent. The subjects that had been so slow to accept her now wept openly for the beautiful woman who had given so much to them and the principality the last twenty-six years.

On Saturday morning, September 23rd, family, friends, and dignitaries said good-bye to Grace Kelly at her funeral mass. Trumpets sounded as a procession led by Rainier, Caroline, and Albert walked with heavy gaits and heads bowed for the wife and mother who had loved them all unconditionally. Directly behind them were Lizanne, Peggy, and Kel, whose grief was apparent for the sister they'd lost. Arm in arm they steadied each other through the streets of her kingdom, proceeding back to the cathedral where one of the world's most beautiful women ever had captured the attention of all humanity with her charm and elegance twenty-six years earlier. Stephanie's injuries prevented her from attending. From her hospital bed, she had to suffer and watch her mother's final farewell.

Over one hundred million people from around the world watched the live telecast as Grace was laid to rest. Royalty from the few remaining monarchies in Europe came to pay their respects. Among these dignitaries were First Lady Nancy Reagan and Princess Diana, who sat together. Fifteen years later, in 1997, Mrs. Reagan would exclaim, "When I heard the news reports about Diana and got over the initial shock and surprise, I immediately thought of Grace Kelly."

At the luncheon following the funeral, Judith was seated at a table in the palace garden near Diana. As Judith told me, "One of the Princess' ladies in waiting came over and asked if I could come to Diana's table." There, Diana told Judith of the time Grace had befriended and comforted her at Goldsmith Hall in London. The remembrance of the reaching-out Grace had given to Diana would now see fifteen years of dedication from the Princess of Wales—until she herself would meet the same fate.

On the Tuesday following the accident, Grace's body was entombed inside the Grimaldi family vault. So ended a life that had experienced both the highest peaks and lowest valleys of endurance. To the end, the inner peace from Grace's faith never wavered. She was a true disciple of Christ, never deviating from the principles set forth at the time Jesus appeared to his Apostles after the crucifixion: "Go, therefore, and make disciples of all nations, baptizing them in the of the Father, and of the Son, and of the Holy Spirit, teaching them all that I have commanded you. And behold, I am with you always, until the end of the age."

The work Grace Kelly accomplished personified the values set forth in the Catechism of the Catholic Church she was devoted to her whole life. Although she was a sinner as we all are, her reconciliations and Catholic doctrine saw Christ in each person she reached out to her entire life, those virtues instilled in her from the time the Holy Water of Baptism was poured over her infant head at Saint Briget's, to the disciplines and philosophies set forth by her family and the Sisters of the Assumption. Now her soul could complete her journey of faith and cross over to the everlasting love and peace Christ promises to all His children.

After the funeral, close friends and family joined Rainier, Caroline, and Albert in the garden of the palace. Sharing their grief and sorrow, Rainier strolled over to the terrace, where he once again became overcome with grief staring out at the tranquil harbor where his princess had sailed from across the ocean to become his bride. From now on, all his voyages would be without the one true thing he could always count on. The love they had given each other in the good times, as well as the neglect and taking-for-granted attitude that had prevailed at times, was also now over. He and the children would have to go on without the wife and mother who dedicated her entire being to their welfare. In the coming years, they would all find out just how important her leadership and devotion had been.

Back at Balmoral, where Charles, Queen Elizabeth, and the boys were staying, the initial news of Diana's accident was phoned in. Charles, awakened from a sound sleep, groggily pressed into action. The first thing he did was to call Camilla, who had become his stalwart pillar. After this, he called his mother's room to tell her. Diana still hadn't been declared dead, and the queen suggested that he not awaken the boys. Charles agreed to wait until morning, when more would be known about Diana's condition. Charles then spent the next two critical hours listening to the radio.

At 3:30 AM, Sir Robert Fellowes called Charles back with the tragic news. As Anderson relates in *The Day Diana Died*, "What the Prince of Wales did then even stunned Robert Fellowes. " Overcome with grief, Charles let out a wail that resonated throughout the castle.

Like so many of the other ironic circumstances that had intertwined the lives of Grace and Diana, a couple more were ready to play themselves out. Like Grace, the first reports of Diana's accident said she hadn't been hurt very badly. For most Americans, and myself, the preliminary reports, beginning at around news-time at 11 PM EST on Saturday, August 30, 1997, only reported Diana injured. However, with the six-hour time difference, she was already dead at the time those first reports came in.

I don't know why, but when I got up that Sunday morning I had forgotten what had happened. It was only when I entered the store that I buy my Sunday paper at that the headlines hit me: "Princess Diana Killed." It was then about 10 AM, and I quickly drove home to find that almost every channel was by then covering the tragedy.

When former President Clinton received the initial report from his vacation on Martha's Vineyard, it was that the princess's injuries were not life-threatening. In fact, he was quoted as saying, "But from the first reports it sounded as if it we were talking at the very worst about a broken bone or two."

When news of Diana's death reached her family and the royal family, arrangements and decisions were begun immediately. After sitting solemnly alone and going for a walk, Charles went to the boys' room at 7 AM to break the news. William had sensed something was wrong; he'd had trouble sleeping. After crying and consoling each other, Charles and William went to Harry's room to tell him the tragic news. As Anderson's account stated, "All three Windsor men wept unashamedly."

Paul Burrell had flown to Paris immediately upon hearing the news. He broke down immediately when he entered the hospital room and saw her body. After attending Sunday morning church, Charles, along with Diana's two sisters, boarded a Royal Air Force jet and flew to Paris to bring Diana's body home. Diana's body was already in its coffin and draped with the traditional maroon, gold and blue Royal Standard of the House of Windsor. Chief nurse Beatrice Humbert recalled how alone Diana's lifeless body looked.

All Diana's clothes had already been sent back to England, so the British ambassador's wife provided a dress, and Paul Burrell gave nurse Jeanne Lecorcher rosary beads which had been given to the princess by Mother Theresa, along with a picture of William, Harry, and Diana's father. These were gently placed in her hands to ready Diana for her final journey home.

Before Charles and Diana's sisters arrived, the crowd outside the hospital had grown angry and agitated when they saw the reporters arriving, and began to shout, curse, and even threaten the people of the media, who they felt were responsible for the princess's death. Thierry Meressa, the hospital's communication director, immediately went outside to calm the crowd. With stunning diplomacy, he sought out the ringleaders and convinced them to show complete respect when Charles and Diana's sisters arrived. From that moment on, the crowd's behavior was exemplary.

When Charles and Diana's sisters arrived, nurse Beatrice Humbert took them to see Diana. When she saw her sister's body, Jane Fellowes immediately broke down, sobbing. In their devastation, the three of them bowed their heads in prayer.

In preparation for Diana's body to leave the hospital, Charles insisted that Diana's coffin leave by the main entrance. Since the accident, the crowd, which had swelled even more behind the barricades, waited with fervent anticipation for the honor-guard to bring the coffin containing Diana out to the awaiting hearse.

Pitie Salretiere Hospital's exterior is old; the St. Louis Chapel on the grounds was built in 1776. On my Saturday afternoon visit to the hospital, I found myself smiling in irony. As people began to stroll in for late afternoon mass, I couldn't help but reflect on this chapel being built the same year America declared its independence from Britain. Now France, the same country that had helped America win its independence, would send home the woman who redefined centuries of England's royal image.

The well-manicured courtyard lined with gardens of salvias and marigolds set a dignified background as the four pallbearers carried Diana's casket out the front of the hospital, with Charles following behind. The crowd's silence became a muffled applause that slowly grew louder. Shouts of love, respect, and praise from various people echoed the adoration and sorrow felt as the People's Princess left for her final journey home.

Back at Balmoral, the queen was clearly showing her jealousy towards Diana. From the moment Elizabeth heard of the tragedy, she made every effort to stonewall the honor all Diana's family, the British people, and everyone around the world had begun to pay homage to their princess. Anderson relates, "While those around her made no effort to conceal their grief, the Queen betrayed an astonishing lack of emotion—even for the notoriously reserved monarch." True to this assessment, the queen insisted that all of them remain at Balmoral for a few more days, while Diana's body stayed in London. Here two innocent boys, who had just lost the most important person in their lives, were being kept away from her.

Whatever conclusions, regards, or reasons the queen had, they were wrong. Sadly, this was just the beginning of a few more decisions Her Majesty would make to show her subjects and the world how callous she could be. At times her shame knew no boundaries. With complete disrespect, she inquired if Diana was wearing any of her jewelry. God forbid if she lost any of the material toys she had at her beck and call. At church on Sunday morning August 31st, not one mention of Diana's name came up in the entire service, even with both her sons sitting there. This snub was apparently not enough; William and Harry were some of the only British subjects who didn't witness Diana's final return to her homeland. This was because the queen forbad any television sets at Balmoral from being turned on as events unfolded.

When Charles finally arrived back at Balmoral on Sunday evening, he was bewildered, confused, and daunted by his mother's attitude. First, he found out his mother wanted to keep all the normal, planned activities in place. This included a hunt. Upon learning this, Charles told his mother in no uncertain terms that the hunt would be canceled.

This was only the beginning, though. Her Majesty still had more cards in her deck. She would trump any and all plays that fed the jealous contempt she felt for Diana's popularity.

Charles and the boys took long walks each day around the grounds of Balmoral, to pass the time and talk while preparations were being made for Diana's funeral. William and Harry didn't understand the many goings-on, but in all their bewilderment, they acted bravely and maturely, including William's decision that he and Harry would follow their mother's coffin during the funeral procession.

Naturally, all flags in Great Britain were flying at half-mast...except for the one at Buckingham Palace. When the public began to question why, the queen gave the excuse that she was not in residence. Again, Charles was put in a very embarrassing position. William also questioned some of his grandmother's motives with regard to the flag issue. He also asked, "Why are we here when Mummy's in London?"

Prime Minister Tony Blair did some covering-up for the queen's conduct, commenting that the queen was acting in the boys' best interest. To even the most casual observer's interest, this appeared to be pure bunk. When Blair got Charles alone, he privately told him, in no uncertain terms, that if he didn't straighten his mother out, irreparable damage would be done to the monarchy. Once again Charles stood up to his mother, telling her flat-out that if she didn't make a public statement, he would take it upon himself to issue one with regard to the queen's malicious behavior. As Anderson observed, "For the first time, Charles delivered a flat ultimatum to his mother."

Finally, this got the queen's attention. The next day she went to London and issued a statement to the nation. In it, she told of all the sorrow and grief the Windsors were feeling. Although it was dubbed as a convincing statement, it was much too little, much too late.

Each night, Diana's body lay in state at the Chapel Royal at St. James Palace. True-blue Paul Burrell stayed with her each night, reading, telling jokes, and just talking to the most popular women of her time, who he had served faithfully.

On Saturday morning September 6, 1997, at 9 AM London time, the casket carrying Diana Spencer passed the gates of Kensington Palace for the final time. The place that the Princess of Wales had called home for so long was now blanketed in a sea of flowers, candles, and testimonials, forming a shrine the size the world had never witnessed before. The tributes extended down the entire road that borders Regents Park. Ten of thousands of bouquets lying between the tall cylinder-shaped hollies, an enormous kaleidoscope of color covering every inch of available pavement, were placed in remembrance of the People's Princess. As I looked back from the gate of Kensington Palace in August of 1999, I was awed by the mental image of what the expanse of floral tributes must have looked like.

In monetary terms, subjects had spent 45 million pounds. The estimated weight of the flowers, a floral expression in remembrance and grief, was ten thousand tons. Even during my visit a few cards and flowers were attached to the gate, as was done each day. Their sentimental messages transmitted the wishes of lives touched by Diana. Even in death, those who knew or admired her reached out to the soul and spirit of the lady whose heart had a limitless perimeter.

The horse-drawn carriage carrying Diana's earthly remains proceeded towards Westminster Abbey, whose bell tower resonated the world's loss. The polished, wooden-spoked wheels of the carriage rotated along the thoroughfare as the somber, steady gait of the disciplined procession focused on its task. Each passing block was filled with subjects weeping, calling out, and mourning their loss. Wails of endearment were shouted from the crowd every so often by the many so touched by her life.

Leading the procession were four officers from the Prince of Wales Company. On either side of the carriage, five palace guards kept in step with the horses. Following immediately behind were representatives from the vast number of charities Diana had dedicated herself to. At the rear of the carriage was a simple wreath of white roses, with a note from Prince Harry attached. Its envelope displayed one word, "Mummy."

As the procession passed Buckingham Palace, the queen bowed her head. From there the funeral carriage continued to St. James Palace. Joining it now were Princes William, Harry, Charles, and Phillip. Diana's brother Charles, who had converted to Catholicism, made the sign of the cross and joined the others. They walked abreast, heads bowed, the remaining way to Westminster Abbey.

At 10:50 AM London time, the coffin was carried into the abbey through the main entrance where Christ's throne in heaven is etched above. As wails of "Diana!" continued outside, the coffin entered the abbey past various statutes of kings and queens that mark each one's crypt. The eight dazzling chandeliers cast light down to illuminate the nave as the coffin was placed in front of the first row of pews. Leaders, dignitaries, family and friends from around the world waited for the service to begin. Among them was Reverend Tony Lloyd, who was one of the leaders of Diana's charities invited to the funeral.

The Reverend Wesley Carr opened the service by handing Prince Charles and the boys flowers, which they placed at the foot of the casket. Reverend Carr then began his oration by giving thanks to Diana for the life she led. He precisely conveyed that: "Although a princess, she was someone from whom, from afar, we dared to feel affection."

Both of Diana sisters gave brief readings, pledging their never-ending love and affection to the sister they had lost.

Next, Prime Minister Tony Blair read from one of St. Paul's most beautiful epistles in the Bible. *The Way of Love,* transcribed so beautifully by the Apostle chosen by Jesus, would journey to reach all the gentiles in the Jesus Movement or People of the Way:

> "Love is patient, love is kind. It is not jealous, love is not pompous, it is not inflated, it is not rude, it does not seek its own interests, it is not quick-tempered, it does not brood over injury, it does not rejoice over wrongdoings but rejoices with the truth. It bears all things, believes all things, hopes all things, endures all things."

Prime Minister Blair's words recalled images of the love Diana had given so endlessly, whether stooping down to show tenderness to a child, or sitting with a dying patient. The two most moving, touching, and candid parts of the service came from Elton John and Diana's brother, Earl Charles Spencer. Elton John beautifully and poetically rewrote the words to his song about Marilyn Monroe,

Candle In The Wind, as a tribute to his lost friend. As the verses reverberated throughout the abbey, handkerchiefs and tissues gently blotted tears the tears of those who remembered the love and affection Diana had given the world. The sons Diana had loved so much cried openly for woman who had given them life.

Now it was Diana's brother Charles turn to pay homage and say good-bye. With a fixated self-determination, the little brother Diana had comforted and protected during their childhood now stood stoically at the podium and, with bold leadership, expressed how tragic this death really was.

His oration was of a quality few could match. His voice was at times emotional; however, most of the text was clear, concise, and capturing. His words conveyed a mature dialogue that hit all its points dead center. While his brilliant tribute tenderly expressed all Diana's flaws and insecurities, it also highlighted how reaching out to all those in need gave her purpose and a reason to carry on.

He told of the sixth sense of intuition she applied so extraordinarily in every situation. One of the most exhilarating descriptions was the humility Diana possessed: "A truly British girl who transcended nationality, someone with a natural nobility who was classless, who proved in the last year that she needed no royal title to continue to generate her particular brand of magic."

This passage wasn't received well by the royal family, and would continue to cause friction between Charles Spencer and the Windsors. The earl also presented some much-needed chastising for the press and tabloids that had given the princess unyielding torment and abuse. To that end, he thoroughly castigated the media with a barrage of many deserved remarks, including, "It is a point to remember that of all the ironies about Diana, perhaps the greatest is this; that a girl given the name of the ancient goddess of hunting was, in the end, the most hunted person of the modern age."

Exactly!

In his final dissertation, Earl Spencer pledged his love and loyalty to the two sons that meant more to his sister than anything. He concluded by thanking Diana for everything she had brought to the world, her family, and him.

At the close of his eulogy, the crowds outside began an applause that soon reached a crescendo throughout the church.

After the service, the Welsh Guards placed Diana's coffin into a black hearse for its final journey back to Althorp. The crowds once again cheered, sobbed, threw flowers, and said good-bye. So many stems and petals fell upon the hearse that the windshield wipers labored just so the driver could see. Broken hearts cried out one final time for the young women who moved the world as no other women of her time, or anyone else's time, ever had.

Only immediate family boarded a train for Northamptonshire, where they would meet the hearse at Althorp and lay Diana's body to rest. Back to her childhood home came the woman whose life symbolized with distinction the renowned gifts she gave to those whose lives she touched. Now she rests in tranquility.

♛ ♛

Diana's brother Charles, who is now the earl of the estate where she is buried, has made the family home a tribute to honor Diana. This final resting-place, if any can, serves as a worthy accolade to her life. Set in the rolling hills and farmland northeast of London, Althorp lies near the town of North Hampshire. Today, visitors from every corner of the globe come in a steady stream each day during July and August to visit Diana's home and grave.

To find out more about her, and try to get a sense of her final resting-place, I visited Althorp in the summer of 1999.

The wrought-iron gates leading into the estate display the family crest, and are open each day for the precisely timed schedule of buses filled with visitors. Acres of gentle hills, silhouetted by oak and cedar of Lebanon trees, line the roadway leading up to the house, and sheep graze contentedly on the abundant grassland that abounds around them.

The estate is rich with heritage and history. The main house holds all the various artwork, china, furniture, and other artifacts of the Spencer family's history. The double-paned entrance doors lead into a large foyer displaying beautifully muraled walls. Various scenes on these murals capture Diana's ancestors engaged in hunting and other leisure activities. The hardwood oak floors, books, lamps, chandeliers, and sculptured ceilings offer a pleasant view at the entrance.

The expansive dining room, parlor, library, and billiard room are noticeably suited for entertainment. The stairway to the second floor is regal in design, with dark, rounded balusters supporting the immense banisters. The second-floor hall is lined with paintings; one of Diana and her brother Charles is surrounded by portraits of the various earls. The final room visitors are allowed to view is filled with fine china; arrays of cabinets hold the delicately crafted gifts from all over the world.

A small island in the middle of a pond holds the grave of the People's Princess. Visitors paying homage to her stroll the circular memorial each July and August. As my wife and I walked down the stone path on the right side of the estate leading down to the oval pond, a gentle rain and soft breeze rippled the water lilies and other aquatic plant life, as well as the green grass bordering the pond's shore. As is usual during each late summer, the lakeside garden temple at the far side of the pond gathers flowers, notes and inscriptions left by those who make the journey. The temple's inscription reads from the princess: "Whoever is in distress can call on me. I will come running, wherever they are."

Yet Diana was not the kind of person who required or even expected a fine memorial. Looking back on the day I visited her grave, I find a line I read in *American Heritage Magazine* most appropriate—the motto on Christopher Wren's tomb in St. Paul's Cathedral: "Si monumentum requiris circumspice (If you seek a monument, look around you)."

However, the memorial at Althorp seems fitting; From beyond the path, sheep graze the peaceful meadows and pastoral surroundings. In the soft and quiet harmony, this brings serenity to her rest.

"Beautiful Princess, open your door,
That I may come in and go out no more."
The Frog Prince

Of all the decisions and choices, both positive and negative, made by Rainier and Charles, the most valuable credit that can be given to them in all their decisions were the ones they made to make Grace and Diana their princesses. In spite of the sad chapters, each of their kingdoms, and then the world, came to love and adore them, and each kingdom came away far better off for having them as their princesses. Although neither Grace nor Diana was born with royal blood, they were as real and authentic as any other princesses throughout the ages. They each opened their hearts to the world, and those who entered were given memories that occupied the sanctuaries of their minds with serene reflections. Had their princes gone the normal route of arranged marriages like other royals, the world as we know it could never had witnessed the sheer and unsurpassed bounty Grace and Diana brought to all they touched.

Though their journeys had many slippery slopes, these two women's focus always remained steadfast in service and commitment. The reiterating aspects of their characters that influence so many can only be measured by the distinction that set them apart from all others.

Now, as the new millennium is still in its infancy, we remember the effect these two princesses had on our world during the last fifty years of the previous millennium. Monaco and England's "roses" will always bloom in the memories of love they left us with.

Even though I have portrayed them in different contexts of their relationship with Christ, they both were disciples through their acts and dedication, as well as seekers of His love, mercy, and salvation. Their immediate families who bear the loss can take comfort in the individual Christian principles that their spirits are with them, and someday they all will be together again in the ultimate Kingdom of God.

As Princess Grace's soul made its journey to heaven, Christ's arms were surely outstretched, embracing her with love and welcome. When Diana joined her, I truly feel that the spirit of her mentor was with the Son of Man, along with a choir of angels singing the hymn which has become synonymous for the dearly departed who have the hope of rising again: "Do not be afraid, I am with you. I have called you each by name. Come and follow Me, I will bring you home; I love you and you are mine."

In the realms and eons of eternity, our lives are measured by the flick of a match or the snap of a finger. Although taken before their time, both Princess Grace and Princess Diana made their marks in the pages of history. Now in their final rest, they find the eternal peace, harmony, and tranquility they deserve.

Chapter XVI - Only the Lonely

The shattered remains and broken pieces of life left behind when death occurs, either expected or not, leaves a void that time heals somewhat, but never replenishes. Those remaining must deal with their grief and sorrow in the vacant emptiness. A gap that narrows over time, but never closes completely.

When the finality of each mortal's life becomes reality, the loss of loved ones tests our resilience, character, and faith. In the cases of Grace Kelly and Diana Spencer, the ones truly close to them dealt with the loss in varying ways and degrees. Some have handled it well, and some have not. However, all of their injured hearts carry the scars. Some of the scars heal as time passes, but the emotional pain is too great to ever completely abate.

Grace's death was only the beginning of suffering, heartache, and aggravation for the family she left behind. Rainier, Caroline, Albert, and Stephanie have all experienced further catastrophes in the years since Grace's tragic death. Some of them were bad luck, or the further devastations of fate that caused more suffering, while others who have written about them conjecture some sort of "Grimaldi curse." Some of their problems, though, were due to their own bad choices and behaviors.

After a vacation to bond and begin to deal with their grief, Grace's family began the process of life without her. Rainier delegated Grace's duties between Caroline and Albert. Caroline became Monaco's first lady, taking over many of her mother's artistic and social responsibilities. This choice was excellent, since Caroline had a true love for the arts just as her mother had, and was well qualified for the position. Albert took over some of his mother's charities, the Red Cross being among them. The closeness of family, combined with the Catholic faith Grace had instilled in her husband and children, was the greatest gift she left behind: Rainier and the children have been able to lean on each other for the past twenty years because of Grace's love, efforts, and work.

Caroline

Of the four members of Princess Grace's nuclear family, Caroline has suffered the most. Grace's death had a definite maturing effect on her oldest child; although she still had some growing-up to do, her partying and carousing ebbed. The most significant thing Princess Caroline did when she became First Lady of Monaco was to look after her father. From her mother's death until now, Caroline has been extremely close and nurturing to her father. Their closeness has seen each of them through some very trying times.

All three of Grace's children have had several romantic relationships since her death. Caroline was no exception. In the past two decades, Caroline has had to deal with grief far beyond the expectations of most people. Some periods of the past twenty years must surely have seemed like a hell on earth for her.

After her divorce from Philippe Junot, Caroline began seeing Robertino Rossellini, who is the son of superstar actress Ingrid Bergman, the dramatic star whose closing scenes in *Casablanca* and *The Bells of Saint Mary* are among the greatest ever. As author John Glatt explains, "The pair, who had been together since Caroline divorced Philippe Junot in October 1980 had been brought closer together by tragedy; Rossellini's mother Ingrid Bergman had died of cancer in August 1982, just fifteen days before Princess Grace's accident." Caroline accompanied Rossellini to Fjallbacka, Sweden, where he scattered the ashes of his beloved mother in her native country.

This relationship became a therapeutic and healing one for the two young adults who had both lost the women that gave them birth. Their relationship became somewhat serious, even to the point of talking about marriage. This was not to be, though, as Caroline caught the eye of Stefano Casirghi, the heir to an oil and construction empire. The handsome playboy and Caroline quickly fell in love.

Caroline's relationship with Casirghi was going to be the first of many problems Rainier would have to deal with after Grace's death. Caroline became pregnant, which caused multiple problems. First, she was divorced. Before her death, Grace had gained an audience with Pope John Paul II to try and get Caroline's marriage to Philippe Junot annulled. The pope hadn't yet rendered his decision when Grace was killed, and this just complicated matters all the more, since Junot had threatened to blow the cover off the entire matter if Caroline was granted the annulment. With this situation, Caroline had really backed her father into a corner.

Finally in December of 1983, with no public display or fanfare, Caroline and Casraghi were married. Without the annulment they had to settle for a civil ceremony, instead of the blessings of the Catholic Church. Some of the public and press questioned all the secrecy. In the end, though, it turned out to be one of the happiest periods in Princess Caroline's life; her relationship with her second husband had love and romance. Although there was some evidence that Casraghi strayed in commitment, Caroline seemed to gain respect from him in their relationship. The oldest daughter of Grace Kelly had inherited her mother's shrewdness.

Other dilemmas still plagued Caroline. She had a child on the way, a child that needed to be baptized into the Catholic faith. She used her name and influence to gain an audience with the Pope. John Paul II was not impressed, however. The pontiff chastised Caroline, reportedly asking her, "Did you ever make a sacrifice to save your marriage?" He refused to grant her an annulment.

Princess Caroline did, however, bring joy and rejuvenation back into her depressed father's existence when on June 8, 1984, her son, named Andrea Albert Grimaldi, was born at the Princess Grace Clinic in Monaco. It was a truly happy moment for Rainier. His first grandchild lit up the gray exterior that had only known darkness in the twenty-one months since his wife's death.

In August 1986, Caroline gave birth to a second child. She and her husband named the girl Charlotte. Again, Rainier was very pleased to be blessed with a second grandchild. One year later a third child named Pierre was born. The three children's births marked a period of relative comfort and stabilization for Caroline's immediate family, a normalcy which was enjoyed...until disaster struck again.

Caroline's husband Stefano was a thrill seeker. Fast cars and boats were second nature to him. Even so, he narrowly escaped some close calls with his daredevil ways. Marriage and family didn't deter him from this passion. In the end, he would pay for it with his life.

After winning as the World Champion of Speedboat Racing in Atlantic City in 1989, he went back to Monaco to defend his title. Stefano promised Caroline he would retire after this last race.

Whether he intended to follow through or not will never be known; this last race would prove to be one race too many. While racing at a speed of about 100 MPH, Stefano and pilot Patrice Innocenti's boat became airborne. The craft flipped over, with Stefano taking the brunt of the impact. He was killed instantly; Innocenti survived.

Rainier was the first to be informed of the tragedy. Knowing what the loss would mean to Caroline and the children, he wailed in grief.

Caroline was in Paris having her hair done at the time of the accident. When she learned of her husband's fate, she immediately returned to Monaco to see him lying in state already. Eight years had passed since her mother had been taken from her. Now, once again, the entire Grimaldi family was suffering. In contrast to the way he had lived his life, Stefano's funeral was profound in its somberness.

The weeks and months following Stefano's death were extremely hard on Caroline: day after day depressions came, numbing and paralyzing her emotionally as if her very being was mortally distraught. This, the second death of a loved one, shattered her heart. Dressed in black for her few public appearances, many people thought she would never overcome the hurt that seemed to envelope her.

Yet Caroline was one of the lucky ones: a great deal of prayer, the needs of her children, and the help of her family led her back up the long dark alley she described so vividly, saying, "Strength comes when you are in a very narrow alley and have no way of turning back, I think. It's circumstances." Finally, by the spring of 1991, the wounds that had remained opened for so long began to heal. Her husband's death, though, brought a noticeable change; now two scars would remain on her heart, and two deaths would leave her emotionally disabled for some time.

In some respects, Caroline became much like Danielle Steel's character Paxton Andrews in *Letters From Nam*. Crushed and subdued by the loss of a parent and lover, Paxton Andrews escaped from the world that had brought her terminal grief. Princess Caroline had endured enough of the world she knew, also—it was time to leave Monaco.

A new man in Caroline's life was the impetus of her decision to leave Monaco. She had seeing a French actor named Vincent Lindon, and he lent Caroline the therapeutic ear she so drastically needed.

While traveling together with Lindon, Caroline found a farmhouse in St. Remy de Provence. The house, with its peaceful, quiet setting for her and her three children, became the refuge she needed to bring peace back to her decimated world.

As their relationship progressed, Caroline and Lindon knew they had to keep their new love as discreet as possible. With the paparazzi piranhas always circling in schools, no amount of effort was sufficient, and the secret didn't last long. Eventually Caroline was forced to set up security around her new domain.

Even so, the people of the town she called home for some time always respected her privacy, and this welcome gift was the greatest gift her neighbors gave to her. The next few years for Caroline were as placid and peaceful as could be expected for someone of her stature. She maintained a warm circle of friends who shared her lifestyles, interests, and concerns.

This wasn't the end of her troubles by any means. Back in Caroline's wilder days, when she'd first fallen for Junot, Grace tried to set her up with Prince Ernst, who was Queen Elizabeth's godson. The young Caroline rejected the idea completely of any arranged marriage. In her eyes, the also-young prince was another flamboyant royal whose money was always spent fast and lavishly. Prince Ernst eventually married Chantal Hochuli. But as things turned out, Caroline and Lindon became friends with them in their royal circle.

By 1996, Lindon was becoming tired of the royal social circle he wasn't comfortable in and never got used to. During a dinner to celebrate Monaco's ballet, Caroline and Lindon had a rift right in front of everyone, which ended their relationship. With the end of their five-year relationship, Caroline turned to Ernst. The result was love...adulterous love.

The reports said that Caroline was enjoying one of her happier times. Naturally, the rumors of Caroline and Ernst's new relationship sent the paparazzi in motion. Walking around Caroline's home in St. Remy, one photographer got his shot. As reported in *People* magazine, "When they kissed, a vigilant cameraman caught the moment."

To make matters worse, the stress and strain of the Grimaldis' whirlwind circle of K-O's gave her a case of Alopecia, a condition characterized by varying degrees of hair loss. The increased pressure of painting her as "the other woman" in the royal circle made so much of her hair fall out that she ended up shaving the remainder off. Naturally, the press immediately began rumors and accusations that Caroline had cancer and was undergoing chemotherapy. In a bold statement of courage, Caroline came out in public displaying her new look.

Prince Ernst and Chantal Hochuli divorced after sixteen years of marriage, and Princess Caroline and Prince Ernst pledged their love for each other. Ironically, Prince Ernst, being related to Queen Elizabeth, had to ask her permission to marry Caroline. Queen Elizabeth said yes, and in a small and very private civil ceremony in Monaco's palace on January 23, 1999, Princess Caroline and Prince Ernst were wed. Someone close to them was quoted as saying, "Ernst is over the moon. I have never seen him so happy." A daughter named Alexandra, born on July 20, 1999, joined Caroline and Ernst's other children.

Still fleeing from the paparazzi at times, Caroline and Ernst are now man and wife. The Austrian Prince Ernst, like his father-in-law Prince Rainier, has lost his temper with the media a couple of times. All in all, though, they have settled down into another royal family life.

Stephanie

Stephanie, still quite the rebellious teenager, wasn't able to handle the trauma of her mother's death at all. Grace's death found various media and gossip echoing the same refrain of blaming Stephanie. But this time, Grace wasn't around to calm the water when the paparazzi and press went on its rampages.

Stephanie made even more mistakes than Caroline in her public and personal life. She was lost within herself, in a catch-22 where she had to deal with the guilt and grief from her mother's death, along with the reality of not having her mother to turn to for comfort. Mired in trauma, guilt, and immaturity, she was a scandal waiting to happen. The French paparazzi took dead aim at Stephanie, who provided them with an arsenal of ammunition.

The eighties' image of sex, drugs, and rock-and-roll fit Stephanie as provocatively as the skintight leather bad-girl outfits that became one of her trademarks. Paris nightclubs strewn with loud music, lewd behavior, and cocaine-infested restrooms marked the spoiled-rich-kids-pack the princess interacted with—a swarm of spoiled deviants whose only mission seemed to be reaching the zenith of irresponsibility.

The publicity had made her an item, though, and the olive-skinned Mediterranean beauty and name did open some doors for her. Modeling became the first of a number of short careers for Stephanie. Along with some acting and singing, the entertainment world provided Grace Kelly's youngest child with short-term fame. Seeking the limelight her mother had known, Stephanie moved to Los Angeles to pursue her dreams. The princess-turned-California-girl gave Hollywood a try, and took acting and singing lessons while trying to follow in her mother's footsteps.

Romantically, Stephanie had a number of relationships after her mother's tragic death. These ranged from liaisons with actors like Rob Lowe to a number of rich playboys, as well as some men who were less-than-desirable in the eyes of her family. A member of the group Stephanie partied with in the late eighties was Dodi Al Fayed. This was years, though, before Dodi and Diana would meet their fate. For the most part, the relationships Princess Stephanie got involved in caused pain and heartache for her, as well as a pain-in-the-derrière for her father.

During her time in California, Stephanie had two serious romances. The first was with Mario Oliver. Oliver was of questionable character. He had a criminal record, which came as a result of a rape that was plea-bargained to sexual assault. Stephanie and Oliver lived together in California, and their relationship caused a great deal of worry and friction between Stephanie and her father. Rainier even asked Judith Quine to keep an eye on Stephanie, because she lived close by in Beverly Hills. The relationship Stephanie and Oliver had did last for a while. Fortunately, though, they eventually went their separate ways. There was no real damage or scandal during their time together, just a great deal of worry for Rainier.

Sony record producer Ron Bloom was the second romance Princess Stephanie had during her time in California. Bloom produced Stephanie's first and last American album. Bloom was older (37) and more mature than Stephanie's other men. He respected her, and in some ways was a positive mentor for the Princess. With Bloom,

Stephanie toned down and put more effort in to the goals she wanted to attain. At the beginning, Rainier approved of the relationship. Stephanie and her father even made up for all the fights they had had. One report stated, "One morning Rainier turned up at the Toluca Canyon house unannounced and armed with gifts, to be warmly greeted by a tearful Stephanie and her new boyfriend."

Stephanie and Bloom traveled to Monaco in June 1989 for Rainier's fortieth anniversary as prince. Once again, the paparazzi were to ruin the celebration when the London *Sunday Mirror* printed some uninhibited pictures of the couple in their backyard. Rainier was beside himself, and this also started a steady descent in Stephanie and Bloom's relationship.

With only limited success in the entertainment industry, Stephanie's short career came to an end. When it was over, like so many young people do when they feel they've failed, Stephanie headed back home. Back in Europe, she recorded another record, no more successful than her first. But it was during this period that Stephanie's heart began fluttering for a new man: her bodyguard, Daniel Ducruet.

Coming from a modest background, Ducruet had married at age nineteen, and was taken on in 1986 as a trainee officer in the Monaco police force. The muscular young man kept his nose clean; Rainier took a liking to him. So impressed was the prince that he promoted him to palace guard, where he was assigned to protect Albert. Albert, however, felt uncomfortable with Ducruet, and this was where Rainier made a very bad mistake—he assigned Ducruet to guard the flighty princess on her record-promotion tour. The rest was as rhetorical as it was predictable.

Ducruet, recently divorced, already had a new girlfriend who was already five months pregnant. It seems that virility and a lack of knowledge of birth control were two of his main attributes: in a short time Stephanie became pregnant. Like so many other situations, Rainier was humiliated once again. The thought of another grandchild born out of wedlock stared the elderly monarch square in the face.

Shortly after National Day in November of 1992, Stephanie gave birth to a son at the Princess Grace Hospital. He was named Louis after Rainier's grandfather. Rainier, Caroline, and Albert all shunned the birth, and chose to leave Monaco for various destinations. As John

Glatt revealed in his study of Monaco's royal family, "Princess Stephanie's current estrangement from her family now became obvious to all when neither Prince Rainier, Albert nor Caroline visited the hospital to see the newest addition to the family."

For the better part of four years, Ducruet and Stephanie lived a fairly simple existence even though—as with Caroline's husband Stefano—Ducruet's main hobby was race car driving. They had another child, a girl named Pauline. Finally, in a simple ceremony kept as quiet and simple as possible by Rainier, Ducruet and Stephanie were married in her mother's beloved St. Devote's Chapel in 1995. In a genuine gesture of love, Stephanie placed a bouquet of flowers at her mother's tomb before the civil service.

Everything rolled along well for a while...at least until Ducruet's eyes began to wander. An old enemy of Ducruet's named Stehane de Lisiecki set a trap for him in the person of a seductive young woman. Her name was Fili Houteman. With a video camera and paparazzi waiting, Houteman snared Ducruet into making love to her at her rented poolside villa. Ducruet had swallowed the bait whole, and put on a superior adulterous performance for the camera.

Two weeks later, the young man who had the world to himself got a rude awakening: An Italian tabloid printed the first set of pictures. Literally caught with his pants down, Ducruet tried to talk his way out of it to no avail. In total humiliation, Stephanie retreated to Roc Agel. Rainier, never liking Ducruet from the beginning of his romance with Stephanie, persuaded his daughter into agree to a divorce. Stephanie still loved Ducruet very much; for once, however, she bowed to her father's advice.

Voted one of the ten most beautiful women in the world by Harper's Bazaar in 1991, as well as making Mr. Blackwell's infamous "ten worst-dressed list" too, Princess Stephanie has definitely gotten around the past two decades. She has since had a third child. Camille Marie Kelly was born July 15, 1998. As of date, Stephanie hasn't revealed who the father is.

Since her mother's death, Princess Stephanie has experienced diverse emotions: periods of happiness, along with cloudy periods that fogged and polluted a potentially content retrospect. It appeared that true happiness was not to be when the one person whose guidance, love, and leadership would have certainly supported her through her trials was taken away.

Albert

The death of his mother didn't affect Albert as it did his two sisters. Not that he wasn't devastated in his loss, but the double standard of the male gender being evaluated, judged, and looked at differently has been notably evident in Albert's case the past twenty years.

The man to who belongs the throne of Monaco took a much different direction than his sisters. Some of the rich playboys Caroline and Stephanie took up with had similar social status and wealth as Albert, yet Albert was more focused—not so much in his destiny or call to duty, rather in getting involved in sports and athletics. Like so many other males, sports became an outlet and passion for the prince. Blessed with good athletic skills, he was free to participate in activities without having to worry about financial costs, and was able to enjoy sports purely for the love of the camaraderie and competition they brought...completely different from the life of a minor league baseball player or Nike golf tour professional whose pocket money comes out in drips. With Albert, his grandeur was an asset that made these interests easily assessable.

Prince Albert became an ambassador for Monaco's sport and athletic programs. He was the youngest active Olympian ever elected to the International Olympic Committee in 1985. Other athletic associations under his leadership include his presidency of Monaco's Yacht Club as well as Monaco's swimming and track federation. The tiny principality became well endowed in athletics by its "jock prince."

The Winter Olympics struck a chord in Albert in 1980. Fascinated by the bobsled races in Lake Placid, Albert founded Monaco's bobsled team after giving it a try at St. Moritz in 1984. Totally enthralled with the sport, he set to the task of having a team ready for Calgary in 1988. There he lived the complete Olympic athletic experience, from marching in the opening ceremonies to living in the Olympic Village. Albert inherited a good deal of the Kelly drive and fierceness in competition. Duties and schedule didn't allow him the devotion he wanted, which showed four years later in Albertville. The

229

experience gave him a perspective of the enormous dedication and focus that must be applied at the top level of competition.

As far as dalliances and romance are concerned, Albert, like all young virile men, has had his fair share. Encouraged to enjoy the opposite sex by both his parents before his mother's death, the gregarious Albert socialized all his abundance of energy regularly. He had his fair share of wild parties and escapades throughout the better part of two decades since his mother's death, and a number of blonde-haired, blue-eyed models and actresses have been with the prince at various times and in various degrees of relationships. Some of these include Donna Mills, Catherine Oxenberg, and Claudia Schiffer. None of these beautiful women, or any of the many others, has gotten Albert within striking distance of an altar though. This prince is intelligent enough to know the strain and pressure any woman would be under who would become his wife. Beside the fact that, like all men of power, fame, and fortune, the pleasure and fun are a hard act to give up.

The only dark cloud on Albert's horizon was the inevitable: With the dozens of women he has had relations with, one of his sperm cells was bound to make a zygote. This happened after a two-week romance with a young California woman named Tamara Rotolo. Albert kept the pregnancy from his father until the baby was born in March of 1992. When Rainier found out, he ordered Albert to go into total denial about the situation.

This was an extremely serious situation as far as the Monaco line of succession was concerned, since Albert's child would take precedence over Caroline or Stephanie's children. With proof of paternity being sought by Ms. Rotolo, Rainier feared the line to the throne would be relegated to an illegitimate child, as had happened with Rainier's mother, or as John Glatt pointed out, "when the illegitimate birth of Prince Rainier's mother irrevocably diverted the path of the Grimaldi dynasty."

Even though a judge threw out the paternity suit, this situation wasn't going to go away. Ms. Rotolo embarrassed Albert at a Wild West show by boldly confronting him with their daughter. To this day, the situation remains in a holding pattern, with Albert neither denying nor confessing to the transgression. According to writer John Glatt, "Now a very independent six-year-old, Jazmin Grace bears a striking resemblance to Grace Kelly with the same fair hair and perfect features. Her mother prays that in time that Albert will stand up to his father and get to know his daughter, who has inherited her grandmother's love of the theater, ballet, and music."

Overall Albert seems like a fine man whose life lies before him with promise. In an interview with Larry King in 1999, he was composed, articulate, and intelligent, demonstrating a significant self-confidence, and who seemed thankful for all the blessings he has received in life. From the questions Mr. King asked him, one concludes that he is ready to take over his father's duties whenever the future presents the inevitable, whether that be within the next year or ten years from now. Albert knows his principality inside and out. Yet he continues to be interested and involved in athletics; now in his forties, he again competed in the 2002 Winter Olympics.

As far as marriage is concerned, he stills seems a bit gun-shy. Although certainly when it is his time to become Monaco's ruler, things will fall into place.

Rainier

The handsome and dashing young man who brought the stunning beautiful star of stage and screen to his kingdom, has worn the years since Grace's death heavily. Grace's departure knocked the wind out of the principality. Since then and until now, both Monaco and Rainier's breathing are still labored.

Problems with the paparazzi and media have plagued Rainier since losing Grace. In the winter of 1983, Rainier had some run-ins with photographers while conducting some business in New York. Rainier hit one photographer and cursed another. One report said, "Rainier punched him to the ground." This didn't help Monaco's tourism industry, as the media immediately flashed these incidents all over the newspapers. That predicament, and many others involving the children, has haunted Rainier. Without the help of his life partner, life has been difficult for him.

Rainier was a textbook case of grieving widower. Two years after Grace's death in 1984, Rainier looked well beyond his years at a state dinner put on by then-President Ronald and First Lady Nancy Reagan. The Princess Grace Foundation, which was being promoted on that visit to the United States, was a sanctuary for the still grief-stricken prince.

Even so, life has not been total isolation for the aging prince. He has even come close to remarrying a couple of times. One thing or another, though, seemed to get in the way. In 1987, Rainier let it be known that, with age sixty-five setting in, he would never remarry.

Yet through the sorrow and anguish of Grace's death, along with his children's problems, Prince Rainier has endured, and his survival has been laden with various misfortunes as well as many good times also. His enjoyment of his grandchildren, the day-to-day running of Monaco, leisure time activities, and hobbies keep him going.

During the past ten years, Rainier has experienced some health problems. In 1994, his doctors discovered a blockage in one of his cardiac arteries, and a double bypass was successful. Other health-related concerns have been off again, on again for Rainier during the last ten years.

In his forty-fifth year as Prince of Monaco, Rainier oversaw the Monte Carlo Circus Festival. The wonderful acrobatics, animals, and clowns breathed new life into the aging monarch, returning him to his boyhood and rejuvenating a great many fond memories. The experience reportedly gave energy and renewed zest to a man who had faced so much heartache throughout his life.

Prince Rainier has lived a long life filled with the material wealth so many people search for their entire lives, as well as tragedies that no amount of money or power can prevent. He has dedicated his life to the responsibilities, obligations, and commitments of Monaco. His keen business-sense has reaped many positive benefits for the principality, and his absolute power weighs a heavy responsibility for Rainier in keeping Monaco's reputation and finances sound. He has met the problems of money laundering as well as losses from the Saving Bank of Monaco head on. No one can question his love or total involvement in his kingdom.

Even in his waning years, he still keeps his finger on the button and is still quite capable of running Monaco. The safety and security of the principality, which has more police-per-capita than anywhere else in the world, keeps its reputation protected. Rainier has a true love and loyalty for his kingdom and family, evidenced by this quote from him: "Our great strength is the union between our family and our people."

His personal life over the years went the way of so many throughout history. Grace was the steel rods in the concrete, binding together the family and social foundation that made Monaco the focal point of the Mediterranean. Since her death, Rainier has wandered and strayed off the steady path the girl from Germantown, Philadelphia was able to keep him on.

Others

In the twenty years since Princess Grace's death, the only one of her siblings still living is her sister Lizanne. Kel died from a heart attack while jogging in 1985. Her sister Peggy died in November of 1991. Her mother, the indomitable Ma Kelly, suffered a stroke in 1975, but lived until 1990.

Although it has been a long time, memories of the times shared by those who loved her are still fresh. Judith Balaban Quine expressed her grief after Grace's death by continuing to write letters to the friend who was like a sister to her, comforting prose to soothe the hurt she felt. Judith began writing Grace on Mother's Day 1984, and continues to do so. Her touching letters can be read in her book, *The Bridesmaids.* In November of 1985, Judith held a reunion in Beverly Hills for all the women she could summon. Included at this affair were most of Grace's bridesmaids: Caroline, Lizanne and various grown children of the ladies. There is a lovely picture of them all in *The Bridesmaids.*

The various people of Grace's generation, along with the succeeding ones, have gone on with their lives. Many of her Hollywood friends including Cary Grant, Frank Sinatra, Bing Crosby, Sammy Davis Jr., and others have passed on. The list of the living is becoming a short one with Marlon Brando and Oleg Cassini still living.

Grace's family and friends—from the most powerful country on earth as well as the small principality that became her domain—still love her, and her memory will surely stay with them until their journey through life ends.

The three left behind by the most famous woman of the twentieth century (and arguably the second millennium) have so far fared much better than Grace's family. Although it has only been five years, Princes Charles, William, and Harry have drawn very close. Their maturity and love for each other has formed a cohesion that seems to steadily progress them all towards their destiny.

There are three critical elements in this alloy. First and most important is the influence of Diana herself. The most significant comparison between the two princesses will always remain the love they furnished. The boys cannot help exhibiting the caring "Mummy" gave them through the heredity and role-modeling they received from her. With so much "water under the bridge," Charles realizes and accepts with gratitude all the influences Diana had on their two sons, and seems to continue to maintain her philosophy for as normal a life as possible for the two boys, along with the respect and caring for those in need.

Second in the family's success is the strong British tie to duty and dedication, which has always been Charles's strongest attribute. His unyielding pledge of loyalty to the United Kingdom is an excellent prototype for the boys to follow.

The third factor is the control and calming of the press, media, and paparazzi. Although the media is decidedly still in business, the frenzy that prevailed while Diana was alive has definitely geared down and changed dimensions. In one report it was said that, "Britain's newspaper editors reached an agreement with St. James Palace." Both the media and royal family have kept to their parts of the agreement, meaning photo opportunities by the royals, as well as the media backing off and allowing the royal family their privacy.

In the checkout lines of America's supermarkets, the covers of various tabloids still try to sell their fabrications of goings-on of England's royal family, especially William. Some still try to conjure up rumors and accusations behind Diana's death. But these rumors simply don't have the appeal or allure anymore. Those two important attributes went to their grave with Diana. This, too, brought a welcome calming effect for Charles, William, and Harry.

William

The handsome young man who is second in line to the throne behind his father is growing in stature and his sense of duty. Characteristics from both father and mother have blended beautifully in every aspect of his personality. Prince William, according to one report and validated by others, "Is increasingly being viewed as his mother's standard bearer." A serious, stoic attitude prevails in his education, as well as his father's involvement. These steer him towards his providence.

The boy who experienced the brunt of his parents' unhappiness seems to have adjusted well in the face of all the adversity. The rough periods of witnessing his mother's pain were soothed a great deal after the divorce, bringing an amicable period for both William and Harry in the time between Charles and Diana's divorce, until Diana's death. This was the most precious gift both Charles and Diana gave their sons; the boys now have a memory of peace and friendship between their parents instead of anger, a combination of fun and carefree times with "Mummy" and the traditional social English pastimes with their father.

Diana's features are transformed into William with true radiance. From brow to chin, William's entire facial structure mirrors his mother's piercing blue eyes with soft cheekbones contouring the smooth skin. The glowing smile his mother blessed the world with completes William's handsomeness. For some time already, he has been turning many female head in England, America, and elsewhere.

In a similar way to his mother, the prince is a prized possession in his own right. His gender, making his succession to the throne assured, matches the allure that Princesses Caroline and Stephanie had at that age. He is a commodity that will make some of the media and paparazzi a great deal of money as time goes on—estimates range from two hundred to three hundred thousand dollars for a first picture of William with his first serious love. (Whether this is done fairly or underhandedly remains to be seen.)

The road before Prince William is a much smoother one than his mother endured. The bickering and conflicts between his mother, the queen, and Prince Phillip are completely transposed with William. Of course, they are his grandparents. More than that, though, William has always been close to his grandfather, especially in the traditional

English cultural activities such as hunting. He and his grandmother share closeness as well—during his days at Eton, he regularly had tea most Sunday afternoons with the queen, who was at nearby Windsor Castle on the weekends. These bonding times were good and positive situations for the young prince, as well as for Queen Elizabeth and Prince Phillip. Too, William has been raised in royalty, not thrown into it like his mother was. That has made a great deal of difference.

An excellent student, the self-confident but sometimes-shy prince enjoys both the academic and athletic programs at school. Like his mother, competitive swimming became one of his accomplishments. He set new school records in the fifty and hundred meter freestyle at Eton. Eton was a completely capable institution for William, with Harry now reaping its benefits as well.

The third week of June 1998 was a very busy time for the press and media in both Great Britain and the United States—it was that week that William's eighteenth birthday was celebrated. His coming-of-age was looked upon and analyzed with both regard and intrigue. As he advances out of his teens, the heir to the throne is moving forward in all areas that will someday become his calling. In assessment of his leap into adulthood, one magazine noted, "Levelheaded and normal are the words most commonly used to describe William."

Before entering St. Andrew's University, which he chose for his higher education, Prince William took a year off to travel and expose himself to different experiences, countries, and cultures. On a ten-week trip to Chile, William hiked, hauled lumber, and taught English to local children. Somewhere, his mother's spirit was surely smiling and proud.

St. Andrew's University, located in the Scottish city known for the invention of the game of golf, quickly became a mecca when William made the choice to pursue his higher education there. Applications for enrollment increased forty-four percent; students were forewarned about the rules of discretion as far as William's privacy is concerned. This is especially important considering that William, who will major in art history, lives in a residence hall on the campus like the rest of his peers.

Socially, William enjoys many of the things other teenagers enjoy. Now able to drive, he tries to take pleasure in the independence and excitement each young man his age longs for. Of course, the normalcy of other English teenagers cannot be granted: the role of whom he is, and what he will become, follows him everywhere. Like all other royalty, he knows it goes with the territory. However, William wants his father to take his rightful place as king before he does, because after University, he will either enter the military or perhaps even work a job in his field of study.

The sense of security Diana always seemed to be searching for is present in William, even though he has inherited his mother's sensitivity. An equilateral triangle between his father, brother, and himself forms a safe, strong, and stable environment, but it is likely that the "call to duty" will progress as William gets older and matures. With his own good attitude and the support of his family, his destiny seems compelling. As his uncle Earl Spencer said about him, "He has some of his mother's magic with people." That, along with his many other attributes, will help bring the royal family of Great Britain into the twenty-first century.

Harry

The younger of the two princes is a study in less pressure. Harry's personality is much more playful, spry, and fun loving than his older brother. His tendency toward horseplay and clowning-around are characteristics that are part boy, and part the influence of his mother. With Diana's death and the closeness that has grown between Harry and his father, it is apparent their love and affection go hand-in-hand with Harry's lively personality. According to one report, "They aren't afraid to be seen having fun together." Nonetheless, Harry's personality goes hand-in-hand with his status, too. There is plenty of time for Diana's youngest son to decide what direction he chooses to go, since he doesn't have the stifling presence of the throne staring down on him. This gives him much more freedom and leeway as he moves through his teen years and into adulthood.

Academically Harry is not the student William is. Harry joined his brother at Eton, beginning there on September 2, 1998, two days after the first anniversary of his mother's death. The decision to have both princes at Eaton was a good one—it has drawn them even closer together since the death of their mother.

Like most male teens, his love of sports is evident. As one source has said, "Harry is shaping up as an all-around sportsman." He loves soccer, and has even had a few injuries that he persevered through in true British style. *People* magazine's report stated of one such injury, "Two days later Harry hobbled on crutches into London's Twickerham Stadium to root for England's rugby team against France."

The cameras don't intimidate the redhead whose looks gravitate towards his father. He has inherited the Windsors' traits more than the Spencers', a softer yet still-compelling resemblance to his father's facial features, if (thankfully) not the bold, protruding ears and piercing eyes that gave Charles such a "geekish" look during his teens.

Harry has also displayed some of his father's artistic talent. One source amplified others by saying, "He sketches and paints with natural skill." The summers give Harry precious time to do things with his father, like watching or competing against his father in a polo match to attending the World Cup of Soccer. So caught up he was in the spirit of England's soccer team during the summer of '98, Harry had his hair buzz-cut to look like his soccer hero, Michael Owens.

Even though bubbly and energetic most of the time, Harry's behavior sometimes drifts to thoughts of his mother. At those times, he becomes quiet and placid. As one source put it, "He's the one showing the effects of the loss."

In January of 2001, the media reported that during the previous summer Harry had engaged in underage drinking and smoking marijuana. While experimentation of all sorts is tried by a great deal of young adults, and this seemed to be the situation with Charles and Diana's younger son, naturally this was big news for the tabloids. Prince Charles handled the situation well, though, by having Harry visit a halfway house to see exactly what the effects of drug use can lead to. Although Prince Harry might still have to perform some community service, I'm sure his father, grandparents, and bodyguards will keep a more watchful eye on him.

Harry, like any other adolescent, is trying to find his way. He has drawn close to his remaining parent, a relationship that will surely see both William and himself through the lonely times that come when the cameras of their minds reflect on the loss of their mother.

Charles

The leadership qualities and complex personality of the Prince of Wales have shone brightly since Diana's death. A feature in *Newsweek* magazine one year after Diana's death talked about the dedication Charles has displayed as a single parent: "By seeming to work hard at fatherhood, the Prince of Wales has turned his image around, and with it, the fortunes of the British monarchy."

Charles' report card of fatherhood is filled with high grades in the way he has handled his relationship with his boys. The memories of his own lonely childhood has manifested a side of him never seen before, and he seems to understand the importance of the love and care his sons need so desperately.

With Charles's help, the normalcy Diana wanted so much for the boys is being executed. Charles has been at the forefront of respecting Diana's memory and what she meant to the world. One source was quoted as saying, "Friends now say that if it hadn't been for Diana's tragic death and Charles' response, the world might never have seen the man inside who was bursting to escape."

The once-stuffy Prince of Wales has a much more relaxed and easy demeanor. Now in his fifth decade, Charles has let himself enjoy leisure and social situations. In the needs and love they have for each other, the boys are a major part of that transformation.

The other ingredient that has helped all three of them so much since Diana's death is the boys' acceptance of Camilla. Through all the hurt and scandal surrounding the triangle between Charles, Diana, and Camilla, a forgiveness and peace has now calmed, healed, and restored a happiness to those left behind. The embers that always remained between Charles and Camilla are now again burning brightly. Back are the romantic times of theater and disco music that was so much a part of their first era of love.

The maturity and love the boys have shown towards the priority of their father's happiness cannot be commended enough. They realize that Camilla is his soul mate. A staged event of Charles and William together with Camilla at London's Somerset House on February 2, 2001, was a show of William's support of his father's relationship with Camilla. The royal correspondent for the British Press Association, Peter Archer commented, "The show of family unity was a measure of maturity that he wants to relate to the woman in his father's life."

Camilla, who understands his complexities, is the woman Charles has always needed. Where Charles and Diana's personalities were battering rams against each other, Camilla's more easygoing nature and stepping back from the limelight are more suited towards Charles' needs. Even the British people have calmed and acclimated toward acceptance of Camilla. In June of 1999, fifty-nine percent of British subjects surveyed felt Charles could marry Camilla and still be king. Whatever anyone's feelings may be, Charles and Camilla are together, spending an average of three nights a week in each other's company, usually at St. James Palace.

The progress of her public acceptance continues, if slowly. During the summer of 1999 Charles, Camilla, and the boys vacationed together in the Greek Isles. In October of 1999, Camilla traveled to New York, a successful public relations campaign to remake her image. At a charity event put on by Camilla in July of 2001, Charles and Camilla exchanged their first public kiss. As of the summer of 2001 there is still no commitment from the Prince of Wales of whether marriage between he and Camilla will ever take place.

Still an extremely busy man, Charles's responsibilities and missions are an ongoing process. He is well versed in all aspects relating to science and the environment, and is a political adversary on most any subject. This man of deep inner mind and fascinating psyche even keeps a dream diary.

Even his passions and hobbies intertwine with his duties. The love of gardening and farming is still one of his greatest pastimes. His organic farming at Highgrove has become a sounding board for his agricultural views, and he has made it clear he is against biotechnical farming. The Prince of Wales advocates more traditional methods of growing, rather than the use of chemicals, pesticides, and other mutations.

Another of the issues Charles has supported in the past few years was in reference to the problems in England's beef industry. The outbreak of what is called "mad cow disease" as well as an E-coli bacteria outbreak crippled beef farmers all over England. Charles once again used his political clout to raise awareness of the safety of England's beef after the dreadful consequences of this misfortune.

His intellectual and writing skills have even taken him into the world of medicine. In January of 2001, Charles wrote an article in the *British Medical Journal* on the importance of the use of traditional and alternative medicine. In part he said, "I strongly believe that the way forward is to create a more inclusive system that incorporates the best and most effective of both complementary and orthodox medicine."

His seriousness about various world problems is always at the forefront of his opinions. His environmental views were critical toward the devastating floods that hit England in the fall of 2000, which he characterized as "Mankind's arrogant disregard of the delicate balance of nature."

Painting, one of his favorite passions and talents, has intertwined in both relaxing social events and diplomacy. At a dinner at St. James Palace with *Charlie's Angels* stars Drew Barrymore and Lucy Lui, Lucy and Charles spent a great part of the social occasion talking about their individual showings. Charles also used his shared passion for painting in building relations between England and Saudi Arabia. The combined talents of himself and Prince Khalid gained a mutual respect and friendship for relations with this important Middle Eastern nation.

As far as the Prince of Wales' destiny is concerned, who knows? With his grandmother's passing after living to one hundred and one and his mother showing no signs of giving up the throne anytime soon, the question of Charles ever becoming king is anyone's guess. The important thing is that Charles has won back the admiration and respect of his subjects. Human nature and the press will always kindle controversies. The media will always stir the political cauldron. Whether that is criticism from animal rights activists about fox hunting, or political strife in Northern Ireland, or the bombing of a gay bar in London, the Prince of Wales always takes a keen interest in each problem confronting Great Britain. When and if he ever ascends to the throne will manifest itself one way or another. Whether that means as king, or the role he now plays, his heart and soul will always be striving to keep the United Kingdom united. More importantly, though, the role of father and the love between Charles and his two sons is a gift more precious than any crown or scepter.

Sarah Ferguson

The Sarah of the twenty-first century is very different from the rousing young woman who burst into the royal family in 1986. The barrage of energy and enthusiasm she exhibited fifteen years ago has taken on a new and more productive persona, and her problems with the media have ebbed with her maturity. The "no nonsense" part of her personality makes her a formidable adversary about any questions she deems inappropriate during interviews.

In the five years since Diana's death, the former Duchess of York has taken stock of herself. She gained control of her weight, and became a spokeswoman for Weight Watchers in the process. The once heavyset Sarah has learned to discipline herself with regular exercise and diet to back up her advertisements for the company she has represented, and the counsel and advice she both talks and writes about have been beneficial to women worldwide.

Sarah has made an amazing comeback in the years since Diana's death. With her divorce from Andrew, she received only 1.7 million dollars, which was way too little for the lifestyle she was used to and expected to maintain. As a consequence, or perhaps in spite of this dilemma, she showed a maturing savvy that helped her market herself well enough to climb out of debt. Besides Weight Watchers, she has done commercials for Ocean Spray, and companies such as Charles Schwab have used her name.

Sarah and Andrew's separation in 1992 lasted for four years. Their divorce became final in 1996. With custody of her two girls, Beatrice and Eugenie, Sarah and Andrew have moved back into Sunninghill Park, the home the queen had built for them. Even after her financial troubles were solved, she and the two girls still share the home with Prince Andrew. Yet what some people might think of as an odd arrangement works quite well for them: Sarah has called her relationship with her ex-husband "the happiest divorced couple in the world." Just recently Sarah and the girls moved into their own home, which is conveniently close to Andrew's house for the girls to stay close to their father.

The center of her life revolves around the two girls, who are fast approaching their teen years. She has a busy schedule and agenda, which, with the aid of her personal assistant, John O'Sullivan, she manages quite well. "You have to be extremely good at multitasking," she has said.

Not all her endeavors have succeeded: a talk show called *Sarah - Surviving Life* was canceled after ten shows. However, her first career (in editing) has blossomed into a writing career. Besides her autobiography *My Story*, she has also published *Reinventing Yourself With The Duchess of York* and a book on Queen Victoria. She also published the children's book *Budgie, The Little Helicopter*. There may be even more children's books in the future.

With a rejuvenated career in place, Sarah has made her charity work the main part of her professional life. This is where Diana's leadership and role-modeling gave positive influence to Sarah's life. Sarah now has two charities, and both concern children. The first is a European-based organization called Children in Crisis. The second, Chances For Children, is based in America. Both are excellent charities dealing with many aspects of the hardships children must endure. Poverty, accidents, childhood disease and parenting issues are some of these organizations' many focuses. Sarah became very close to a boy she met during her work with Chances for Children. P. J. Allen was one of the many victims of the Oklahoma City bombing, burned badly in one of the cruelest crimes in history before September 11, 2001. Sarah has done a great deal of work making sure his medical care and recovery went as well as possible.

The queen and Sarah are trying to patch up their relationship. The public seems to have come back to her in the wake of Diana's death, both in England and America. In a Newsweek interview, she thanked the people of America for their renewed interest in her, saying, "They've given me a second chance."

Although a bit apprehensive with the media after all her problems, she has exhibited a new confidence. In promoting her Weight Watchers and charity work in January of 2002 on *Larry King Live*, she was confident, candid, and at ease with all Mr. King's questions, and answered numerous questions from callers with confidence and humility.

Sadly, the day that shook the world on September 11, 2001 affected Sarah, too—one of her offices was located in one of the twin towers of the World Trade Center. Fortunately, she wasn't there;

however Sarah, like so many others, knew many of the victims who lost their lives that day.

Another wound that is going to take a long time to heal is the loss Sarah feels for Diana. The bitter grudge Diana wouldn't let go before her death left no closure for Sarah, so she lives without the forgiveness she so desperately wanted from Diana. The tabloids, along with other quotes in Sarah's biography about Diana, combined with the mistake Sarah made to the press of saying she contracted a plantar wart from wearing a pair of Diana's shoes, never saw any reconciliation.

For Sarah, Diana's loss is like a chronic illness; improvement may come over time, but she will never be symptom free. Still in the various stages of grief for the best friend she'd been through thick and thin with, she will never be able to say good-bye, or forget all the happy times she had with "Dutch." During her interview on *Larry King Live,* she conveyed her feelings how she and her girls miss "Auntie Dutch."

Nonetheless, the new Sarah Ferguson is a vibrant, caring, and mature woman who will play a positive role in all aspects and endeavors she commits herself to in the future.

Paul Burrell

The faithful servant and "rock" of the Princess of Wales has gone on to a quiet and more peaceful life with his family. Gone are the exciting days of fanfare and journeys he had with the most popular woman of her day. Along with his wife Maria and two boys, Alexander and Nicholas, they now live in Fardon, Cheshire, 180 miles northwest of London.

On the fateful night of August 30, 1997, Paul had gone to see *Beauty and the Beast* with his family, and was relaxing in his Kensington Palace apartment with his brother when, "An hour later a policeman knocked on the door with chilling news."

With Diana's death, his years of serving the royal family ended. He now holds two Titles of Events, and is the fundraising manager for the Princess of Wales Memorial Fund, along with being a member of the Governors Memorial Committee. He receives a salary for these two jobs. He still writes some articles on etiquette and cooking from the expertise he gained over his years of service. His book, *In The*

Royal Manner, which deals specifically with his training in cuisine and entertaining, was very successful.

He is willing to talk about some of his experiences with Princess Diana as far as his working relationship was concerned, but never divulges any personal information. This is the thing I admire most about Paul Burrell—his unwavering loyalty to Diana after her death. He could have made himself a very rich man with any information he knew about her. This isn't in his character though, and the working relationship between the Princess of Wales and her faithful servant will always remain aboveboard.

Jerry White, the director of the Landmine Survivors Network, once said, "He [Paul] had an uncanny ability to read her." Paul Burrell will go down as the right hand of Princess Diana, as intricate a part in service to her as any famous celebrity, president, general, king, queen…or princess.

In an article in *People* magazine in late November of 2000, Paul Burrell told of the excitement of the coming Christmas for him and his family, saying, "The first weekend in December, the whole family heads to nearby Delamere Forest to chop down a spruce or pine." Part of his duties for Princess Diana during Christmas was to wrap an average of two hundred gifts each year. He is now able to spend more time with his own family, although all the busy moments throughout the year during his tenure with Diana were labors of love that were both gratifying and fulfilling.

My thank-you note for the letter Mr. Burrell sent me in the fall of 2000 included one of the personalized Christmas sled ornaments I make for people who help me each year. Along with the angel for his treetop, which Diana had given him during one of their years together, I hope the ornament I gave him was there too, and will be for many more years to come.

Frances Shand-Kydd

Diana's mother, who always had a distant relationship with her youngest daughter after the breakup of their family so many years ago, also lives a quiet and secluded life. In June of 1997, only weeks before Diana's death, the private mother of the most famous woman in the world broke her silence and admitted how traumatic her first divorce had been on the children.

Since her divorce from Peter Shand-Kydd in 1990, she spends most of her time at her home on the Isle of Seil in Scotland. So remote a figure was she in her daughter's life, Frances actually mingled outside Kensington Palace with mourners after the fatal accident without even being recognized. The day after her burial, Diana's mother rowed out from the pond to Diana's island resting-place to gain closure and peace from the loss of her third child. Of that experience she said, "I could feel my beloved Diana was at peace."

In April of 1998, the Catholic Frances Shand-Kydd led a pilgrimage to Lourdes for disabled children. This was a follow-suit for all the humanitarian work her daughter had done, a way of keeping her memory alive.

The allegations of sabotage and conspiracy in the death of Diana and Dodi by Mohamed Al Fayed have been traumatic for Shand-Kydd. In June of 1998, she had to appear in court with Mr. Al Fayed during the inquiry into the accident. One account described the situation as, "She was ignoring him in a dignified fashion, which annoyed him." Mr. Al Fayed was angry at her attitude, and made some disparaging remarks about her.

She sees very little of her two princely grandsons, but did go to Highgrove in July of 1998 to spend two days with Charles and Harry. (William was away at school during her visit.) Now approaching her mid-sixties, she spends her days enjoying various activities, especially fishing, in which she is a competent and gifted angler.

Lady Jane Fellowes and Lady Sarah McCorquodale

The five years since Diana's death have had several moments of grieving and pain for her two sisters. The two have gone on with their lives with their two families, and like their mother did, spend some of their time carrying on their younger sister's memory and work.

Each of them tries to stay in touch and involved in the lives of their two prince-nephews. They have attended some of each prince's activities, both academic and athletic. Sixteen days after Diana's death, one of Sarah's first acts to stay connected with her sister was to drive to Harry's school, Ludgrove, to give him a gift his mother was going to give him.

Part of Sarah's work and therapy is serving as president of the Princess of Wales Memorial Fund. This is quite a time-consuming chore, as she travels three hours to and from her home to London twice a week.

Jane Fellowes was left with a similar fate as Sarah Ferguson after Diana's death. Being married to the queen's personal secretary, there was still a great deal of friction in her relationship with Diana before her death. This of course was due to all the jousting that had occurred during and after Diana and Charles' divorce. Perhaps partly because of this, Jane took Diana's death very hard. Hopefully, her guilt will ebb more and more each year, and she will remember all the love, support, and good times she saw her famous sister through during her life.

Charles Spencer

The little brother Diana comforted and protected after their parents' divorce has been in the news and on television a great deal in the five years since her death. Various talk shows like *Oprah Winfrey*, *Regis Philbin* and *Larry King Live* have had his insight and memories of Diana. People so love Diana that Charles once commented "I often have to fight with taxi drivers to get them to accept my fare."

Althorp is his estate. Even though he has received some criticism for his handling of it, it is clear from my research, including my personal visit, that he's done a marvelous job. As Althorp is now, it exists as a beautiful tribute to the People's Princess rather than a capitalistic exploitation, as some have unfairly charged. It is well organized and kept up beautifully for those who visit the estate each summer.

Unfortunately, Earl Spencer has had some problems in his personal life. He was divorced from his wife, Victoria, in December of 1997, shortly after Diana's death. Like most divorces, it was a messy affair with allegations of adultery by Charles and alcohol and substance abuse by Victoria. In addition, his criticism of the royal family during his eulogy at Diana's funeral didn't sit well with the Windsors, and left a strain on their relationship.

The gregarious earl has written two books since his sister's death. They are: *The Spencers*, a five-hundred-year history of the family tree, and *Althorp: The Story of an English House*. Neither book received first-class reviews. Charles would now like to write a novel having nothing to with any of his famous family.

Like everyone else in his family trying to stay connected to Diana and the work she did, Charles returned to Cambodia to see the landmine campaign that was so dear to her. He was very moved by the victims of this horrible practice, who his sister gave so much for at the end of her life.

Earl Charles Spencer, single father and articulate man, will remain in the public eye for some time to come. Of all memories, memorials, and tributes to Princess Diana, Althorp is the center. The final resting-place of the woman who redefined popularity is and should be Charles Spencer's main responsibility during the remainder of his professional life. No matter what shortcomings others might feel for him, I feel he is doing an outstanding job of running Althorp in keeping with, and as a tribute to, the love he feels for his famous sister.

They found themselves reaching for what they surely felt.
They found themselves seeking for others
whom they would surely help
The altruisms they performed could only be compared
to those whose seek the love and service the Son-of-Man declared.
When troubled times came upon them like a raging stormy sea,
the refuge that they sought was more than any plea.
For when two damsels dreamed of fame, fortune, and aspirations,
they quickly learned that the reality is filled with reservations.
Though boldly faced with tasks that never seem to end,
each princess always gave their hearts with tenderness genuine.
For fairy tales are written, with intentions that are sincere.
In the case of Grace and Diana, their storyline is clear.
Two little girls grew up and moved the world we know.
When disaster ended the two lives, a canyon void was bestowed.
The story doesn't end there, though, for when they were with us,
the legacy they left behind will forever be in trust.

A few final thoughts:

Through the research and writing of this book, a labor of love I can only convey with the joy, pleasure, and therapy it gave me, one thing stands out that I feel compelled to make clear: Of the people who knew each princess and were gracious enough to share their experiences with me, one of the characteristics that came out of some of their retrospects was that the princess they shared their lives with was the superior one to the other in some way. I realize this is human nature and only natural. For the most part, this was positive and harmless; however, one person's thoughts—who wanted to and will remain anonymous—were disturbing to me.

The purpose of this book was to give perspective and celebration to these two extraordinary women. No contest or competition in any way, shape or form ever entered into the text of this work. If I could put Princess Grace and Princess Diana on pedestals that would rise like elevators, I would vault them above the twin towers of the World Trade Center as it stood before September 11, 2001. Both of these mementos of grandeur would be even in height, without so much as a millimeter separating them. And I believe that if the honor and glory of such a magical tribute was possible, that they would turn and face each other, join hands and hug each other with love and respect.

I hope you enjoyed this book and found it a good read, perhaps in the quiet and warm comfort of your cozy home on a cold winter night, or on the beach on a beautiful summer day. If you did, it only adds to the compliment and delight I attained in its writing.

The Triumphs and Trials of Grace Kelly and Diana Spencer

**Princess Grace's baby picture
credit: Corbis Photographs**

**Princess Diana as toddler
credit: AP Worldwide Photographs**

**Althorp-Princess Diana's home, where she grew up and is buried.
Personal photograph of author- 1999**

**Grace Kelly and Cary Grant arriving at premier of,
To Catch A Thief. Credit: Temple University Libraries, Urban Archives,
Philadelphia Pennsylvania 1955**

**Headlines of Princess Diana's
engagement.
Credit: Temple University Libraries,
Urban Archives, Philadelphia
Pennsylvania - 1981**

**Colhere Court, Princess
Diana's flat in London
Credit: Personal
photograph of author- 1999**

Princess Grace with wedding dress designer Helen Rose
Credit: Corbis Photographs- 1956

Princess Grace's wedding
Credit: AP Wide World Photos- 1956

St. Paul's Cathedral London, place of wedding of Princess Diana and Prince Charles
Credit: Personal Photo of Author 1999

Princess Diana and Prince Charles on Buckingham Palace balcony after their wedding
Credit: AP Worldwide Photos 1981

**Princess Grace with husband Prince Rainier and children,
Princess Caroline and Prince Albert
Credit: Temple University Libraries, Urban Archives, Philadelphia
Pennsylvania 1956**

**Prince and Princess of Wales
with Princes William and
Harry in Sicily
Credit: AP Wide World Photos**

**Princess Grace and Prince
Rainier
Credit: Temple University
Libraries, Urban Archives
Philadelphia, Pennsylvania
1956**

**Princess Grace and Princess Diana at Goldsmith Hall in London
Credit: AP Wide World Photos 1981**

**Princess Grace and family with audience before Pope Paul VI.
Credit: AP Wide World Photos 1974**

Shrine depicting Princess Diana with Mother Theresa: outside Kensington Palace

Credit: AP Wide World Photos 1997

**Kensington Palace summer People still leaving cards and flowers two years after Princess Diana's death
Credit: Personal photo of author 1999**

Shrine over tunnel (Place de l' Alma) where Princess Diana was killed
Credit: Personal photo of author 1999

Shrine beside pond of Princess Diana's Grave
Credit: Personal photo of author 1999

**Princess Diana and Dr. Tony Lloyd at annual fundraiser for Leprosy Mission
in London
Credit: PA photo London 1996**

**Invitation to Princess Diana's funeral
Credit: Dr. Tony Lloyd 1997**

Author's Notes

Research for this book was begun in September of 1997 and completed in January of 2002.

Introduction and Chapter One - They'd Only Just Begun

Research for this chapter comes from several books in bibliography, as well as my visits to Philadelphia and North Hampshire, where each princess grew up.

1. 'Fate does not...' *In My Own Fashion*, Cassini, p. 239
2. 'Sarah and Jane...' *Diana In Private*, Campbell, p. 5
3. 'When the oars...' *Yankee*, June 2000, p. 118
4. 'In the halls...' Comedian Lenny Bruce
5. 'We daughters who...' *The Bridesmaids*, Quine, p. 44
6. 'Every faith journey...' *The New Catholic Vision*, Mark Link, S. J., p. 1

Chapter Two - Different Roads Traveled

Research for this chapter comes from a few books in the bibliography, along with my visit to London in 1999.

1. 'Diana fell badly...' *Diana: Her True Story*, Morton, p. 41

Chapter Three - Young Star

Research for this chapter comes from several books in bibliography and all the films of Grace Kelly.

1. 'I wanted somebody...' *Grace*, Lacey, p. 111
2. 'She had played...' *Grace*, Lacey, p. 111
3. 'The right leading...' *The Life of Alfred Hitchcock*, Spoto, p. 342
4. 'I met Grace...' *The Bridesmaids*, Quine, p. 31
5. 'Judybird, she said...' *The Bridesmaids*, Quine, p. 45
6. '...hovers over James Stewart, in white chiffon and pearls.'...*In Style* magazine, Fall 1997
7. 'But I can't...' *Audrey Hepburn, an Intimate Portrait*, Maychick, p.105
8. 'Soon, Conant...' *Grace*, Conant, p. 9
9. 'Grace Kelly trusted...' *Grace*, Conant, p. 9
10. 'She is going...' *In My Own Fashion*, Cassini, p. 238
11. 'I want to...' *In My Own Fashion*, Cassini, p. 239
12. 'I have made...' *Grace*, Lacey, p. 224
13. 'Grace became the...' *Princess Grace*, Robyns, p. 18

Chapter Four - Princely Pursuits

Research for this chapter came from books in bibliography and my interview with Judith Balaban Quine.

1. 'The taffeta dress...' *The Bridesmaids*, Quine, p. 107
2. 'I think he's...' *Grace*, Lacey, p. 201
3. 'If he asked...' *A Princess and Her Troubled Marriage*, Davies, p. 88
4. 'They looked bored...' *A Princess and Her Troubled Marriage*, Davies, p. 87
5. 'All young women...' Judith Balaban Quine, Interview, 9/18/00
6. 'You're all dropping...' *The Bridesmaids*, Quine, p. 124
7. 'Gracie, I noted...' *The Bridesmaids*, Quine, p. 121

8. 'I want all...' *The Bridesmaids*, Quine, p. 122
9. 'But I want...' *The Bridesmaids*, Quine, p. 122

Chapter Five - Engagements Festive and Volatile

Research for this chapter came from bibliography books, *People* magazine and my interview with Judith Balaban Quine.

1. 'Oh my God...' *Royal House of Monaco*, Glatt, p. 30
2. 'I'm engaged to...' *The Bridesmaids*, Quine, p. 129
3. 'She spoke when...' *The Bridesmaids*, Quine, p. 129
4. 'She would have...' *Diana: Her True Story*, Morton, p. 47
5. 'Camilla evaluated...' *Diana: A Princess and Her Troubled Marriage*, Davies, p. 93
6. 'She had strong...' *Diana In Private*, Campbell, p. 96
7. 'For once Buckingham...' *Diana: Her True Story*, Morton, p. 53
8. 'he had something important...' *Diana: Her True Story*, Morton, p. 55
9. 'And then simply...' *Diana: Her True Story*, Morton, p.56
10. 'I pined for...' *People*, Oct. 1997, p. 102
11. 'might act again...' Interview, *Los Angeles Times*, 1/22/56
12. 'We were all...' *The Bridesmaids*, Quine, p. 127
13. 'Jay tapped his...' *The Bridesmaids*, Quine, p. 148
14. 'The day we left...' *Grace: An Intimate Portrait*, Conant, p. 42
15. 'Grace never liked...' *Grace*, Lacey, p. 245
16. 'This was the birth...' Judith Balaban Quine, Interview, 9/18/00
17. 'Stationing themselves in...' Judith Balaban Quine Interview, 9/18/00
18. 'Once the announcement...' *Diana In Private*, Campbell, p. 107
19. 'I just want...' *People*, Oct. 1997, p. 102
20. 'Her head and...' *Diana: Her True Story*, Morton, p. 64
21. 'Whatever Happens...' *People* Oct. 1997, p. 104

Chapter Six - I Do

Research for this chapter comes from books in the bibliography along with my visit to London in August 1999. Also history of St. Paul's Cathedral from PBS series, *Crown and Country*, January 2001.

1. 'It was all...' *Grace: An Intimate Portrait*, Conant, p. 60
2. 'Still, no sketch...' *The Bridesmaids*, Quine, p. 198
3. 'Having all of...' *The Bridesmaids*, Quine, p. 201
4. 'Listening to the...' *Diana: Her True Story*, Morton, p. 65
5. 'All I want...' *Diana: A Princess and Her Troubled Marriage*, Davies, p. 116
6. 'As she walked...' *Diana: Her True Story*, Morton, p. 66
7. 'Another Time...' *People*, Oct. 1997, p. 106
8. 'Their honeymoon gave...' *Diana: Her True Story*, Morton, p. 68

Chapter Seven – Reality

Research for this chapter comes mostly from books in bibliography, with short references from interviews and magazines.

1. 'Both Grace and'...Judith Balaban Quine, Interview, 9/18/00
2. 'In this capacity...' *Grace*, Lacey, p. 259
3. 'Grace was more...' Judith Balaban Quine, Interview, 9/18/00
4. 'Palace officials drilled...' *Royal House of Monaco*, Glatt, p. 39
5. 'How many times...' *Grace*, Lacey, p. 265

6. 'A European husband...' *Royal House of Monaco*, Glatt, p. 40
7. 'They were coming...' *Royal House of Monaco*, Glatt, p. 43
8. 'The honeymoon period...' *Diana In Private*, Campbell, p. 126
9. 'Darling Judybird...' *The Bridesmaids*, Quine, p. 213
10. 'I'm going to...' *The Bridesmaids*, Quine, p. 225
11. 'My cries for help...' *Diana: Her True Story*, Morton- Chapter V Title, p. 73
12. 'Standing on top of the...' *Diana: Her True Story*, Morton, p. 73
13. 'You have so...' *Time*, 11/9/98, p. 93
14. 'At the same...' *Diana: Her True Story*, Morton, p. 77
15. 'Thank goodness he...' *Diana: Her True Story*, Morton, p. 79

Chapter Eight - Parenthood Priorities and Problems

Research for this chapter comes from various books in the bibliography.

1. 'Shortly after Caroline...' *Grace: An Intimate Portrait*, Conant, p. 122
2. 'Their strongest characteristic...' Judith Balaban Quine Interview, 9/18/00
3. 'She also liked...' *Grace: An Intimate Portrait*, Conant, p. 94
4. 'She and the...' *Grace: An Intimate Portrait*, Conant, p. 9
5. 'Grace studied her...' *Grace*, Lacey, p. 284
6. 'I know you...' *The Bridesmaids*, Quine, p. 320
7. 'Some of us...' *The Bridesmaids*, Quine, p. 322
8. 'I rose from...' *The Bridesmaids*, Quine, p. 322
9. 'For Grace this...' *Grace: An Intimate Portrait*, Conant, p. 84
10. 'Caroline, thrilled...' *Royal House of Monaco*, Glatt, p. 89
11. 'My baby Stephanie...' *Royal House of Monaco*, Glatt, p. 72
12. 'She believes that...' *Diana: Her True Story*, Morton, p. 79
13. 'She turned against...' *Diana In Private*, Campbell, p. 180
14. 'She [Diana] was furious...' *Diana In Private*, Campbell, p. 175

Chapter Nine - Looks and Fashion

Besides books in the bibliography, a great deal of the research for this chapter came from Grace Kelly's archives, which are at the Temple University Library in Philadelphia (All articles from *Philadelphia Bulletin*). Also, Diana's Dresses for Humanity, which I saw on display in Lowell, Massachusetts in December 1998.

1. 'But I want...' *In My Own Fashion*, Cassini, p. 246
2. 'You are becoming...' Ibid. p. 246
3. 'I thought of...' Ibid. p. 246
4. 'There was a...' *The Life of Alfred Hitchcock*, Spoto, p. 348
5. 'Like an untouchable...' *A & E's Biography*, Edith Head, 3/23/01
6. 'I have never...' *Grace of Monaco*, Enklund, p. 81
7. 'Best tailored women...' *Philadelphia Bulletin*, 4/7/55, p. 13
8. 'Their auras are...' *In Style*, Fall 97, p. 54
9. 'Glamour doesn't have...' Ibid. p. 54
10. 'a woman looking...' Ibid. p. 55
11. 'Her looks were...' *Time*, 6/14/99, p. 141
12. 'Lots of us...' *Harpers Bazaar*, 11/97, p. 45
13. 'The photographs taken...' *Diana: A Princess ad Her Troubled Marriage*, Davies, p. 177
14. 'When Jane approached...' Ibid. p. 224
15. 'Not long after...' *Vanity Fair*, 7/97, p. 72
16. 'Dresses Saves Lives...' *Diana's Dresses: Dresses For Humanity*, Rorech, p. 3
17. 'She provided unending...' *Diana: a Tribute to the People's Princess*, Donnelly
18. 'Like Princess Grace...' *Time*, 6/14/99 p. 136109.

19. 'Before the lionization...' Judith Balaban Quine Interview, 9/18/00

Chapter Ten - Giving Back: Charities, Causes and Commendations

Besides various books in the bibliography, the research for this chapter came from my interviews with Judith Balaban Quine, Reverend Tony Lloyd and my correspondence with Paul Burrell.

1. 'Rich the treasure...' Alexander's Feast, John Dryden (1631-1700)
2. 'When she was...*Prince Grace*, Robyns, p. 25
3. 'Grace had a...' *Royal House of Monaco*, Glatt p. 61
4. 'It was a...' Judith Balaban Quine Interview, 9/18/00
5. 'Probably don't know...' Ibid.
6. 'Each year, she...' *Grace: An Intimate Portrait*, Conant, p. 99
7. 'They appreciated her...' Ibid. p. 116
8. 'To interact with...' Judith Balaban Quine Interview, 9/18/00
9. 'It went against...' Ibid.
10. 'Sometimes at night...' *Diana: The Secret Years*, Simmons, p. 130
11. 'Secret nocturnal visits...' Ibid.
12. 'I've had difficulties...' *Diana, A Tribute To The People's Princess*, Donnelly, p. 96
13. 'She is not...' *Diana: A Princess and Her Troubled Marriage*, Davies, p. 27
14. 'Diana went where...' *Diana: The Last Year*, Spoto, p. 73
15. 'Diana, Princess of...' Centrepoint patron document, 1992-97
16. 'She would stoop...' *Diana: The Secret Years*, Simmons, p. 151
17. 'Then she insisted...' *Diana: A Tribute to The People's Princess*, Donnelly, p. 103
18. 'I first met...' AIDS Trust pamphlet, Adler, p. 4
19. 'After reading his...' *Diana: Her True Story*, Morton p. 137
20. 'The Princess became...' AIDS Trust pamphlet, Adler, p. 5
21. 'The Princess of...' Ibid. p. 6
22. 'Don't do it...' Tony Lloyd Interview, 2/11/01
23. 'That one picture...' Ibid.
24. 'For the son...' *The New American Bible for Catholics*, Mark 10:45
25. 'I can't do...' Tony Lloyd Interview, 2/11/01
26. 'She came in...' Ibid.
27. 'Her mere presence...' Ibid.
28. 'Her goodness at times...' Ibid.
29. 'She was Professional...' Ibid.
30. 'Jesus, remember me...' *The New American Bible for Catholics*, Luke 23:42
31. 'Are you not the Messiah?...' Ibid, Luke 23: 39
32. 'That is was some...' Ibid.
33. 'It will do...' Tony Lloyd Interview, 2/11/01
34. 'Her visit was...' *Diana: A Tribute to The People's Princess*, Donnelly, p. 104
35. 'The most poignant...' Letter from Paul Burrell, 11/10/00
36. 'The landmine campaign...' Ibid.
37. 'Being put on...' *Diana: A Tribute*, DeLano, p. 66
38. 'She gave too...' *Princess of Wales Memorial Lecture*, 6/25/99, p. 7

Chapter Eleven - Friends and Colleagues

The research for this chapter comes from various books and magazines about the Two Princesses, as well as my correspondences with those who worked with The Princess of Wales.

1. 'I remember at...' *Princess Grace: A Biography*, Robyns, p. 240
2. 'Someone had recently...' *The Bridesmaids*, Quine, p. 446
3. 'There were lesser...' *Princess Grace: A Biography*, p. 235
4. 'Sarah was a...' *Duchess: An Intimate Portrait*, Morton, p. 54
5. 'Throughout her difficult...' Ibid. p. 51

6.   'The Princess of...' Ibid. p. 51
7.   'The article, which...' *Diana: A Princess and Her Troubled Marriage*, Davies, p. 314
8.   'Despite Diana's affection...' Ibid. p. 316
9.   'How can you...' Ibid. p. 318
10. 'For six years...' *Maclean's*, 10/21/96 p. 38
11. 'I cried all...' *Diana: Her New Life*, Morton p.13
12. 'No one was...' *Diana: The Last Year*, Spoto p. 163
13. 'I am proud...' Letter from Paul Burrell, 11/10/00
14. 'A real friend...' *Readers Digest*, 5/01, p.152A

Chapter Twelve – Smothered

Research for this chapter comes from various books in bibliography, along with some of the interviewed who were friends of the two princesses.

1.   'It was Grace...' *Grace*, Lacey, p. 127
2.   'I've never known...' *Princess Grace*, Bradford, p. 88
3.   'Chipping away at...' Ibid p. 103
4.   'There was a...' *Grace*, Lacey, p. 135
5.   'She had come...' Ibid. p. 137
6.   'Out! I have...' Ibid. p. 137
7.   'Bill Holden's highly...' *Princess Grace*, Bradford, p. 89
8.   'As long as...' Ibid. p. 90
9.   'Grace would only...' *Royal House of Monaco*, Glatt, p. 25
10. 'Day after day...' *Princess Grace*, Bradford, p. 130
11. 'By the time...' *The Bridesmaids*, Quine, p. 153
12. 'In Dublin itself...' *Princess Grace*, Bradford, p. 181
13. 'Without ever bothering...' *The Bridesmaids*, Quine, p. 288
14. 'Grace and Rainier...' *Grace*, Lacey, p. 272
15. 'Nothing to see...' Judith Balaban Quine, Interview, 9/18/00
16. 'Tall and graceful...' *Royal House of Monaco*, Glatt, p. 90
17. 'With anyone else...' Judith Balaban Quine Interview, 9/18/00
18. 'These explicit photographs...' *Royal House of Monaco*, Glatt, p. 99
19. 'Every day an...' *Diana In Private*, Campbell, p. 86
20. 'The story was...' *Diana: A Princess and Her Troubled Marriage*, Davies, p. 95
21. 'While once she...' *Diana: Her True Story*, Morton, p. 54
22. 'Editors all ordered...' *Diana: A Princess and Her Troubled Marriage*, Davies, p. 135
23. 'But she had...' Ibid. p. 137
24. 'Gossip columnist Nigel...' *Diana: Her True Story*, Morton p. 82
25. 'Malice In the...' Ibid. p. 82
26. 'Photographers captured the...' Ibid. p. 96
27. 'We editors listened...' *The Real Diana*, Campbell, p. 222
28. 'They scream obscenities...' Ibid. p. 228
29. 'How Diana felt...' Tony Lloyd Interview, 2/11/01
30. 'It was sad...' Ibid.
31. 'She became very...' Ibid.
32. 'In one of...' *Diana: The Secret Years*, Simmons, p. 113
33. 'One writes of...' *Tender Is The Night*, Fitzgerald, p. 181
34. 'Grace told me only recently...' *The Bridesmaids*, Quine, p. 467
35. 'It's hard for...' *Diana: The Secret Years*, Simmons, p. 129

Chapter Thirteen - Nothing Lasts Forever

Research for this chapter comes from various books in bibliography, along with magazines, my interviews with Adele Richards and Tony Lloyd, as well as my visit to Paris in the summer of 1999.

1. 'Grace had begun...' *The Bridesmaids*, Quine, p. 439
2. 'She made my...' Interview Adele Richards, 10/29/00
3. 'The Princess still...' Ibid.
4. 'See you Grace...' Ibid
5. 'She [Grace] had grown...' *Royal House of Monaco*, Glatt p. 91
6. 'When she was...' Ibid. p. 120
7. 'I remember meeting...' Ibid. p. 121
8. 'We smiled for...' *The Bridesmaids*, Quine, p. 351
9. 'Why would you...' Ibid. p. 358
10. 'but there was...' *Grace*, Lacey, p. 328
11. 'That she was...' *Grace*, Lacey, p. 319
12. 'So walking down...' Ibid. p. 106
13. 'Something inside me...' p. 110
14. 'He said I...' *People* 10/20/97, p. 106
15. 'They tried to stop me from going downstairs...' Ibid.
16. 'Camilla I'd love...' Ibid. p. 106
17. 'I'd done something...' Ibid. p. 107
18. 'She took his...' *Princess In Love*, Pasternak, p. 18
19. 'These meetings, she...' Ibid. p. 22
20. 'All she could...' Ibid. p. 26
21. 'delighted by the invitation...' Ibid. p. 48
22. 'The relief at...' Ibid. p. 77
23. 'As he heard...' Ibid. p. 123
24. 'Diana would creep...' Ibid. p. 159
25. 'For now that...' Ibid. p. 166
26. 'How many times...' *People*, 10/20/97, p. 108
27. 'She became very...' Interview, Tony Lloyd, 2/11/01
28. 'William and Harry...' *The Day Diana Died*, Andersen, p. 131
29. 'Why do you...' *Time*, 3/11/96, p. 51

Chapter Fourteen – Accidents

Research for this chapter came from various books in the bibliography, some periodicals, as well as my own research in Paris in 1999.

1. 'her mother...' *Grace*, Lacey, p. 346
2. 'It's just easier...' Ibid, p. 347
3. 'Grace was clinically...' *The Royal House of Monaco*, Glatt p. 9
4. 'I'd heard she...' *The Bridesmaids*, Quine, p. 453
5. 'It was also...' *Grace*, Lacey, p. 355
6. 'Step on It...' *The Day Diana Died*, Andersen, p. 164
7. 'I'm having a...' Ibid. p. 167
8. 'When Dodi came...' Ibid. p. 164
9. 'The ring was...' Ibid. p. 172
10. "Furious that his...' Ibid. p. 174
11. 'A second analysis...' *Time*, 9/22/97, p. 30
12. 'Now look, don't...' *The Day Diana Died*, Andersen p. 184
13. 'Paul, who made...' Ibid. p. 185
14. '[Reports] put the motorcycle at thirty...' *The Day Diana Died*, Anderson
15. 'The entire trip...' *The Day Diana Died*, Andersen, p. 198
16. 'On doctors orders...' *Death Of A Princess*, Sancton & MacLeod, p. 25

Chapter Fifteen - Grief, Sorrow and Comfort

Research for this chapter came from various books in the bibliography, periodicals, and newspapers, my interview with Judith Balaban Quine, as well as my trips to London, Althorp, and Paris in the summer of 1999.

1. 'On hearing the...' *The Royal House of Monaco*, Glatt, p. 9
2. 'Up, Up, Up...' *The Bridesmaids*, Quine, p. 455
3. 'Mom, my Amy...' Ibid, p. 455
4. 'It's not fair...' Ibid, p. 455
5. 'She was over...Ibid, p. 457
6. 'It doesn't seem...' Ibid, p. 457
7. 'When I heard...' *Newsweek*, 9/15/97, p. 65
8. 'One of the...' Judith Balaban Quine Interview, 9/18/00
9. 'Go therefore, and...' *The New American Catholic Bible*, Matthew Chapter 28: 19-20
10. 'What the Prince...' *The Day Diana Died*, Andersen, p. 217
11. 'But from the...' Ibid, p. 215
12. 'All three Windsor men...' Ibid, p. 225
13. 'While those around...' Ibid, p. 218
14. 'Why are we...' *Good Housekeeping*. 9/98, p. 92
15. 'For the first...' *The Day Diana Died*, Andersen, p. 259
16. 'Although a princess...' *Newsday*, 9/7/97, p. 4
17. 'Love is patient...' *The New American Catholic Bible*, 1st. Corinthians Chapter 13: 4-7
18. 'A truly British...' *Newsday*, 9/7/97, p. 4
19. 'It is a...' Ibid, p. 4
20. 'Whoever is in...' Visit to Althorp, 8/99
21. 'Si monumentum requiris circumspice' *American Heritage*, July/August 2001, p. 11
22. 'Beautiful Princess, open...' *The Frog Prince*, Bates, p. 14
23. 'Do not be...' Hymn, *You Are Mine*, Haas, 1991

Chapter Sixteen - Only The Lonely

Research for this chapter comes from various books in the bibliography, along with magazines and television shows.

1. 'The pair, who...' *The Royal House of Monaco*, Glatt, p. 129
2. 'Did you ever...' Ibid, p. 134
3. 'Strength comes when...' Ibid, p. 214
4. 'When they kissed...' *People* 5/12/97, p. 218
5. 'Ernst is over...' *People* 8/9/99, p. 88
6. 'One morning Rainier...' *The Royal House of Monaco*, Glatt, p. 202
7. 'Princess Stephanie's current...' Ibid, p. 241
8. 'when the illegitimate birth of...' Ibid
9. 'Now a very...' Ibid, p. 253
10. 'Rainier punched him to the ground...' *The Royal House of Monaco*, Glatt, p. 128
11. 'Our greatest strength...' *Time*, Australia 1/20/97, p.,44
12. 'Britain's Newspaper Editors...' *Maclean's*, 8/31/98
13. 'Is increasingly being...' *Ladies Home Journal*, July 2001, p. 96
14. 'Levelheaded and normal...' Ibid, p. 98
15. 'He has some...' *Biography*. December 2000, p. 71
16. 'They aren't afraid...' *People*, 6/21/99, p. 134
17. 'Harry is shaping...' *Ladies Home Journal*, July 2001, p. 99
18. 'Two days later...' *People*, 5/7/01, p. 139
19. 'He sketches and paints with natural skill...' *Good Housekeeping*, March 1999, p. 28
20. 'He's the one...' *Newsweek*, 9/17/98, p. 46
21. 'By seeming to...' Ibid, p. 48
22. 'Friends now say...' *Good Housekeeping*, March 1999, p. 28
23. 'The show of...' *People*, 2/26/01, p. 89

24. 'I strongly believe...' *British Medical Journal*, 1/20/01, p. 181
25. 'Mankind's arrogant disregard...' *New Statesman*, 11/31/00, p. 8
26. 'The happiest divorced...' *People*, 1/22/01, p. 86
27. 'You have to...' *Christian Science Monitor*, 7/6/01, p. 20
28. They've given me...' *Newsweek*, 12/18/01, p. 4
29. 'An hour later...' *People*, 11/10/97, p. 4
30. 'He [Paul] had an...' *People*, 8/31/98, p. 48
31. 'The first weekend...' *People*, 11/28/00, p. 46
32. 'I could feel...' *People*, 12/29/97-1/5/98, p. 37
33. 'She was ignoring...' *People*, 6/22/98, p. 56
34. 'I often have...' *People*, 6/25/01, p. 96

Bibliography

Andersen, Christopher. *The Day Diana Died*. New York: William Morrow and Co., 1998.

Bates, Katherine Lee. *Once Upon A Time: A Book of Old Time Fairy Tales-The Frog Prince*.
New York: Rand McNally, 1986.

Bradford, Sara. *Princess Grace*. New York: Stein And Day, 1984.

Campbell, Lady Colin. *Diana In Private*. New York: St. Martin's Press, 1992.

Campbell, Lady Colin. *The Real Diana*. New York: St. Martin's Press, 1998.

Cassini, Oleg. *In My Own Fashion*. New York: Simon & Schuster, 1987.

Conant, Howell. *Grace: An Intimate Portrait of Princess Grace*. New York: Random House, 1992.

Davies, Nicolas. *Diana: A Princess and Her Troubled Marriage*. Carol New York: Publishing, 1992.

Delano, Julia. *Diana: A Tribute*. New York: Crescent Books, 1997.

Donnelly, Peter. *Diana: A Tribute to The People's Princess*. Philadelphia. London: Courage Books, 1997.

Dryden, John. *Bartlett's Familiar Quotations*. Boston, Brown & Co., 1992.

Englund, Steve. *Grace of Monaco*. New York: Doubleday, 1984.

Ferguson, Sarah. Budgie: The Little Helicopter, with John Richardson (Illustrator) New York: Simon & Schuster (1989)

Fitzgerald, F. Scott. *Tender Is The Night*. New York: Charles Scribner's Sons, 1933.

Glatt, John. *The Royal House of Monaco*. New York: St. Martin Press, 1998.

Grace, Princess-Robyns, Gwen. *My Book of Poetry and Flowers*. Doubleday & Co.

Lacey, Robert. *Grace*. New York: G.P. Putnam's Sons, 1994.

Maychick, Diana. Audrey Hepburn: An Intimate Portrait. New York Carol Publishing Group, 1993.

Morton, Andrew. *Duchess: An Intimate Portrait of Sarah, Duchess of York*. New York: Contemporary Books, 1989.

Morton, Andrew. *Diana: Her True Story*. London, Simon & Schuster, 1992.

Morton, Andrew. *Diana: Her New Life*. New York, Simon & Schuster, 1994.

Pasternak, Anna. *Princess In Love*. New York: Dutton Books, 1994.

Quine, Judith Balaban. *The Bridesmaids: Grace Kelly, Princess of Monaco, and Six Intimate Friends*. New York: Weidenfeld & Nicolson, 1989.

Robyns, Gwen. *Princess Grace: A Biography*. London: W. H. Allen, 1982.

Rorech, Maureen A. *Diana's Dresses: Dresses for Humanity*. Toronto: Zeppelin Communications, 1998.

Sancton, Thomas & MacLeod, Scott. *Death of A Princes*. New York: St. Martin's Press, 1998.

Simmons, Simone. *Diana: The Secret Years*. New York: Ballantine Books, 1998.

Spoto, Donald *Diana: The Last Year:* New York: Harmony Books, 1997.

Spoto, Donald. *The Dark Side of Genius: The Life of Alfred Hitchcock*. New York: Ballantine, 1984.

Index

Printed in the United States
752000001B